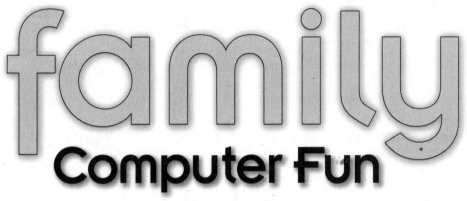

Computer Fun

Digital Ideas Using
Your Photos,
Movies, and Music

800 East 96th Street,
Indianapolis, Indiana 46240

Family Computer Fun:
Digital Ideas Using Your Photos, Movies, and Music

International Standard Book Number: 0-7897-3378-1

Library of Congress Catalog Card Number: 200522652

Printed in the United States of America

First Printing: June 2005

08   07   06   05   4   3   2   1

Trademarks

All terms mentioned in this book that are known to be trademarks or service marks have been appropriately capitalized. Que Publishing cannot attest to the accuracy of this information. Use of a term in this book should not be regarded as affecting the validity of any trademark or service mark.

Warning and Disclaimer

Every effort has been made to make this book as complete and as accurate as possible, but no warranty or fitness is implied. The information provided is on an "as is" basis. The author and the publisher shall have neither liability nor responsibility to any person or entity with respect to any loss or damages arising from the information contained in this book or from the use of the CD or programs accompanying it. *The views expressed by Ralph Bond are his personal views and are not the views of Intel Corporation.*

Bulk Sales

Que Publishing offers excellent discounts on this book when ordered in quantity for bulk purchases or special sales. For more information, please contact

U.S. Corporate and Government Sales
1-800-382-3419
corpsales@pearsontechgroup.com

For sales outside of the U.S., please contact

International Sales
international@pearsoned.com

Associate Publisher
Greg Wiegand

Acquisitions Editor
Todd Green

Development Editor
Todd Brakke

Managing Editor
Charlotte Clapp

Team Coordinator
Sharry Lee Gregory

Senior Project Editor
Matthew Purcell

Production Editor
Heather Wilkins

Indexer
Lisa Wilson

Technical Editor
Greg Perry

Multimedia Developer
Dan Scherf

Designer
Ann Jones

Page Layout
Stacey Richwine-DeRome

Contents at a Glance

Table of Contents

8   ENJOY YOUR PC'S DIGITAL MEDIA IN THE FAMILY ROOM 239

GLOSSARY **255**

INDEX **269**

About the Author

In his role as consumer education manager for Intel Corporation, **Ralph Bond**'s mission is to travel North America, sharing with radio and television audiences how a home computer and the Internet can help families learn, create, communicate, and have fun. A twenty-four year veteran of the computer industry, Ralph began his career as a technical writer in 1981 while teaching night and weekend courses at Saddleback Community College (Mission Viejo, California).

Ralph has shared his home computing expertise via print and broadcast outlets for more than 10 years. His broadcast résumé includes appearances throughout the United States and Canada, averaging nearly 100 TV and radio interviews each year.

Regular media stops for Ralph include the nationally broadcast radio shows *Into Tomorrow*, *Computer America*, *Computer Outlook*, and *The David Lawrence Show*. Ralph also appears frequently on the NBC, CBS, and ABC television affiliates in Chicago, and in Canada he has appeared on the nationally broadcast *City TV* show. On the print side, Ralph has been quoted on the pages of *USA Today*, The *New York Times*, *Esquire*, the *New York Post*, the *Boston Globe*, *Miami Herald*, *St. Petersburg Times*, and the *Globe and Mail*, among other top newspapers.

His writing experience began in the 1970s when he served as a contributing editor in southern California with such publications as *Art Week*, *Orange Coast Magazine*, and the *Orange County Metropolitan Journal* where he served as a home computer products reviewer. During his years as one of Intel's PC Dads, Ralph authored numerous articles, and co-authored with Mark Ivey *The PC Dad's Guide to Becoming a Computer-Smart Parent* (1999).

Ralph received his bachelor's degree in art history with a minor in education in 1975, and in 1981 earned a master's degree in art history from California State University, Long Beach. Ralph lives in Hillsboro, Oregon with his wife and seventeen-year-old son. His twenty-one-year-old daughter is a student at the University of Oregon.

Dedication

This book is dedicated to my wife Carolyn, and millions of fellow home computer owners who, like her, are ready to do more with their PCs than just surf the web, write email, and do a bit of word processing.

Until recently, my wife was content to have a strictly business relationship with her PC. All that digital photo editing, movie making, and music CD stuff was something my son Jeff, daughter Christina, or I handled. About a year ago I noticed a big change. She became increasingly interested in digital photography as her friends started showing off their digital cameras and creative photo projects. And as our neighbors and friends continued to ask her if I could help with computer projects, such as creating a DVD with home movies to be sent to a son serving in Iraq, she wanted to learn how to do more for herself.

Most important of all, it was her request, whenever asking to learn the ropes of a task such as cropping a digital photo, to cut the techno babble and get right to the essentials that guided the structure and tone of this cookbook-like collection of step-by-step digital family fun projects.

Acknowledgments

This book became a reality largely due to huge contributions from a host of talented friends and colleagues.

First and foremost, I'd like to thank the team at Que Publishing for their editorial and content contributions, starting with Todd Green, who believed from day one in the potential of a family computer project book and worked tirelessly to guide me through the entire creation and production process. In terms of content, the able fingerprints of Todd Brakke are all over many segments as he contributed solid ideas and input that, on all counts, improved the text. And sage tech guru Greg Perry made sure all the high tech *i*'s were dotted and *t*'s crossed, with Heather Wilkins ensuring the text went from my input to proper English.

The desire to demystify home computing underpins every word in this book. I owe a debt of inspiration to a host of print and broadcast media pioneers who showed me how to make technology accessible and fun for general audiences, including Walt Mossberg of the *Wall Street Journal*; David Gussow of the *St. Petersburg Times*; *USA Today*'s Ed Baig; Michele Marriott of the *New York Times*; Robin Raskin, the Internet Mom; Dave Graveline, host of the *Into Tomorrow* radio show; Craig Crossman, host, and Mark Lautenschlager of the *Computer America* radio show; John Iasiuolo, host of the *Computer Outlook* radio show; David Lawrence, host of *The David Lawrence Show*; Dan Dubno, CBS TV New York; Art Norman and Charlie Wojciechowski of NBC TV Chicago; David Onley, Citytv Toronto; and so many others I could list for pages and pages!

I'd certainly be remiss if I failed to recognize my friend Mark Ivey, who toured the United States with me as one of Intel's PC Dads. Mark's gift for simplifying technology and sprinkling humor along the way to help illustrate points started me on a solid path nearly 10 years ago.

Next I'd like to acknowledge the remarkable company I work for and the encouragement and support I've received from so many teammates. Robert Noyce, one of the co-founders of Intel, once said, "Don't be encumbered by past history; go off and do something wonderful." That spirit of thinking out of the box creates within Intel a culture that openly embraces new ideas. It's that willingness to experiment that moved my management to give me the freedom to explore ways to reach everyday consumers and to ultimately create my position as Intel's consumer education manager. Topping a list of Intel experts who are all ninja masters when it comes to looking at the world through a consumer's eyes is Larry Bozman, head of Intel's broadcast team and my current manager; Ken Kaplan, Intel broadcast; Steve Short, Consumer Education; Linda Bonniksen, who heads up Intel's consumer media relations team and was my manager during the formative years of the consumer education program; and Linda's fellow consumer technology gurus, Shannon Love, Claudine Mangano, Alison Wesley, and Ken Epstein.

And finally, I'd like to acknowledge that many of the projects in this book are based on show-and-tell demos developed in collaboration with a team of fellow Intel road show warriors, including Phil Lowrey, and Sean Foster.

We Want to Hear from You!

As the reader of this book, *you* are our most important critic and commentator. We value your opinion and want to know what we're doing right, what we could do better, what areas you'd like to see us publish in, and any other words of wisdom you're willing to pass our way.

As a publisher for Que Publishing, I welcome your comments. You can email or write me directly to let me know what you did or didn't like about this book—as well as what we can do to make our books better.

Please note that I cannot help you with technical problems related to the topic of this book. We do have a User Services group, however, where I will forward specific technical questions related to the book.

When you write, please be sure to include this book's title and author as well as your name, email address, and phone number. I will carefully review your comments and share them with the author and editors who worked on the book.

Email: feedback@quepublishing.com

Mail: Greg Wiegand
Associate Publisher
Que Publishing
800 East 96th Street
Indianapolis, IN 46240 USA

For more information about this book or another Que Publishing title, visit our website at www.quepublishing.com. Type the ISBN (excluding hyphens) or the title of a book in the Search field to find the page you're looking for.

Introduction

Are you stuck in a computing rut? Is your family computer only serving as an appliance for email, web surfing, and checking your stocks? Do you have the basics of PC operation nailed but feel left behind when it comes to all the cool digital photo, music, and video projects you see other people doing with their PCs?

If the questions above have your head nodding "yes" like a spring-loaded bobble doll, this is *the* book for you.

As Intel's consumer education manager, I've traveled throughout North America for the past 10 years, staging workshops and making hundreds of TV appearances demonstrating home computer projects. My time on the road has shown me that the overwhelming majority of home PC owners want to do more with their computers, but have little time to spare for in-depth hobbies. They know a modern PC can be a remarkable tool for personal creativity and expression, but constantly asking for help from tech-savvy friends, spouses, or even their kids doesn't seem to work. They're more than willing to learn new tricks, but they don't want to invest a ton of money or time pursuing an activity only to discover that it's not their cup of tea. Most importantly of all, they want to test drive a wide variety of rewarding activities and see tangible results quickly, all without having to become a computer engineer.

Am I talking about you? If yes, *Family Computer Fun* can be your guide to entry-level entertainment, communications, and personal expression projects including

- Taking your digital snaps to the next level of creativity using photo-editing software
- Creating animated photo album scrapbooks with pictures, text, and narration
- Transforming your Web-connected PC into a worldwide radio jukebox, karaoke machine, or recording studio
- Preserving your precious home movies by converting tapes into entertaining digital CD or DVD heirlooms
- Using the Internet to conduct video conferences and make phone calls across the street or around the world
- Accessing your digital photos, music, and even videos stored on a PC and playing them back via your home stereo and TV

Family Computer Fun offers a collection of home-tested, low-cost projects handpicked in response to what thousands of nontechie folks have told me are top items on their want-to-try list. Some projects require less than an hour to complete, while others are great half-day or weekend adventures ideally suited for a family team effort. And best of all, each project can be explored solo or with a spouse or friend, or shoulder-to-shoulder with your kids or grandkids.

Think of *Family Computer Fun* as being like a beginner's digital cookbook full of recipes you can enjoy in any order you like. Scan the table of contents, pick a chapter, and thumb through a project. You'll see that most projects open with a brief description and contain these key help elements flagged with handy icons:

 Time—Estimate of the time you'll need to complete an activity

 Open Wallet Alert— Estimated budget to purchase hardware or software ingredients

 Materials—An ingredients list of software and hardware

 Are You Hooked Yet?— Ideas and suggestions at the end of a project for growing your experience and skills

And like a good cookbook, each project offers step-by-step instructions enhanced by illustrations, tips, and notes that will make your PC more than just a mundane tool for balancing your checkbook.

Worried about being left in the dark by techno babble? Rest easy! Technical words and acronyms only appear if absolutely necessary and each is explained when it appears in the text or in a comprehensive glossary provided at the back of the book.

Stop! *Family Computer Fun* is *not* for everyone. To use this book you should have

- A personal computer with Microsoft's Windows XP operating system (Home, Pro, or Media Center edition). All operating system and browsing illustrations are based on a Windows XP personal computer. If your PC uses Windows 95, 98, or Me, many of the projects here will work, but operations tied directly to the Windows XP OS might not. The overall assumption is you have a modern PC with the horsepower and features, such as USB 2.0 ports, that might or might not be present in PCs four years of age or older.

- A command of *basic* PC operation. You should know how to turn on a PC, connect to the Internet, navigate drop-down menus using a mouse, create folders, and manage files.

- A high-speed DSL or cable modem connection to the Internet. Downloading free trial software and interactive activities via the Internet underpins most of the projects. A slow dial-up connection to the Internet might quickly turn the projects from fun to frustrating.

Have you got what it takes? If yes, bring this book home and get ready to embark on an adventure to unlock the fun that's waiting inside your home computer. But as any Boy or Girl Scout knows, you shouldn't hit the trail or head to the campground without first making sure you're prepared. That's the job of Chapter 1, "Is Your PC Ready?," which contains quick exercises to ensure your computer is ready to go and its web surfing protection is up-to-date. With that bit of homework under your belt, you'll be set to explore any of the chapters in any order you like.

Is Your PC Ready?

To reap the full benefits of the projects in this book, your PC and Internet link must meet certain minimum performance requirements. The stage-setting topics in this chapter will check to ensure that your PC is equipped to deliver a rewarding experience as you explore each project and that it is protected when accessing the Internet.

In this chapter you'll

- Determine if your home PC has what it takes for you to enjoy the projects
- Review a list of products, which you might already own, needed for some of the activities
- Review a guide of suggested features to look for if you are shopping for a new desktop or laptop PC
- Follow some steps to ensure your PC is protected against viruses, spyware, adware, and adult content before you surf the Web to download software used in many of the projects

A Quick Gear Check

For many of you, your PC is already rip-roaring and ready to go, so this chapter might not be necessary for you. How do you know if you need this chapter? Overall, nearly any desktop or laptop PC purchased since 2002 that includes the

Windows XP operating system does the trick. If you've got what it takes, skip ahead to the second portion of this chapter, which deals with protecting your PC and then feel free to dive right into Chapter 2, "Get Creative with Digital Pictures."

For a more in-depth set of suggested home computer features, check out the section "PC Shopping Guide" in this chapter for tips on buying a new desktop or laptop computer. Even if you are not looking for a new system, compare the suggested features to those of your present PC to see if it meets or exceeds the items listed.

Beyond a good PC, there are some key additional ingredients needed for many of the projects. In each chapter, project-specific materials lists are provided, along with buying tips for any hardware or software you might need to purchase. These key additional ingredients include

- A CD or DVD burner
- A high-speed DSL or cable link to the Internet
- An email account
- A digital camera or scanner
- A webcam
- A PC microphone
- A digital camcorder
- A DVD player connected to a TV
- Optional home network

The purpose of the list above is not to send you on an immediate unbridled shopping spree. Many of these items are only needed for a couple of projects in just one chapter of the book. Take it one step at a time. The materials list associated with each project leverages free trial software whenever possible and offers options at varying price points for any hardware needed.

That said, if the last time your PC was considered cutting edge was circa 1995, you might already be thinking of buying a new one. In the next section I offer a few buying tips that should help simplify the experience.

PC Shopping Guide

The PC shopping experience for novices can feel like an overwhelming trek into the unknown. To lend a hand, this section provides plenty of tips and suggestions for what to look for when you embark on the journey. The shopping tips are divided into three parts:

- Buying a desktop PC designed for multimedia creativity
- Selecting a laptop aimed at home multimedia versus on-the-go business use
- An introduction to a new and exciting life form in the world of consumer computing, the entertainment PC (also called a Media Center or Digital Entertainment PC)

Buying Tips for a Home Desktop PC

Here lies one whose name was writ in water.

The early nineteenth century English poet John Keats asked to have these words inscribed on his tombstone. This resigned acknowledgment of impermanence and the fleeting nature of life is not unlike the feeling I have offering advice on what features to look for when buying a new PC. Technology advances at such a blinding pace that any nugget of advice given is instantly obsolete. Although some technical specifics change on a daily basis, there are enduring basic strategies to use when shopping for a desktop PC. These include high performance (if multimedia creativity and gaming are important to your family), a large hard disk to store audio and visual digital files, and lots of system memory (RAM).

For up-to-date buying advice, try doing a search via Google (http://www.google.com) using the terms *PC buying advice*. Check out recent articles or websites including any tips from reputable sources, such as *PC World Magazine*.

Another helpful resource is the handy web tool Intel maintains to help consumers analyze what microprocessor they need to match their home computing environment. To find the Intel microprocessor selection tool, visit http://www.intel.com and on the opening page, enter `PC decision tool` in the search box located at the top of the screen. When the search results return, find and click the link for Intel Helps You Find the Right PC. This animated web resource recommends a microprocessor for a desktop or laptop based on your responses to friendly, nontechnical questions, as shown in Figure 1.1.

FIGURE 1.1

Intel's animated web resource recommends a microprocessor for a desktop or laptop based on home usage model questions.

Here's my two cents on what features I suggest you look for in a new home desktop PC that will complement the projects in this book:

note Windows XP and XP Pro were the latest versions of Microsoft's operating system for personal computers at the time this book was written. A new version of Windows is on the roadmap for 2006, so check to ensure the system you are buying has Microsoft's latest and greatest.

- Windows XP operating system (required for the projects in this book). If you can swing the few extra bucks for Windows XP Pro, go for it. This version of the operating system contains additional features especially attractive for home networking.

- Lots of RAM. I consider 256MB of RAM a minimum, with 512MB recommended especially for demanding multimedia tasks.

- A good microprocessor. Any PC with a processor operating at 1.5GHz or higher can be used to do the projects in this book.

- USB 2.0 and FireWire ports. These are high performance ports used to link a PC to peripherals, such as printers, digital cameras, and external hard drives. If you have a digital camcorder, buy a PC with a built-in FireWire port because this gives you a huge advantage when it comes to using the video-editing software discussed in Chapter 4, "Lights, Camera, Action!"

- A DVD burner that can burn DVD and CD blanks is a great investment. You'll be able to play music CDs and DVD movies and, more importantly, burn standard CDs and blank DVDs for home movies or large storage backups. Ask for a dual-layer model that can accept either + or - DVD blanks.

A Lot of Brains to Pick

A host of brain chips are used in today's home desktop PCs. To match the multimedia and creativity projects in this book I suggest buying a PC with a high-performance microprocessor, such as a Pentium 4, or comparable brain chip, operating at 2.8GHz or higher. I'm not saying this is an absolute minimum by any stretch. Budget models using an Intel Celeron D, or comparable processor, operating at or above 2GHz are viable, albeit lower performance, alternatives.

In the end, it's all about what your budget can swing and making sure you have enough horsepower to make doing the projects fun and not frustrating.

If you opt to buy a system with a Pentium 4 processor, look for a model featuring Hyper Threading Technology. *Hyper Threading Technology* refers to a feature that makes the Windows XP operating system think it has two virtual microprocessors at its disposal to divide and conquer demanding tasks.

For the best long-term investment, see if PCs with dual-core microprocessors are available. At the time of this writing, Intel and others in the chip industry were announcing plans for dual-core processors that essentially give a home desktop computer two actual brains. Initial offerings may be available by the time you read this. A PC with two brains would be ideally suited to tackle any of the multimedia projects in this book while simultaneously managing other tasks, such as web surfing, email, you name it.

- 100GB or larger capacity hard disk. If you really get turned on by the photo, video, and music creativity projects in this book, you'll soon find yourself working with huge files. For example, a file created by recording video from a digital camcorder at the highest quality setting (DV-AVI) can require more than 4GB of disk storage to accommodate one hour of action!

- Local area network port (Ethernet port) for home wired networking. This is a must-have minimum, and fortunately is rapidly becoming a standard feature on desktop PCs, even bargain basement models. Check to see if the model also offers wireless (Wi-Fi) networking, which eliminates the need to string a cable to the PC to have it join a home network (assuming you have a wireless network in place).

Buying Tips for a Home Laptop PC

When shopping for a laptop, use the features outlined above as a general guide. Budget laptops using a Celeron M, or comparable brain chips, are available for about $1,000. For a system that will best match the projects in this book, consider a laptop based on Intel Centrino Mobile Technology. *Centrino Mobile Technology* incorporates a tuned set of ingredients, including a microprocessor designed specifically for laptops and to deliver a balance of performance and good battery life. Another hallmark of Centrino Mobile Technology is a built-in wireless network transceiver (to make it easy to join a home wireless network or access public Wi-Fi hotspots).

Additional features to consider for a home multimedia-enhanced laptop include a large widescreen format display to make DVD movie watching like a mini theater experience, and a Bluetooth wireless transceiver to support the growing number of peripherals, such as advanced keyboards and mouse devices, that use this short-range wireless technology.

Introducing the Entertainment PC

In Chapter 8, "Enjoy Your PC's Digital Media in the Family Room," I'll show you how to link your Internet-connected PC to your home TV and stereo. You'll learn about adapters that leverage a home wireless or wired network to deliver all the digital photo, video, and music files sitting on your PC's hard disk to the consumer electronics gear in the family room. If the notion of bringing your TV, stereo, personal digital video recorder, home network, the Internet, and personal computing together to create a hybrid experience sounds intriguing, you're a candidate for a new breed of cat called an *entertainment PC*.

Entertainment PCs, which also go by the names of Media Center PCs or Digital Entertainment Centers, represent an entirely new way to bridge the gap between consumer electronics entertainment gear and the world of the PC and Internet. These amazing boxes, some of which look like sleek stereo components, combine the functionality of a home's stereo, TV tuner, personal TV digital video recorder (DVR) with all of the features a high-end, Internet-connected computer brings to the table. You can pop one of these babies into your family room to augment your existing entertainment gear or to start fresh with an all-in-one box solution.

The Shuttle XPC entertainment PC shown in Figure 1.2 and the HP Digital Entertainment Center shown in Figure 1.3 are remarkable on several counts. Designed for the family room and to be connected to a TV and stereo, these systems can function as a full PC, play and digitally record TV programs (a TiVo–like function), display digital photo albums, tune in to FM radio, and play music and DVD video discs. If linked to a home network and a DSL or cable connection to the Internet, an entertainment PC can open the door to enjoying Internet streaming music and Hollywood movie download services.

FIGURE 1.2

The Shuttle XPC is one example of the many forms of entertainment PC available today. Measuring 9×8.5×13 inches, it is well suited for placement in a family room cabinet along with the home stereo.

FIGURE 1.3

Hewlett–Packard's Digital Entertainment Center is a good example of an entertainment PC that looks like a piece of traditional stereo gear.

And last, but certainly not least, most entertainment PCs use Microsoft's remote control, menu-driven Media Center Edition of the Windows XP operating system. Menus that are easy to see, easy to operate, and designed for a family room environment make running an entertainment PC a breeze using either the wireless remote control or keyboard.

In terms of cost, expect to pay from $1,200 to $2,500 for an entertainment PC.

Make Sure Your PC Is Protected

Most of the projects in this book require surfing the Web and downloading trial programs, which, in turn, means repeated exposure to the wonders as well as the pitfalls of today's Internet. Every week it seems there's a story in the newspaper about the latest computer virus scare.

Unfortunately, viruses are not the only spooky things flying around the Internet looking for vulnerable targets. There are worms, malware, and tons of spyware and other parasites your PC can pick up on the information superhighway that can drag your PC's performance to its knees.

Although I would never put any projects in this book that would put your PC in danger, the fact is you'll be downloading a lot of programs from the Internet to do the activities in this book. And because any PC connected to the Internet is a potential target, it's important to follow the steps below to ensure your PC has a good suit of armor.

Update Windows XP

The folks at Microsoft have been taking it on the chin for many years for the security weaknesses found in the Windows operating system and the Internet Explorer browser. I've had my share of unfortunate experiences with viruses, worms, and other nasty bugs infecting my Windows-based PCs. But Microsoft's efforts in the past few years to build a more secure Windows XP environment are steps in the right direction.

The Windows XP operating system (both Home and Pro editions) offers automatic updates and reminders to help keep your PC safe. But it's up to you to respond to reminders and allow Windows XP to automatically handle updates. At the time of this writing, the most important update you can possibly make to Windows XP is to install Service Pack 2. This update to the Windows XP operating system provides numerous tweaks, fixes, and new features that plug many security holes.

There are several easy ways to determine if your Windows XP system already has Service Pack 2 installed. On the Windows XP desktop, click the Start button and select the Control Panel link. Assuming you are in the default Control Panel display mode with a screen stating Pick a Category (as opposed to the optional Classic View mode),

note Skip to the next step in this section if you have already successfully updated your Windows XP operating system and you know you have Service Pack 2 installed.

look for a multicolored shield marked Security Center. If you see the shield, you have Service Pack 2 installed. If you don't, you should strongly consider upgrading.

If you have ignored past Windows XP prompts to update your system and need to install Service Pack 2, follow these actions:

1. With your PC powered up and connected to the Internet, you can quickly access the Windows Update service by pointing your browser to http://www. windowsupdate.com. Follow the onscreen instructions to begin the update process.

2. Windows XP now checks to see if you have the latest version of the operating system's update software program. If it's not found, you'll be directed to download and install the utility program. After installation, the program offers multiple options, as shown in Figure 1.4. In most cases I recommend using the Express Install wizard to identify and install any needed updates.

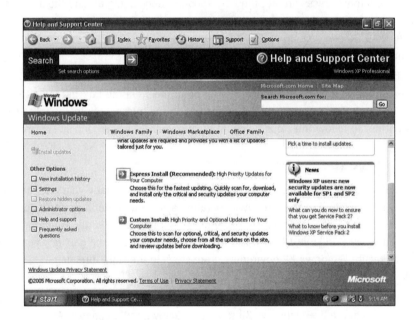

FIGURE 1.5

The Windows Update screen serves as an information resource and launch pad for updating the operating system.

3. At this stage it's very difficult to predict what your report will determine and recommend. If you have not been running the update utility on a regular basis, you will most likely be asked to download and install Service Pack 2 from Microsoft. If this is the case, step 4 is for you.

4. After Service Pack 2 is installed on your system, you are guided through a series of steps managed by the Security Center program to enable firewall protection and automatic updates (so that Windows XP can keep itself up to date with the latest fixes and features). I encourage you to pursue all of these services.

After all the settings are in place, the status of your system's protection is displayed by the Security Center master program, as shown in Figure 1.5. Does the Security Center display on your now-updated PC show Virus Protection as being on? If yes, you're set to surf the Web. If not, and you see a warning stating that virus protection is not installed, follow the actions in the next section.

> **caution** If you receive an update request to install Service Pack 2, carefully read any information provided advising you to backup your data and so forth in preparation for this operation. For a comprehensive tutorial on what you should do before installing Service Pack 2, go to http://www.microsoft.com and on the opening page enter **Service Pack 2** in the search box at the upper-right area of the screen display.
>
> When the next page displays the results of your search, find and click the link labeled Download Windows XP SP2. When the screen refreshes, read all of the documentation associated with the alert titled Important: Follow These Steps Before Installing Windows XP SP2 to prevent potential conflicts with other software on your computer.

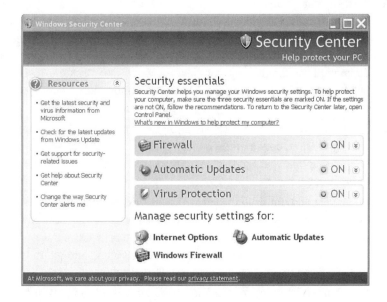

FIGURE 1.5

The main Security Center program screen shows the status of three levels of protection—firewall, automatic updates, and virus protection.

Protect Your PC from Viruses

Because you'll be directed to do a lot of web surfing and file downloading throughout this book, it is absolutely necessary to have virus protection installed. PCs shipped in the past three to four years have routinely come out of the box with a time-limited trial version of one of the major virus protection software products. If you elected to install and update one of these included programs or you have purchased antivirus software separately, you can move on to the next section.

If your PC is without any protection start fresh by following the steps below to download and test drive a major virus protection software package. Many choices are available, but we'll use the free trial of McAfee's virus protection software as a model.

tip *Firewall* protection helps make your PC invisible to other computers and hackers lurking in cyberspace. The firewall protection offered by Service Pack 2 is not the only game in town. Other popular firewall programs to help guard your PC from outside attackers and snoops include ZoneAlarm (http://www.zonelabs.com), BlackICE PC Protection (http://www.networkice.com), Norton Personal Firewall (http://www.symantec.com), and McAfee Personal Firewall Plus (http://www.mcafee.com).

To find and download the free trial version of McAfee's virus protection software, follow these steps:

1. Turn on your PC and point your browser to http://www.mcafee.com. On the opening page, find the Download Product Updates & Upgrades section and click the Home User link. When the page refreshes, find and click the downloads dropdown menu and click the Free Trial Software link. When the page refreshes, scroll down until you find the entry for McAfee Virus Scan. Click the 15-Day Free Trial button, followed by clicking the Add to Cart button. Next, when the screen refreshes, click the No Thanks—Don't Upgrade My Order button.

2. The next screen shows the Create an Account page. Fill in the information and click the I Agree button at the bottom of the screen. A new screen displays announcing that your order is being processed. When that completes, click the Go to My Account button.

3. When your account page displays, scroll down and find the Download/Install/Update associated with the McAfee VirusScan trial listing. This directs you to look for an email message sent to activate your account. Find the email, follow the instructions to activate your account, and return to the McAfee website to log in and download your free trial software.

4. From here it's your job to follow the onscreen wizards and instructions to install and activate the McAfee virus protection software. After installation you'll see a small shield symbol in the lower right of your Windows XP desktop.

Yikes! I realize that was a lot of work just to get a free trial software download. But you now have a virus protection software package faithfully standing guard over your PC's health. If you like this product, you can opt to purchase it at any point during the 15-day trial. Other virus protection packages to consider include Norton Internet Security (http://www.symantec.com), Trend Micro PC-cillin Internet Security (http://www.trendmicro.com), and Panda Antivirus Platinum (http://www.pandasoftware.com).

note When you visit the McAfee website, you might find the specific steps for finding and downloading the free trial software have changed from those cited here. The key is to search for a link to free trial software.

Protect Your PC from Spyware and Adware

If you already know about spyware and adware and have blocking and cleaning software installed, you may skip this step. If you have no idea what spyware and adware are, hang on to your hat and get ready for a shock!

Have you noticed your PC and Internet surfing response time getting slower and slower? Do you have random pop-ups appearing on your screen, even when you're not surfing the web? It's possible the problem is spyware and/or adware. Five or six hidden spyware or adware programs can have a negligible hit on your system's performance, but what happens when hundreds are hanging on like barnacles weighing down your PC?

With a firewall in place and virus protection software on patrol, it's time to fight debilitating *spyware* and *adware*. Believe it or not, these little programs are downloaded and installed on your PC without your permission! These annoying and performance-draining pests find their way to your PC's hard disk as you surf the Web and especially when you download software.

The purpose of a spyware program is to monitor your actions and report them to an advertiser or, much more alarming, a hacker. The advertisers want to know where you surf and what you do as a tactic to sell products and services or to determine what websites and activities are most popular with consumers. And you can just imagine what a hacker might be up to! As time goes on, your PC might be accumulating a horde of spyware programs humming along in the background without your knowledge.

Adware programs are unannounced hitchhikers that come along for the ride when you download trial software or free programs from the Internet. They can run when you are on or off the Internet, popping up randomly to clutter your screen with unsolicited promotional messages.

I don't mean to freak you out. The overwhelming majority of spyware and adware do not pose a fatal threat to the health of your PC. But it's time to park your PC in the dry dock and see what's possibly hiding below the water line!

Lots of great anti-spyware and adware blocking and cleaning programs are available. For illustration purposes, follow the actions below to download the free anti-spyware program I use weekly to scrape the hull of my PC:

1. Point your browser to http://www.download.com (this is one of the many web clearinghouses for shareware, trial software, and free programs that is used extensively throughout this book). On the opening page, look at the upper-left area and find an empty horizontal box labeled Search. Enter **Spybot** and make sure the search term box is set to In Windows. Click the Go button.

2. When the page refreshes to show a list of products, scroll down and find Spybot–Search and Destroy. This is a free program that nearly 50 million people have downloaded from the Download.com site alone! Click the Download button associated with this program and when the Windows File Download dialog box appears, save the program file to a directory you'll remember.

3. When the Download Complete dialog box appears, click the Open button to install the program. Follow the onscreen dialog boxes to select the language, file directory, special features, and the addition of a desktop icon to run the program. Leave the Use Internet Explorer Protection (SDHelper) box checked, click the Next button, and then click Install.

4. When the installation is done, click Finish to start the program. A Legal Stuff dialog box appears explaining that if you clean out the spyware planted by advertisers, you might not be able to use the host programs. So far, I've never had any program I want to run fail because I cleaned out spyware from my PC (see Caution regarding TurboTax 2002 and AIM). Click the OK button and a compatibility technical warning appears (read it over if you like) followed by a dialog box announcing that a backup of your PC's registry will be created in the event you need to restore your system to its state prior to running Spybot. Click the Create Registry Backup button and wait until the Next button turns green.

5. Click the Next button and then the Search for Updates button. The program now goes to its home base to ensure that the latest filter and detection files are downloaded to your PC.

caution If you are using TurboTax 2002, you might find that a spyware cleaner such as Spybot will detect and recommend eliminating elements required to run the program. TurboTax 2002 used an online registration/validation process that embedded some behind-the-scenes software monitoring utilities that Spybot and other similar programs might flag as bad guys. TurboTax 2003 and beyond does not have this feature. Some spyware cleaners, such as Webroot's Spy Sweeper, have the smarts to warn you before removing TurboTax 2002 monitoring programs and files. The free Spybot program does not. If you are not sure, consult the TurboTax support webpage at http://www.intuit.com/support/.

If you use America Online's Instant Messenger service (AIM), it often installs background software called WildTangent to support games hosted by the service (see http://www.wildtangent.com). Spybot might detect the WildTangent entries and suggest they be removed. If that happens, unclick the box associated with the WildTangent entry after Spybot flags it.

After any needed update has been installed, click the Next button and then click the Immunize This System button. A message appears announcing that your PC is now protected from thousands of spyware entities.

6. Click the Next button and a dialog box gives you three options: Read Tutorial, Read Help File, and Start Using the Program. Select the button to start the program.

Don't let this program's humble, retro look fool you. It's a relentless hunter and killer of spyware. Because you just installed the program and no updates were probably required, use the following steps as a reference to detect and remove the spyware that might be lurking inside your system:

1. Click the Search and Destroy icon in the upper-left corner of the screen, followed by clicking the Check for Problems button (has a magnifying glass icon), as shown in Figure 1.6. In future sessions you'll start by clicking the Search for Updates icon.

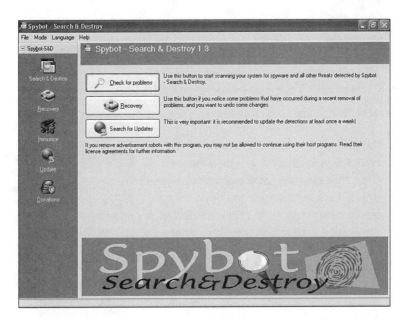

FIGURE 1.6

Spybot might lack flare and a stylish interface but it packs a punch when it comes to finding and destroying spyware.

2. Grab a cup of coffee or take a brief walk around the block. A first-time Spybot scan can take a few minutes or up to 30 minutes or more (depending on the depth of your parasite build up and the amount of data stored on your hard drive).

3. After an exhaustive scan of your entire system, Spybot displays a list of all the spyware detected, as shown in Figure 1.7. If spyware is present, click the Fix Selected Problems button at the top of the screen.

FIGURE 1.7

Did your screen look something like this mess after running Spybot for the first time? It's a real eye opener when you discover all the crud that's been hitchhiking on your system.

4. Clicking the Fix Selected Problems button causes Spybot to create a system restore point. This ensures that you can restore your system back to its current pre–Spybot state before eliminating hidden spyware. You may never need to restore your system, but if an anti-spyware program happens to eliminate something that a legitimate program installed on your PC needs, then you'd be able to restore your computer back to its previous state and be no worse for the wear.

5. It might take a few minutes for the restore point to be set via Windows XP, but when this action ends you will be prompted to delete all the spyware detected.

Don't you feel better now, knowing you just blasted away a ton of spyware tartar that's been clogging up your PC's engine? Chances are good you'll immediately notice improved performance and

note Using multiple spyware and adware programs helps increase your chances of eliminating as much crud as possible. Another free program I use in parallel with Spybot is Ad-aware (http://www.lavasoftusa.com).

At the time of this writing, Microsoft was making its initial contribution to the battle with the beta version of its Windows AntiSpyware technology that the company claims blocks 50 ways spyware attempts to enter your system via the Internet. To find and download this program, go to http://www.microsoft.com and key in **AntiSpyware** in the search box in the upper-right corner of the opening page. Find and click the link for Microsoft Windows AntiSpyware home page. By the time you read this, the full release version should be available.

responsiveness. To keep your PC in tiptop running order, get into the habit of updating and running Spybot, or whatever spyware you select, every week.

Are Your Adult Content Shields Up?

If you plan to pursue the projects in this book as a family activity involving the kiddies, you might want to investigate Internet adult content filtering programs. These programs work by intercepting your browser addresses and search engine requests to block access if they match known adult content sites. These programs, under your control, can also be directed to avoid hate group sites and other material you deem inappropriate.

caution Using Spybot, Adaware, and even Microsoft's new Windows AntiSpyware together does not guarantee that every possible bit of junk is cleaned off your PC. Just like viruses, new spyware and adware entities are being created and turned loose every minute. At best, experts tell us that you'll nail from 60%–70% of the stuff that's out there. As with virus software maintenance, it's important to update your spyware and adware protection at least once a week.

Many Internet filter and access management programs also offer features to control when and for how long a child may access the Internet, as well as tools to track email exchanges and chat room activity.

Loads of good filtering software is available and many makers offer free trials. Check out the following product websites:

- CYBERsitter at http://www.cybersitter.com (10-day free trial available)
- Net Nanny at http://www.netnanny.com (15-day free trial available)
- KidsWatch at http://www.kidswatch.com (15-day free trial available)

For general advice on managing your child's access to the Internet, see http://www.safekids.com, http://www.safeteens.com, and http://www.software4parents.com.

What's next? Do you own a digital camera? Are you thinking of purchasing one? Are your friends and family emailing digital snaps to you but you're not sure how to get pictures on a PC, edit them, and share via the Internet? Are you interested in getting creative with your digital snaps?

The next chapter covers the basics of how to use a digital camera and home computer to capture, edit, and share your digital photos. Using a flatbed scanner as an alternative way to get photos on your PC is also explored, along with just-for-laughs projects, such as one to make a portrait photo talk or another to put your face on the cover of a mock sports magazine.

Get Creative with Digital Pictures

My first digital camera experience came when I purchased a Sony Mavica camera in 1998. It was heavy, bulky, cost a whopping $600, and the digital snaps it took were stored on a floppy disk. It was a miracle in its day. I could get a fairly decent 3×5 inch print from the pictures I took, and it could even capture a few seconds of postage stamp size digital video you could play back on a PC!

In the years and digital cameras that followed that Mavica, I've had a blast pushing the edge of all the fun things you can do. So it is frustrating when I discover that most of the audiences I work with are stuck in a rut. They own a digital camera, have learned how to get pictures on a PC, and they know how to share their pictures with friends and family using email. But that's it. They know there's so much more to do, but don't know where to start. If I'm talking about you, you've come to the right place.

This chapter is designed to take your digital photography to the next level of creativity. We'll start with the basics of editing and attaching a photo to email. The remaining projects will introduce you to some really unusual fun, including putting your digital mug on a magazine cover or making a digital portrait talk.

Skills and Gear Check

Before you jump into the projects, take a quick look below at the list of assumptions I'm making about your skills and gear. If you happen to be in the market for a digital camera or scanner, check out the "Shopping for a Digital Camera or Scanner?" sidebar.

Key assumptions:

- Your personal computer has a connection to the Internet (high-speed DSL or cable is preferred, and for some of the projects, it is required).

- You have an Internet email service account (such as America Online, MSN, Yahoo! mail, and so on) and you know how to send an email message.

- You own a digital camera or scanner and you have installed any software the manufacturer has provided.

- You have a color printer or you are familiar with photo print alternatives, such as online services (Snapfish, Ofoto, and dotPhoto) or photo CDs made from your film rolls.

- You are using Microsoft Windows XP. All onscreen illustrations, dialog boxes, and pop-up menu samples are based on Windows XP. If you are using an earlier version, such as Windows 95 or Windows 98, I strongly recommend you consider upgrading before doing any of the projects in this chapter, and the entire book for that matter. Windows XP offers a host of features designed to support multimedia. It is well worth the approximately $70 required to purchase the upgrade software kit from your local computer or office supply store.

- Your PC has one or more USB connectors (this includes most any PC purchased new since 2000).

Shopping for a Digital Camera or Scanner?

The number one question I get about buying a handheld digital camera centers on the mysterious megapixel performance numbers (2.0, 3.2, 4.0 megapixels). I've found that most families are very pleased with a 3.2–4 megapixel camera that takes pictures that look good as 4×6 inch prints. Expect to pay between $200 and $300.

Digital cameras today use solid state chip technology to store your snapshots. Postage stamp-size Secure Digital (SD) mini cards are the most popular, along with CompactFlash, MCC, and Sony's memory stick. I recommend a digital camera that uses SD cards for storage. If the camera comes with a small capacity SD card (32MB, for example) buy a 256MB SD card to ensure you'll have lots of storage capacity.

You need to know about two things when buying a scanner—bit depth and dots per inch (DPI). Go for a scanner offering 24-bit depth and at least 600 dots per inch resolution. And if digitizing slides is important to you, go for a model with a slide/negative film adapter.

Expect to pay $80 to $150 for a good home scanner. For example, the Microtek (http://www.microtek.com) ScanMaker 5900 offers 48-bit technology and 4800×2400dpi resolution. It goes for about $150. And, for around $80, you can get an HP Scanjet 3670 flatbed scanner with up to 1200dpi and 48-bit technology.

Project: Get Digital Pictures on Your PC from a Digital Camera

Using the step-by-step instructions that follow, I'll show you how to transfer pictures from a digital camera to a PC using a standard USB cable. In the next section I'll also show you how to scan printed photos onto your PC.

Step 1: Connect Your Camera

Before you do anything, get out your digital camera, find the USB cable that came with the product, and pull out the instruction booklet.

Using your camera's manual as a guide, find the USB connector on the body of your camera. Figure 2.1 shows the location of the USB port on a typical HP digital camera. After the cable is inserted into the port, connect the other end of the USB cable to an available USB port on your PC.

note Not all digital cameras offer a USB port and cable. Consult your camera's instruction booklet if your camera uses another method for transferring photos to a PC. In all likelihood you will be asked to remove the camera's memory card and use a USB cable-connected or built-in solid state card reader.

FIGURE 2.1

As is the case here, for many cameras the USB port is located on the side. However, the port location can vary depending on the camera model and manufacturer.

At this point you should place your camera in photo review mode and turn it on.

Step 2: Transfer Pictures to Your PC

I really like the simple way the My Pictures portion of Windows XP handles this task. I have several photo-editing packages on my PC and each tries to jump in and offer help when I connect my camera. Frankly, when the dialog boxes for these programs appear, I cancel them out and take advantage of the clean and universal solution that Windows XP offers. Here is how it works:

tip Most cameras also allow you to eject the memory card with your stored photos from your camera and connect it to your PC through a USB connected multicard (SD/CompactFlash/memory stick) reader. Just remove the card from your camera, pop it in the reader, and Windows XP transfers them to your PC using the same steps as when transferring directly from a camera.

External USB card readers go for about $30 to $50 and can be easily found at your local office or computer supply store. Many new PCs also come with a card reader built into the front panel.

1. After your camera is connected to your PC and powered on, a Camera Detected dialog box should appear, asking which program listed in the box you want to use to transfer your photos. For this exercise, select/highlight with your mouse pointer the Microsoft Scanner and Camera Wizard—Download Pictures from a Camera or Scanner and click OK.

2. Now your photos are transferred from the camera's memory and the Welcome to the Scanner and Camera Wizard page appears. Click Next.

3. The Choose Pictures to Copy window appears, showing thumbnails of the photos stored on your camera's memory card (see Figure 2.2). You may transfer all the images or deselect the check boxes next to any of them to block the transfer as you like. Click Next.

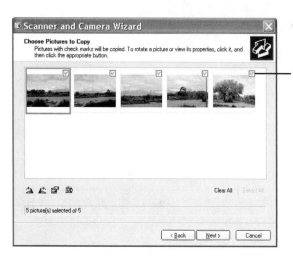

A picture's check box must be enabled (checked) for Windows XP to transfer it to your PC.

FIGURE 2.2

The Choose Pictures to Copy window presents thumbnail images of the photos on your camera's memory.

4. The Picture Name and Destination dialog box appears and presents two input fields. In the top field, type the base name you want for all photos in this group. For example, if the photos are of your summer vacation, you might type Summer in the top box. Windows XP applies that name along with a number to each picture (Summer001, Summer002, and so on). The second field shows the location (path) of the folder where the pictures will be stored. You may accept this default (usually the My Pictures folder), but I like to put my photos in folders with names that help me quickly find them in the future.

5. Click the Make New Folder button to create and name a new folder in which you can store your pictures. Also take note of the Delete Pictures from This Device After Copying check box (see Figure 2.3). If you'd like to clear out your camera's memory after copying all the photos to your hard disk, make sure to enable this check box. Click Next when you're ready to proceed.

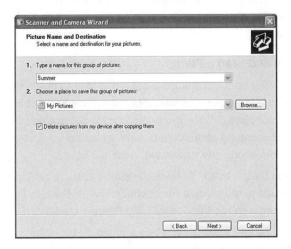

FIGURE 2.3

The Picture Name and Destination dialog box enables you to assign a group name to your imported photos, direct where they are to be stored, and gives you the option to clear your camera's memory following the transfer of images.

6. A progress bar shows the digital photos being transferred to your folder. When this is completed, an Other Options window appears. Select Nothing, I'm Finished Working with These Pictures.

7. The Completing the Scanner and Camera Wizard window appears. Click Finish and you are automatically taken to the folder in which your photos are stored to see thumbnails of them.

Project: Get a Digital Scan on Your PC

The same concepts with the digital camera example I showed you in the previous section apply here, also. Although your scanner might include a program to transfer and edit images, I recommend using Windows XP's Scanner and Camera Wizard, which is accessible through the My Pictures folder.

Step 1: Connect Your Scanner

Make sure your scanner has been properly installed and is connected to the PC using the cable type provided. Most scanners automatically turn on when the host system's PC is powered up. If, however, your scanner includes an on/off switch, make sure the unit is turned on.

Turning on the scanner may automatically fire up the management software provided with the product. If that happens, follow the onscreen instructions. For now, cancel any program dialog box that appears because we'll use the Windows XP Scanner and Camera Wizard.

Step 2: Place and Scan a Photo

Before you actually scan anything, it's not a bad idea to check the glass surface of your scanner to ensure it's clean. A clean scanning surface helps ensure that you get a nice, clear scan of your photos. Once you're ready to begin, position the photo in the upper-left edge of the scanning area. (Consult your operating manual to identify that location.) When your photo is properly positioned, close the lid.

Some scanners have a button to manually start a scan. In most cases you'll use software to start and manage the process. To illustrate how this works, let's walk through how to use your scanner with the Windows XP My Pictures utility:

1. With the PC and scanner on, place a photo on the scanner's glass plate, close the lid, and then bring up the My Pictures window by opening the Windows Start menu at the lower left edge of the screen and clicking the My Pictures icon.

2. On the Picture Tasks menu at the upper left of the My Pictures screen, click on the Get Pictures from Camera or Scanner button. Next, the Which Device Do You Want to Use? dialog box appears. Among the listed devices is an icon for your scanner. Click on the scanner icon and enter the Scanner and Camera Wizard program, as shown in Figure 2.4.

note Did you know you can still go digital and not buy a scanner or toss your trusty film camera? Next time you turn in a roll of film for development, ask about getting a photo CD. Your snaps are burned on a disc you can load into your PC's CD or DVD drive and copy or transfer to your hard disk. From there, you can do anything the digital camera crowd can enjoy.

FIGURE 2.4

Here is what the Scanner and Camera Wizard opening screen looks like after the print photo has been scanned.

3. Using the menu choices, you can preview a scan, decide to scan as a color or black-and-white photo, set the resolution, and even do preliminary cropping. Unless you know specifically what you want to change, you should leave all the settings alone for now and accept the defaults. Click Next.

4. Tell the wizard where you want to save the scanned photo and click Next.

5. At this point, the scanning process begins to transform your print into a digital image!

6. Now you can use any photo-editing program to further work on the scanned image to your heart's content.

Project: Send a Photo Using Email

Sending one or more digital photos as an attachment to an email is, as I noted at the beginning of the chapter, the basic skill most consumers master within hours of using their first digital camera. Not sure how it works? Then read on.

Nearly all email services I've encountered use an *attach file* routine to link a photo to an email message. We'll use my Yahoo! free email account to illustrate. Note that I'm not advocating that you use Yahoo! email in lieu of your existing email service. Instead, glance over the steps below to give you a feel for what the process involves. In all likelihood you'll discover that your email service uses similar steps and options.

Materials

To complete this project you'll need

- Some way to access the Internet (dial-up regular phone line, high-speed DSL, or cable modem service)
- An email account with a service provider, such as America Online, MSN, or EarthLink, or a free email account such as Yahoo! Mail
- Email address of the person(s) who will receive your photo

Time

Less than 30 minutes if you have an email account established and you've sent text emails.

Step 1: Start Your Email Application

The process for starting up your email program varies with the type of client software you use. America Online users typically have an icon on their desktop. Outlook and Outlook Express users can usually activate those programs from the Windows Start menu. Finally, users of web-based email clients like Yahoo! Mail or MSN Hotmail should use their web browser to open their online email account. If necessary for your email service, be sure to log in using your name and password.

Step 2: Construct a New Email Message

Before you can attach pictures to an email message, you need to create it. Usually this is done by clicking a button or menu item labeled Compose or Write Mail. When I open my Yahoo! email account, I'm presented with an opening screen with Check Mail, Compose, and Search Mail as my key options. Clicking Compose opens a new mail message. All email message windows have fields for entering the recipient's email address, a subject, and a message. You can fill these in either before or after attaching your photos.

Step 3: Attaching Your Photos

Most email programs also have buttons or menus that allow you to access other functions, including one for attaching files (photos in this case). Yahoo!, for example, has an Attach Files option button.

Clicking the Attach Files button presents a new screen, allowing you to find and attach files to your email (see Figure 2.5). You'll find most web-based email services use a similar format and approach.

In the case of the Yahoo! Mail service, clicking the Browse button opens the Choose File pop-up dialog box. If you used the Windows XP defaults, your photos should be found in the My Pictures folder (located in My Documents) or a subfolder of My Pictures.

Select the photo (or photos, if your email service allows you to select more than one file at a time) you want to attach to the email.

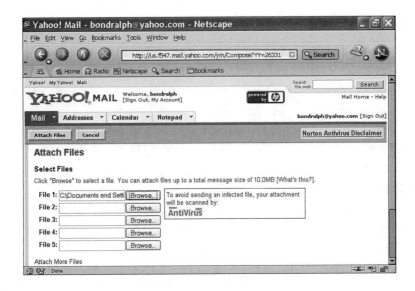

FIGURE 2.5

The attach files screen for Yahoo! email uses a format similar to most email programs.

With the target photo highlighted, click the button (usually labeled Open or Attach) to attach it to your email. Yahoo! requires that you click the Open button, which returns you to the Attach Files page. To complete the process, you need to click the Attach Files button once again to attach your selected files to the email and return to the email's message body.

At this stage, most web-based email services show you a progress bar as the file is sent via the Internet to your email service's computers. From there, you can attach more files or specify that you're finished with attachments (click Done in Yahoo!), which returns you to the main email message window. From there you need only click Send to send the message to its destination.

And that's it!

> **note** If you use a Windows-based email program (such as Outlook Express), after the file is attached to the email you need to click the Send button to place the completed message in your outbox. In some configurations the message is then sent to its recipient automatically. In others you may need to click the Send/Receive button to complete the process.

Project: Adjust, Crop, Rotate, Get the Red Eye out, and Add Text to a Digital Photo

I never tire of using my PC to edit digital photos. This project will help you master the classic steps of auto-adjusting, rotating, cropping, reducing/eliminating red eye, and adding text to a digital photo. These skills will help you fully exploit the remaining projects in this chapter.

Materials

To complete this project you'll need

- Personal computer connected to the Internet.
- Digital photos on your hard disk (from a digital camera, scanner, or Photo CD).
- Photo-editing software. This project uses a free and charming basic photo-editing program from http://www.snapfish.com, ideal for the first-time editor. In fact, it's a downright great little tool for quick fix actions on your digital snaps.

Time

About 2 hours to download the free Snapfish PhotoShow program, install it, and try the exercises on multiple test photo images. Add 30 minutes if you use a regular dial-up line to connect to the Internet.

Step 1: Download Snapfish PhotoShow Express

Use the following steps to download and install the Snapfish PhotoShow Express program to your PC:

1. Turn on your PC and connect to the Internet.

2. Type `http://www.snapfish.com` into your browser's address bar.

3. Look at the bottom of the opening web page and find the Snapfish PhotoShow Free Software button. Click it and a new illustrated screen appears, explaining what the program can do. Look for the Download button and click it.

4. Next, the Windows operating system fires up a File Download dialog box asking what you want to do with the file. Click Save and then use the browsing capabilities of the Save In drop-down menu to find your `Snapfish` folder under the Downloads folder.

5. Now you are ready to download and store the `SnapfishPhotoShow.exe` file on your hard disk. Click Save and the downloading process begins.

    If you are using a DSL or cable link to the Internet, this process will be fast because the file is small. Dial-up download time can vary wildly.

6. When the download is completed, a new dialog box appears with multiple choices. Click Open.

7. The Snapfish PhotoShow installation process begins. Follow the onscreen instructions to accept the license.

8. Next, you are asked to enter your Snapfish account. Don't worry, it's *free*. The folks at Snapfish are giving you this program hoping

> **tip** You are about to download data from the Internet. I like to store downloaded program files in special folders. So I recommend you use the My Computer interface (open the Start menu and click My Computer) to create a folder on your hard disk and name it Downloads. You can further organize things by creating a sub-folder and naming it Snapfish.

you'll order prints from them online. And I encourage you to do so after you edit a couple of keepers using the exercises below.

After you've registered with your email address and password, you'll find an icon on your Windows desktop to fire the program up.

Now it's time for the fun to start!

> **tip** The Snapfish PhotoShow editing program searches for photos in the My Pictures folder, so it's best to keep all your digital snaps in this folder.

Step 2: Launch Snapfish PhotoShow Express

To open PhotoShow Express, go to your Windows desktop and find and double-click the Snapfish PhotoShow Express program icon. If you can't find the icon on the desktop, open the Windows XP Start menu and select All Programs, Snapfish PhotoShow Express.

The program opens with a colorful, simple screen including a box on the left listing all the things you can do with the program including viewing and editing snaps, creating online photo albums, ordering prints, sharing images via the Internet, and creating photo gifts. Click the Organize button and you'll see a display on the right side showing photos and subfolders currently in your My Pictures folder. On the left side are two vertical tab areas, one called Albums, the other Shows, as shown in Figure 2.6. SnapFish PhotoShow uses a super simple tab and button navigation scheme that makes it possible to do nearly all operations with the click of a mouse.

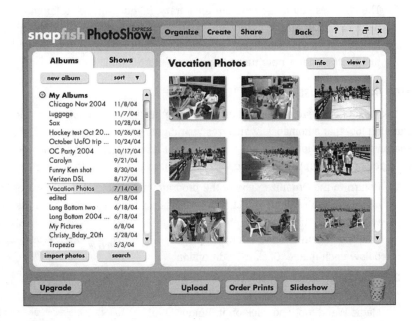

FIGURE 2.6

When you click the Organize button on the opening screen of Snapfish PhotoShow, you see a screen displaying an Albums and Shows area.

After you digitally edit a photo and save it, that's it. There's no going back. One rule of thumb in our family is to preserve all original digital snaps and edit only copies. This optional step does add extra work up front, but it's something that gives me piece of mind. The easiest way to make backup copies of your pictures before editing them is to use the My Pictures window (open the Windows Start menu and click My Pictures) and create a new folder (experiments, for example). Select the photos you want to work on, and, holding down the right mouse button, drag them to this new folder. On the context menu that appears, select Copy. This safety tip should be applied to all of the projects in this chapter.

Step 3: Rotating a Photo

Now that you've got PhotoShow up and running, let's find the photos you want to edit.

1. Use the vertical scrolling bar on the right edge of the My Albums section to find the photo you want to edit.

2. When you find the photo to edit, move your mouse pointer over it, or as the techies would say, mouse over the item. Automatically (without any clicking) a little menu appears below the photo with these choices: rotate right or left, print, email, delete, or edit.

3. With the photo still highlighted, click one of the rotate curved arrow symbols. In a flash, you'll see the photo displayed in its new orientation (a slower PC might take a few seconds). Go ahead, click at will. You can always return your photo to its original position.

4. The changes you make here are temporary. If you want the rotation to be permanent, click Edit on the little menu window and, presto, you'll go to the edit screen. At the bottom you can select Save a Copy. Doing this gives you the option to save the photo under a new name to preserve the original.

Step 4: Auto-adjust a Photo

Auto-adjust is one feature you find on nearly all photo-editing software packages. It's a stunning tool that automatically analyzes your digital photo to adjust color, brightness, and sharpness. I always let a program show me what it thinks should be done and then decide if I agree or not. Snapfish PhotoShow Express makes this a snap (no pun intended).

1. Return to the Organize page of the program and click on a photo folder listed in the My Albums tab. When you click a folder its photos are displayed in the right side work area. Mouse over the photos and note that once again a menu window appears below each image. Click the Edit option.

2. When your photo is displayed on the master editing page, look to the left, find the Auto-fix Magic Wand tool and click on it. Bingo. All of a sudden your photo might brighten and look better overall. This still gives me a rush!

note Rotating a digital photo works because the entire image is broken down into pixels. Each pixel, in turn, is represented by a code of zeros and ones. Your PC's brain can be used to re-order those codes to rotate an image and much more!

3. Now it's time to decide to keep the auto fixes or return to the original. Click the Undo button on the lower-left area or click Save. If you click Save a Copy, the Save Photo As dialog box gives you the option to provide a new name and direct where you want the altered photo to be stored on hard disk.

Step 5: Crop a Photo

With your sea legs now firmly planted on the deck of the good ship Snapfish PhotoShow, let's use it to crop a photo.

1. Find and highlight the photo you want to crop. The one I have selected for this example shows my sister Carol and my brother-in-law Chuck.

2. Click the Edit command in the small pop-up menu that appears below the photo when you mouse over it. This takes you to the editing page.

3. Find the set of tools on the far left and click the Crop tool. In a flash, an outline frame appears over the photo, as shown in Figure 2.7.

Note how the area outside of the frame is darkened. This is a visual clue that the darker area will be discarded after you set the frame boundary. I use lots of photo-editing tools and I really like the elegant and visual way Snapfish PhotoShow sets the stage for the cropping process.

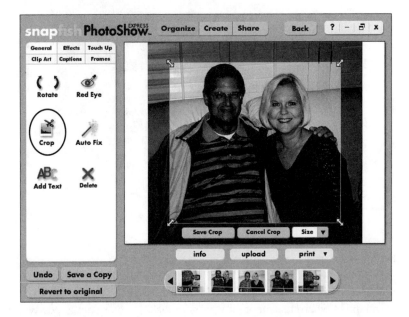

FIGURE 2.7

Click the crop icon and a frame is laid over your photo. The darkened area around the frame represents the areas to be cropped and discarded.

4. Using the mouse pointer (which now looks like a hand), place it anywhere inside the frame. By clicking the left mouse button, you can move the whole frame around with wild abandon.

5. You can also make the frame larger or smaller. Look at the corners of the floating frame and note the diagonal double arrow symbols. Grab one of these babies with your cursor and you can move the overall frame in or out to adjust the target area.

6. In addition to using the cropping tool to create a freehand trim job, note the three choices that float below the cropping frame (refer to Figure 2.7). You can save the cropped version of your picture, cancel the crop, or automatically crop the photo to fit a standard photo size. Click the down arrow on the Size button and you see a list of standard photo sizes. Try out several. This is a great tool for cropping images to a print size that will slip easily into standard photo frames.

7. When you are happy with the cropping frame click the Save Crop button. Just like that Snapfish PhotoShow Express crops your picture (see Figure 2.8).

FIGURE 2.8

After clicking the Save Crop button the new trimmed image is displayed.

8. If you're happy with the final result, click the Save a Copy button to name the file and direct where to store it on your hard disk. (If you're not happy with the result you can click the Revert to Original button.)

Step 6: Get the Red Out!

Here's one place where digital photography has it all over traditional film and prints. I have boxes and boxes of childhood family photos populated with otherworldly beings sporting spooky, glowing red eyes. Eliminating the eerie red glow from eyes caught in a camera flash is right up there with cropping and auto-adjusting as a key benefit of having your PC become a personal photo lab. Snapfish PhotoShow, as with all the programs I use, makes this process painless:

1. Click a folder from the My Albums tab that contains an image with the dreaded red-eye effect. Mouse over the image and click the Edit link.

2. With the image in the editing area, I suggest you first use the Auto-fix Magic Wand to tune up the overall image.

3. Next, find the Red Eye tool on the left that looks like a red outline symbol for an eye with an eye dropper pointing at the pupil. Click this icon and the messages "1. Click and Drag to Select a Red Eye" and "2. Fix a Red Eye" appear at the bottom of the photo.

4. This next part is a bit tricky. You need to click the Red Eye tool, move your mouse pointer to the eye, and hold the left mouse button down. As you hold the left mouse button down, drag it to create a box to frame the eye. Don't worry about being super accurate with the creation of the box or its position. SnapFish PhotoShow's Red Eye tool is remarkably forgiving and smart. Just draw a box over the entire eye area. Or, if you photo is a close up, concentrate on the pupil area. In either case it looks like you are creating a tiny cropping box. Instead, this is the area the program automatically scans to find and change bright red tones. Draw a tight box over the eye. The more on-target you are, the more accurate the result.

5. Repeat the process for the other eye and click the fix button.

6. Happy with the results? Then just click Done and Save.

Feel a sense of god-like power over your photos now? Let's tell the world all about it by adding some text to your photo.

Step 7: Adding Text to a Photo

Here's something that drives me nuts and makes me sad at the same time. It's looking at old photos of ancestors going back to the Civil War and up through the 1940s and having no clue who all these folks are or when and where the photo was taken. Adding text is one trick you can use with digital photos that will leave a record for the future. And on a lighter note, you can have devilish fun embedding silly messages, too.

1. You know the drill by heart now. Select a photo and go into the edit page.

2. This time click on the Add Text tool and up pops a text box over your photo and a bunch of drop-down menus full of choices: Font, Size, Color, Align, and Effects (see Figure 2.9).

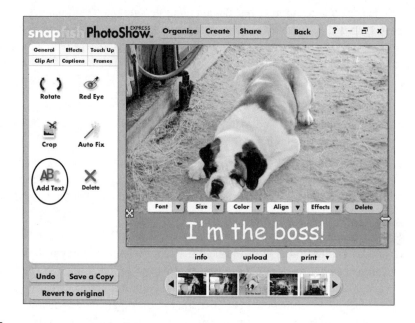

FIGURE 2.9

You may position the text box shown here anywhere on the photo.

3. These controls are very intuitive. Start clicking around and you'll get the hang of it fast.

4. Key in `I'm the boss` and have fun by changing the font, size, color, and alignment. Note the X icon with arrow heads on each end at the upper-left area of the text box. Grab this icon with your mouse pointer to drag and position your text anywhere on the image. When you are happy with the content and position, click outside the text box and the text is embedded into the image. To make the addition permanent, click the Save a Copy button. Figure 2.10 shows you the final product.

If you think this project was empowering, wait till you jump to the next one and take a leap into the world of artistic photo special effects!

note You'll find the Effects button is not activated in the free version. If you want access to those features, you'll need the full version, which costs $49.99. I don't recommend you make that decision right away. There are lots of photo tools out there and you should only spend money on the one that's right for you.

FIGURE 2.10

Here's what it looks like with the text embedded on the surface of the photo.

Project: Turn Your Photo into a Color Charcoal Drawing, an Impressionist Style Painting, or an Antiqued Photo

Your family photos don't always have to be about keeping a "realistic" record of snapshots. You can add some panache. Some style. All you need is a decent photo–editing program that allows you to render your digital pics using various special effects, including styles that replicate charcoal drawings, impressionist paintings and antique photos.

Materials

For this project you'll need

- Personal computer connected to the Internet via a high-speed DSL or cable link.

- Digital photos on your hard disk (from a digital camera, scanner, or Photo CD).

- Photo-editing software—For this project we need editing software more sophisticated than the free Snapfish software we used earlier. Before you download and install the software suggested below, take a close look at the photo-editing software that might have come bundled with your digital camera or scanner. You might find the software you already have is up for the special effects fun we're going to explore. If you're not sure, follow the steps below to download and install the free trial version of Ulead's PhotoImpact 10.

Time

About three to four hours (a great afternoon project) to download the free 30-day trial of Ulead's Photo Impact 10, install it, and perform the tasks below.

Step 1: Download Ulead PhotoImpact

Let's get to it. Follow the instructions below to download and install the Ulead PhotoImpact trial software:

1. Connect to the Internet and point your browser to http://www.ulead.com. Go to Products and click the drop-down menu. With your mouse, highlight the Digital Imaging box and a pop-up menu appears on the right. Ulead PhotoImpact should be the first selection. Click the PhotoImpact box and a new page appears, promoting the product. Look around the page and find the Free Trial button. Clicking this button presents a download page. Look for the Download Now button. You'll see a notice that the file to be downloaded is a whopping 80MB in size.

2. Clicking the Download Now button takes you to a register or log-in page. You need to complete the free registration process to download PhotoImpact.

3. Start the downloading process. When the download is complete, close down your browser, go to the file folder you created, and double-click the file.

4. The automatic installation wizard should now kick in to begin the process of installing the software. Click the Next button on the welcome screen. Read and accept the terms of the license agreement that appears next and click the Accept button.

5. Allow the program to install to the default hard drive and directory.

6. Next, you are asked what version to install. Select the Standard mode and allow the program to install to the default folder. Click Next to start the file copy process.

7. Now you are presented with a screen asking you to look at the Read Me file. When you download files, it's always a good idea to take a peek at the Read Me files. These documents contain tips that might help you run the program on your specific system. Also, go ahead and let the installation program copy the Palette samples.

8. When the installation process completes, you see a screen explaining that the program is updating system settings. When this is done, click the Finish button.

9. Okay, now you are ready to explore Ulead's PhotoImpact 10! Close out any remaining windows on your screen and look for the new PhotoImpact icon that should be on your Windows desktop.

caution Don't bother downloading PhotoImpact if you only have a dial-up connection to the Internet. The file is huge and would take an enormous amount of time. In fact, it took my DSL link at home about 30 minutes to download the 80MB file. If you don't have DSL or cable at home but work in an office with high-speed Internet, check with your company's IT department to see if they will permit you to download and burn it to CD so you can take it home.

note A Softwrap install menu may appear on your screen. If it does, just wait. It should disappear in a few seconds.

10. Double-click the PhotoImpact icon and you are presented with a notice that you have 30 days to enjoy the program free of charge. The menu choices are Try Now, Buy Now, or Reinstall. Select Try Now.

I know that was a lot of work and a chunk of time, but it's going to be worth it. You'll be amazed at what a modern consumer photo-editing package like PhotoImpact can do. Move now to the first exercise—turning a photo into a simulated color charcoal drawing.

note After you download the software, an email from the Ulead support team will come to the address you used when you registered. The message directs you to three helpful resources: a downloadable copy of the instruction manual for the program, a link to a PhotoImpact tutorial website, and a helpful tips web page.

Step 2: Creating a Charcoal Drawing

Follow these steps to turn your photo into a simulated color charcoal drawing:

1. Take a moment to look over the program toolbars and layout (see Figure 2.11). This is what more sophisticated consumer photo-editing programs typically look like. For this exercise, go to File, Browse and find a photo with which you want to work (make sure you've made a backup copy first). I recommend a portrait image. Highlight the photo you want and double-click to open the image in PhotoImpact.

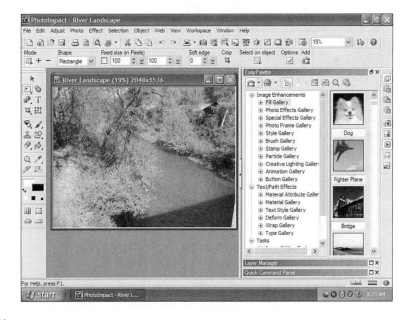

FIGURE 2.11

PhotoImpact's opening screen is packed with an array of tools. Drop-down menus and icons make it easy to access hundreds of features.

2. With your photo now on display, look at the top horizontal toolbar. Click the Effect menu, select Artistic, and then Color Charcoal. A new dialog box appears, showing your original photo side-by-side with a color charcoal effect version on the right, as shown in Figure 2.12. You can opt to have a split view (see the tab) but I prefer a full side-by-side comparison.

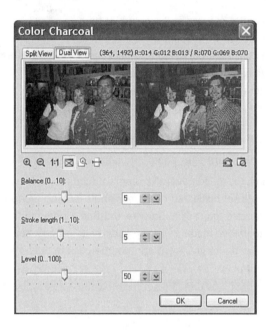

FIGURE 2.12

When you create a color charcoal drawing, PhotoImpact presents a dialog box showing your original photo side-by-side with a view of the image with the special effects applied.

3. Notice the Balance, Stroke Length, and Level control sliders. What I like to do is randomly experiment with each to see what they do, and then select the setting that achieves the desired overall effect. The range of control is absolutely astonishing and it's easy to get carried away. I find that mild effect applications result in the best end product.

4. After you find the right mix of color charcoal effects, click OK on the dialog box and your photo will now be saved with the new effects. It might take a few seconds for the effects to be applied to the image. You'll see a progress bar at the bottom of the screen.

Now that you have a simulated color charcoal version of your photo, you can print it, frame it, and create a unique gift.

Step 3: Morph Your Photo into an Impressionist Painting

For this activity, I recommend you select a landscape photo. Remember to use a copy photo from your `experiments` folder to avoid permanent changes to the original photo.

1. As in Step 2, use the Browse feature in PhotoImpact to find your digital landscape snapshot. When displayed on the program's screen, follow the same steps as above to activate the Effect drop-down menu and select Artistic, Impressionist.

2. The Impressionist drop-down menu knocks me out. It gives you a taste for how your digital snap will look in the Impressionist painting style.

tip Creating simulated Impressionist paintings from your digital snaps opens the door for a fun gift idea. First, be sure to select a photo taken at the highest resolution your camera can handle. Apply the Impressionist effects, save the file, and then print out an 8×10 inch photo on matte photo paper. You can find packs of glossy and matte photo paper for inkjet printers at your local office supply store. Or use one of the online photo print services, such as Snapfish.com, to have a print made and sent to you in the mail. Take the print and frame it to make a unique and personal gift.

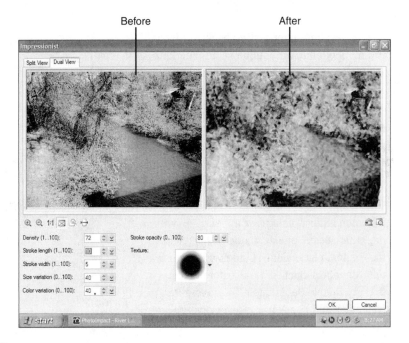

FIGURE 2.13

The Impressionist painting effect screen allows you to control the density and size of the brush strokes.

3. No great rocket science here; just start having fun playing around with the seven control options. And as before, when you are happy with the settings, click OK to apply the effects.

Step 4: Give Your Digital Snap an Antique Look

In Oregon, we have a super state fair each summer. One of the most popular attractions is the Old West photo booth. For a fee, you can dress up in nine-teenth century period pioneer clothes or cowboy gun slinger outfits. As you strike a rigid pose, the photographer fires off a digital snapshot. In seconds, using photo-editing software, she applies a brownish sepia tone effect to the photo and prints it out.

With PhotoImpact and other editing packages, you can turn any photo into an antique sepia tone faux heirloom. It's fun and a great party activity gim-mick, too. So find some costumes and follow the steps below:

1. Repeat the instructions in Step 2 to find your photo, open it, and display it on the PhotoImpact screen.

2. Look at the top-most horizontal toolbar and select Photo, Enhance, Duotone Effect.

3. A Duotone Effect dialog box appears. As with the other special effects dialog boxes, you see the original photo side-by-side with a version with the effect applied. Look carefully and find the Enable Sepia Effect Colors and Range check box and check it using your mouse pointer.

4. Next, look for the box below the Preset call out. Click the down arrowhead portion of the box and a list of settings appears. I've found the setting Duotone04 best approximates the

tip Each Duotone number represents a different form of the effect, with some creating a gray tone and others the amber tone I usually associate with old Wild-West era photos. Try all the numbers to see what works best for your photo.

Are You Hooked Yet?

You may want to purchase the Ulead program. Other good, general purpose consumer photo-editing software packages in the sub $50 range include

- ACDSee, $49.99—Free trial available to download at http://www.acdsystems.com.

- Roxio Photo Suite 7, $49.95— For information, see http://www.roxio.com.

Willing to invest more? Here are solid performers for less than $150:

- Microsoft Picture It! Premium 10, $54.95—You find information in the products area of http://www.microsoft.com/products/imaging/.

- Adobe Photoshop Elements 3.0, $99.99—Free trial available at http://www.adobe.com.

- Paint Shop Pro, $129.00—Free 60-day trial available at http://www.corel.com.

For a great listing of photo editing and other kinds of home multimedia creativity software, go to the featured software section of the personal computing area of the Intel website (http://www.intel.com) and click the Photography link. You'll find listings and links to loads of great programs the personal computing team suggests for average consumers to try.

old west antique brownish sepia tones I prefer. Of course, you can experiment with all the settings to find what works for you.

5. Apply the settings and start your creative juices flowing as you imagine the possibilities—from gag gifts to a great party activity.

These exercises tapped a tiny fraction of what a program such as PhotoImpact offers. You can spend hours and hours exploring such a program by simply trying out icons and drop-down menu items. Or, of course, and I know this is hard for us guys, you could check out the tutorial or read the on-disk manual for more ideas. Click Help on the top toolbar to access the on-disk manual.

Project: Use Your Photos to Make a Personal Screen Saver and Slide Show

If you own a PC, you know what happens when the machine is on but unused for 10 or more minutes. Typically the monitor screen goes into what the geeks call *screen saver mode*. On most recent PCs, Windows XP controls this function.

Screen savers include patterns that appear on the screen, photo slideshow-like presentations, and sophisticated multimedia productions. Did you know screen savers once had a serious purpose? Back in the day, it was important not to have a static image remaining on the screen of a tube-type monitor for hours and hours. This resulted in a permanent burn of the screen's inner surface. Today's tube monitors are resistant to this problem, but years ago, the screen saver was born to prevent this from happening.

In this exercise I'll show you how to make a simple screen saver using the built-in services of Windows XP.

Materials

For this project you'll need

- PC with Windows XP operating system
- Digital photos on your PC's hard disk (from a digital camera, scanner, or Photo CD)

Time

You'll need about 15 minutes to configure the Windows XP screen saver.

Step 1: Open the Display Properties Window

To make it easy to find the photos you want to use for your screen saver, I suggest you create a folder in My Pictures and name it Screen Saver Photos. You can transfer (drag and drop) photos to the folder or place copies of images in the folder. For the purposes of this project, place about 10 photos into that folder.

Now, find an empty area on your Windows XP desktop. By empty I mean a zone with no icons or open windows. Position your mouse pointer in a free zone and click the right button on your mouse. Select Properties from the context menu that appears.

Find and click the Screen Saver tab.

Step 2: Select the My Pictures Slideshow

When the Screen Saver tab area is fully displayed, look at the horizontal box-like area below the representation of your monitor screen. Click the little down arrow under the words Screen saver to open a drop-down menu of options. Find and click the My Pictures Slideshow (see Figure 2.14).

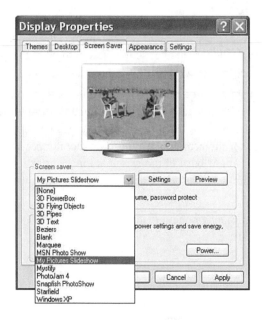

FIGURE 2.14

Select the My Pictures Screen Show to create a custom screen saver using your personal digital photos.

After you select My Pictures Slideshow, a preview of a slideshow screen saver using the photos stored in your My Pictures folder runs. The simulated monitor display gives you an idea of what your screen saver will look like. You can leave the settings alone and all the pictures in your My Pictures folder will be displayed in random order. For this exercise, however, I want you to use the photos you placed in the Screen Saver Photos folder you created in Step 1.

Step 3: Customize Your Slideshow

Click the Settings button and the My Screen Saver Options dialog box appears. Find the Browse button, click it, and find your Screen Saver Photos folder. Click OK and you return to the My Screen Saver Options dialog box. Before we finish, check out all the controls on the Options window, as shown in Figure 2.15. You can regulate the size of images, duration of display, and other actions. Click OK and you are returned to the main Screen Saver tab display.

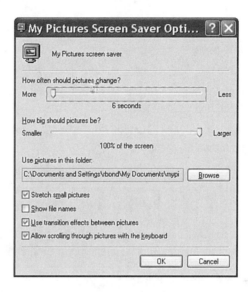

FIGURE 2.15

The My Pictures Screen Saver Options dialog box offers lots of controls. Use the Browse button to find the folder and photos you want to display.

Step 4: Testing Your Slideshow

Click the Preview button on the Screen Saver tab display and a full screen preview of your screen saver kicks into gear. If you like what you see, you're done. Just click Apply and close out the Properties dialog box. And, of course, you can always go back to select other folders and make adjustments.

Project: Stitch Photos Together to Create Stunning Panoramas

As a road warrior who spends up to 50% of my life away from home, I love to send photo postcards to my family. A single snapshot just can't capture the sense of place and scale of a scene such as Times Square, or the experience of looking at the long stretch of beach in San Clemente, California, where I grew up. Nothing beats a panorama photo for re-creating the feeling of being there.

In this project, we'll use ArcSoft Panorama Maker 3 to create breathtaking panoramas using photos from your digital camera. You'll learn how to line up and stitch together a series of horizontal landscape photos to create a single panorama. And that's just the start. Using this program you can create 360° panoramas you can move around in using your mouse and you can save photos as email-friendly files to share or print out.

Materials

For this project you'll need

- PC connected to the Internet using a high-speed DSL or cable service.
- Handheld digital camera to take a series of four shots panning a single location horizontally from left to right.
- Panorama-making software—For this project, we'll download the free trial version of ArcSoft Panorama Maker 3.
- Tripod—Highly recommended to ensure the best input for your panorama.

Time

About two hours to download the free trial software, install it, take a series of landscape photos with your digital camera, transfer them to your PC, and create a panorama.

Step 1: Download ArcSoft Panorama Maker 3

Follow the steps below to find and download Panorama Maker 3 from the ArcSoft website.

1. Connect to the Internet and point your browser to http://www.arcsoft.com. On the main ArcSoft screen, find the Home and Office button and click it. A new menu appears. Click Photo Software, and scroll down the new page to find Panorama Maker 3.

2. Click on the bold Panorama Maker 3 and the main product page appears. Find and click the Download Now button. Look for Panorama Maker 3 Trial (English version) and click on the product name.

3. You now enter the Download Description page where you can download a 15-day free trial of the program. Note that the file you are about to download is 20.8MB in size, which a DSL or cable connection can easily manage, but will take several hours over a dial-up. Look for the bold Download and click it. Next look for a bright red button labeled Download Now and click it.

4. Use the browsing feature on the dialog box that appears to direct the download to the Downloads folder you created. Start the download.

5. When the download is completed, a dialog box gives you the option to fire up the install process. I prefer to close out at this point, close down my browser, and then find and run the downloaded installation program from the folder on the hard drive. Why? This cleans up your desktop and prevents a confusing mess of layered windows you no longer need.

6. Follow the Panorama Maker onscreen instructions and menus to install the program.

Step 2: Take Four Landscape Digital Photos

1. To create your first panorama photo, you need a series of landscape shots of a single location. Grab your digital camera and pick any location (it can be indoors or outside).

2. For the best results, use a tripod if you have one. Stand in one spot or set your tripod and camera up, and take your first snapshot. Start with the furthest left area you want for your panorama. Move your camera to the right and snap another photo. Be sure that the left edge of your new photo overlaps with the furthest right area of the previous view you captured (this sets the stage for the stitching process which requires objects to align). Repeat this process for four snapshots. For this exercise we'll use four images. You can, of course, use two, three, or more than four images when making future panoramas.

3. Create a folder on your hard disk called Panorama Photos and transfer your images from the camera to the new folder.

Step 3: Start Panorama Maker 3

To start the program, open the Windows Start menu, click All Programs, and then find and click the ArcSoft Panorama Maker 3 icon.

When the program opens, a greeting page appears with the choice Evaluate This Program. Note the number of days remaining for your free trial period. Highlight Evaluate This Program and click Finish to start the program. After a brief title splash screen appears, the first main screen is displayed (see Figure 2.16). Note the multiple project options, including horizontal, vertical, 360°, and tile. Click the option buttons to see a visual representation of what each function can do with a set of photos taken at a single location.

> **tip**
> When selecting a location to shoot a series of photos go for one with little or no rapidly changing action. For example, a busy street scene or seascape with violent waves would not be good candidate locations.

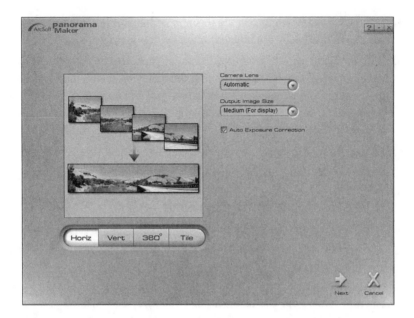

FIGURE 2.16

Following an initial splash screen Panorama Maker 3 offers four project options: horizontal, vertical, 360°, and tile.

Step 5: Make a Panorama Using Your Four Photos

Follow the steps below to create a panoroma using your landscape photos.

1. Open the Panorama Maker 3 software and click Start. When the screen showing four images merging to one appears, just click Next in the lower-right corner.

2. The next screen shows the test images as before. Now we're going to add our four landscape snapshots. Look for the open book icon with the word Add underneath. Click it and a dialog box labeled Open appears. Use the conventional Windows file browsing tool (the file folder symbol with the up arrow) to find the folder you created called Panorama Photos.

3. When you find the folder, thumbnail images of the photos appear. Place your mouse pointer on the first thumbnail image of the four photos and highlight it. Hold the Shift key down and highlight the remaining three

> **tip** When selecting the images for your panorama, sometimes they do not appear in the program window. To select multiple, non-adjacent images, select the first image in the series you want to build and hold down the Ctrl key on your keyboard. Then select, in any order, the remaining photos. Finally, click the Include icon to place them in the lower filmstrip-like work area.

images. Then click Open. This action loads the selected photos into the slide show boxes in the upper area.

4. Look carefully at your four images and begin dragging and dropping them into the lower filmstrip area, starting with the far left image (see Figure 2.17). Double-check to ensure you have the correct left-to-right order, as the images might or might not be loaded in the proper sequence when first transferred to the upper strip.

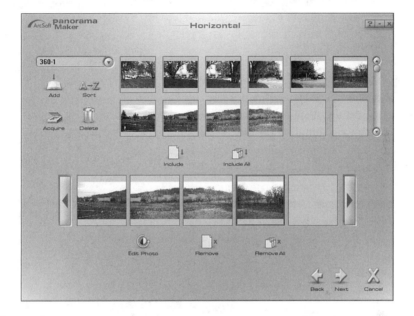

FIGURE 2.17

The main panorama building screen presents a collection of source photos in the upper area and a filmstrip-like row of boxes to be filled with the photos to be stitched together.

5. When you are satisfied with the line up, click Next and a processing bar appears, showing you how long it will take as the program stitches the photos together. When this process completes, you see a new screen showing your panorama. Note that there is an Auto Crop box with a check in it. Do not uncheck this box. This feature analyzes the stitching job and cleans up edges.

note The miraculous blending of multiple digital photos to create a single panorama image takes a lot of your PC's brainpower to accomplish. I'm glad I have a desktop with lots of memory and a Pentium 4 processor with Hyper Threading technology. Did it take your PC a long time to accomplish? An incredible amount of operations take place to compare the codes that represent each photo, identify the overlays, and combine the photos to a continuous image. This kind of digital photo manipulation is an example of where power pays off in a home PC.

6. Click Next again and you return to a display of your new panorama in all its glory, with several option buttons displayed below (see Figure 2.18). Repeat the same steps as in your test photo and then save the image as a new single JPEG photo. This time, however, note the Quality setting at the bottom of the program's Save As dialog box. I like to move it all the way up to 100 percent.

There's a great deal more you can do with this remarkable little program. Spend some time exploring its advanced editing features and output options, including the creation of playable movie-like files you can share with friends as email attachments.

Are You Hooked Yet?

If you want to continue using Panorama Maker 3 after the trial period expires, start the program, click the Purchase Product option, and follow the instructions to buy via the Internet or phone. It's $35.99, plus any taxes that might apply.

Another program to check out is Ulead's COOL 360 photo panorama software ($39.95, free trial download available from http://www.ulead.com/cool360/).

FIGURE 2.18

When you complete a panorama, you can save it as a picture file, edit or crop the image, create a movie file, or print it.

Project: Put Your Digital Mug on the Body of a Sports Star, Caveman, or Cover of a Glamour Magazine

Several face manipulation programs can take your digital portrait snaps to a land of huge laughs. One is ScanSoft's SuperGoo ($19.95, http://www.scansoft.com/supergoo/) and another called Funhouse comes from ArcSoft, the makers of the Panorama software used for the previous project.

SuperGoo is super fun. In a nutshell, you inject a close-up digital photo of your face (or any face, of course) and apply hilarious fun house mirror effects. You can stretch, bend, and warp a face to add an absurd grin, pointy eyebrows, you name it. Unfortunately, ScanSoft does not offer a free trial download of this very entertaining program. If you're looking for an engaging party activity for kids of all ages, you should purchase it and give it a try.

Fortunately, ArcSoft makes their face activity program available as a 15-day free trial. Remember my story about the Oregon State Fair and the booth where you could dress up in old Wild West clothes and get a sepia tone simulated antique photo? Another popular digital photo attraction at this and many fairs around the nation is the stand where they take a quick digital close-up of your face and place it on the body of a superstar, muscle man, bikini beauty, athlete, movie star, and so forth.

ArcSoft's Fun House program does just that, and like any good fair or amusement park, it's worth the price of admission! Jump ahead and look at Figure 2.21. That's me as a cave man and my daughter Christina as a surfer on the cover of a simulated sports magazine. These kinds of photos make for a fun gag gift and are a source of hours of family entertainment.

Materials

To complete this project, you'll need

- PC connected to the Internet using a high-speed DSL or cable service
- Handheld digital camera or webcam to take close-up face shots, or a collection of good portrait digital snaps
- The free trial version of Fun House

Time

About two hours to download the free trial software (85.52MB file), install it, take a few portrait photos, and go wild with a couple of the funny templates.

Step 1: Gather Your Photos

Take or collect several close-up facial digital shots. Once again, I strongly advise you to make backup copies of your photos and put them in a new folder. I suggest naming the folder Funhouse Photos.

Step 2: Download, Install, and Run ArcSoft Funhouse

Since ArcSoft Funhouse comes from the same source as the panorama software (http://www.arcsoft.com), just follow the same steps in the panorama section but apply them to the Fun House download and installation.

With the program installed on your system, look for the FunHouse icon on your main Windows desktop area. Double-click it and you get the Evaluate the Product opening screen. Highlight Evaluate and then click Finish.

Step 3: Select a Background Template

Take a moment to study the work area screen (see Figure 2.19). Note the five numbered steps to the far left. This program does a stellar job of guiding you through the process. The first highlighted number opens libraries of templates. The templates include faux magazine covers, action sports scenes, comical role-playing scenes and characters, and a time warp set of retro 1940s and 1950s black-and-white photos.

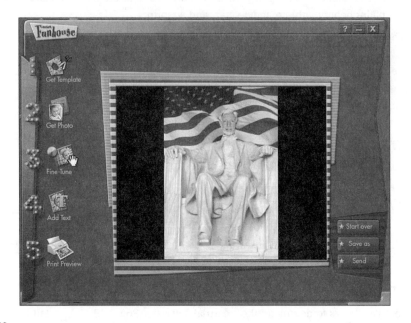

FIGURE 2.19

Arcsoft's Funhouse lets you run wild with your digital picture collection.

Play around with the template libraries until you find one that strikes your fancy and then click OK in the lower-right corner of the display. For me the cave man was a natural (see Figure 2.20). Heck, that guy has the really full head of hair I dream about!

Step 4: Insert Your Digital Mug Shot

Click the Number 2 icon and up comes a new screen with a vertical filmstrip lineup of stock photos that come with the program. Click the Open button and browse your hard disk to find and select your photo. The photo(s) are now added to the vertical filmstrip area.

Insert the face shot into the character template by clicking on your photo in the vertical strip. This places a red frame around the image and automatically inserts it into the face zone on the human form. Don't worry if the face is not aligned; that's our next step.

Click OK and then the Number 3 icon to start up the Fine-tune screen. Study this new screen. Play around with all the tools on the far left edge. You can increase the size of the image, rotate it slightly, and even adjust the color tones to match the human template character (see Figure 2.20). You may also move your inserted face image within the template head by grabbing it with your hand-shaped mouse pointer.

Face from digital photos inserted into template

FIGURE 2.20

The Fine-tune screen offers a wealth of tools to adjust position and color matching.

Step 5: Finish the Job

The Number 4 and 5 steps allow you to add text to the image and adjust and control printing respectively. In most cases you'll save the image as a JPEG photo file as your last step. Note the Save button on the lower right corner. Click it and save the file in the directory of your choice, but leave it as a JPEG file (with the `.jpg` extension). JPEG files are compressed and make good email attachments (see Figure 2.21).

FIGURE 2.21

It can be goofy or uncanny, but whatever the result, Fun House makes great gag photos.

Project: Make Your Digital Photos Talk, Blink, and Come to Life

By now it should be very clear that after you go digital with your photos, *you* are in control. In the previous project, you saw how a portion of a digital photo can be inserted into another digital image. Here we're going to take digital photo manipulation to the extreme. You're going to learn how to make a digital photo of a human or animal talk!

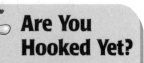

Are You Hooked Yet?

If you get to like Arcsoft's Funhouse and want to continue using it after the trial period expires, return to the ArcSoft website (http://www.arcsoft.com) and buy the program for $39.99.

Another very interesting program for manipulating facial digital photos is FaceFilter Standard by Reallusion (http://www.reallusion.com). Search the site and you can download a seven-day trial of FaceFilter Standard.

Materials

To complete this project you'll need

- PC connected to the Internet using a high-speed DSL or cable service
- Digital photos of faces (human or animal) from a digital camera or scanner
- Webcam with built-in microphone connected to your PC or a microphone plugged into your PC (or built-in microphone if you are using a laptop)
- Free seven-day trial version of Reallusion's CrazyTalk Home Edition software

Time

About three to four hours to download the free trial software (a 16.8MB file), install it, take a few portrait photos, and go explore the many activities this amazing program offers.

Step 1: Gather Your Photos

Before you jump into using the CrazyTalk software, take or collect several close-up facial digital shots. Your best results will be if you have straight-on frontal shots. You might also want to use the Snapfish PhotoShow or PhotoImpact editing software to get a tight, cropped close up. Once again, I recommend that you make copies of these photos and put them in a new folder. I suggest naming the folder `Crazy Talk Photos`.

Step 2: Download and Install the CrazyTalk Home Edition Software

Follow the steps below to find, download, install, and start the CrazyTalk program.

1. Fire up your PC, get connected to the Internet, and point your browser to http://www.reallusion.com/crazytalk. When the page is loaded, click the View Quick Demo button. In a few seconds you'll get the essence of what this program can do with a digital portrait photo. When the demo ends, click the Free Trial link.

2. The next page appears, listing various products. Go to the CrazyTalk Home Edition zone and click Download. Next you'll see two paths available for the download—CNET's http://www.download.com or http://www.tucows.com (two wildly popular trial and free software sites you might want to explore). Let's go with Download.com. Click the Download Now underlined words and stand back for a couple of seconds. Your browser will now shift gears to the CNET site and then settle on the download page for CrazyTalk Home Edition.

3. When the dust settles, you should see a page including an animated arrow Download Now button. Click this button and you get the File Download dialog box that should be very familiar to you by now. Click Save and before downloading, create a folder called `CrazyTalk Program` to receive the data.

4. You're a veteran now, you know the drill. When the download is done, click the program file and follow all onscreen instructions to complete the installation process.

5. At the end of the installation routine, you are asked to look at the Read Me file and then launch the program. Do both as the Read Me file might contain useful information. When the program fires up, the opening screen notes that you have a free seven-day trial. To start the program in the future, simply find and click the Funhouse icon on the desktop, or follow the usual sequence of clicking Start, All Programs and then the icon for Funhouse.

Step 3: Introduction to CrazyTalk Home Edition

The opening screen of CrazyTalk Home Edition is well laid out and instantly hits you with the full range of fun things to explore (see Figure 2.22) .

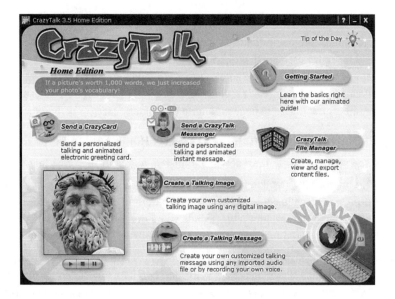

FIGURE 2.22

CrazyTalk Home Edition allows you to create a talking digital image, send a talking greeting card, send a talking instant message, and much more.

Run, don't walk, to the image of the Greek god-like statue at the lower-left portion of the screen. Click the Play button. The statue begins to talk, demonstrating the special effects the program can apply. I rest my case! Did it blow your mind to see a digital figure talk, blink, and convey expression? You can do this to any digital portrait, and it's not hard.

Step 4: Make a Digital Photo Talk, Blink, and Get Emotional

For this one I'm off the hook as your guide. The designers of CrazyTalk Home Edition have built some of the best step-by-step tutorials I've seen, so I'm going to show you how to use them to your full advantage:

1. From the opening screen of the program, find and click the Getting Started button. Scroll down and click Create a Talking Image.

2. The next screen starts a very clear tutorial that holds your hand every step of the way. If you're not concerned about going through some paper and ink, you might want to print out the guide. It's much easier to look at the steps on paper as you run the program on your PC's screen.

3. You can use the sample photo of a dog provided or open one of your own photos.

4. For my test I used a close-up photo of yours truly. Following the tutorial, I selected the semi-auto fitting routine as shown in Figure 2.23. Here you are directed to place four key action points for the eyes and edges of the mouth.

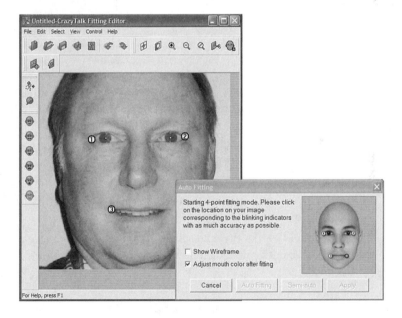

FIGURE 2.23

CrazyTalk's semi-auto fitting routine makes it easy to pinpoint key animation areas on the face by targeting four points.

5. After applying the semi-auto fitting settings, you should try goofing around with the various facial expressions you can activate on the far left vertical area of the display.

6. Next click the Set TTS Voice Attributes icon directly above the first emotion face icon called Bright. Test having your photo talk using the synthetic voices provided.

7. When you finish with the Create a Talking Image exercise, I suggest you go through the Create a Talking Message tutorial to put your own words into action. Following the tutorial, you can record and save your own audio message.

8. Next, you can associate the recorded greeting with the talking image you've been working on. It's a real kick to see your digital face speak a message for you. For me, the laughs really happened when I heard my words coming out of the mouth of the Greek god statue image and other characters in the stock collection.

9. Now that you've created a talking digital image and embedded your own personal audio message, the program gives you four options:

   - **Send CrazyCard**—Initiates a wizard to build an electronic postcard with your talking photo and text greeting embedded in one of several templates

   - **Send Messenger**—Kicks off a wizard to create a small, self-playing video file ideal for email attachments

   - **Add from file**—Allows you to substitute another recorded speech file for the current one

   - **Export to file**—Allows you to save the final composition as a CrazyTalk project you can edit in the future

I recommend you try the Send a CrazyTalk Messenger. This routine helps you email a self-playing animated talking digital image to a friend (see Figure 2.24).

Are You Hooked Yet?

Hands down, I think this little gem of a program is well worth the $49.95 to buy. If you agree, go back to http://www.reallusion.com/crazy talk and follow the onscreen instructions to purchase the program.

If you had fun with CrazyTalk, you might really enjoy one of the fashion and hairdo makeover programs available today. For years my family has loved the Cosmopolitan Virtual Makeover series. It is a wonderful program that allows you to import a digital headshot snap and give yourself a complete makeover. You can try on loads of hair styles, eyewear, makeup, and even jewelry. And hey, it's not just for the ladies. Men's hairstyles and facial hair samples are included in most editions of the product series.

Unfortunately, a free trial download is not available, but you may purchase the product at http://www.amzaon.com. Click on the Software tab and then do a search with the keywords *virtual makeover*. Several versions are available for under $20. Other similar products include YM Makeover Magic and YM Digital Makeover Magic (also available via Amazon.com for less than $30).

Click Play to test drive your talking photo

FIGURE 2.24

The Send a CrazyTalk Messenger screen walks you through simple steps to share your talking digital image.

What's next? In Chapter 3 we'll explore the world of digital photo albums.

3

Share and Preserve Your Photos

Ever talk to an insurance claims adjuster? I did as part of my research for a TV segment on the topic of how to use a PC and scanner to digitize and preserve family print photos. I wanted to know what people grab on the way out the door when disaster strikes. He told me that after ensuring their loved ones and pets were safe, his clients, with very few exceptions, rushed back inside to retrieve family photo albums and home video tapes as their top priority. Not jewelry, not computers, and not even clothing took top billing.

In this chapter I'll show you how to use a personal computer, the Internet, and a scanner to digitize, protect, and preserve your family photo heritage. After you get a grip on the basics of photo restoration, I'll show you how to store family photo albums online for safekeeping. And finally we'll use several creative album-making programs to produce lasting digital heirlooms.

You'll learn how to

- Store family digital photos online using a free photo processing service
- Digitally spruce up old, faded, or damaged photos
- Use multimedia software programs to make animated and music-enhanced digital photo albums

- Explore a variety of digital album output options, including CDs you can play back on a PC or a DVD player connected to a TV

- Use an online service to make professional quality, annotated paperback or hardcover albums based on your digital snaps

As with the previous chapter, the projects use free trial software downloaded from the Internet.

If you have a ton of family video tapes at home, stand by. In Chapter 4, "Lights, Camera, Action!," we'll look at how your home PC can help digitize and preserve them.

Skills and Gear Check

Before you jump into the projects, take a quick look below at the list of assumptions I'm making about your skills and gear.

Key assumptions:

- You have a high-speed DSL or cable link to the Internet. You will be uploading numerous photos using the Internet and downloading large program files, as you did in Chapter 2, "Get Creative with Digital Pictures." A dial-up connection will be too frustrating and unreliable.

- You own a digital scanner and you know how to scan a print photo (if not, see Chapter 2).

- Your PC uses Microsoft's Windows XP operating system. All onscreen operating system illustrations, dialog boxes, and pop-up menu samples are based on Windows XP.

- You have a CD or DVD disc recorder (also known as a *writer* or *burner*) built into your PC, and you know how to make a data or music CD.

tip

Here are some tips I learned from the claims adjuster you might want to consider. First, gather all your family photo albums and videos in one location in the house you can easily access.

Next, keep a large duffle bag nearby that can be stuffed, on the fly, with your albums and home video tapes for a quick escape. Keep critical financial and legal documents in the same location too, and pack a suitcase with a change of clothes for each family member.

And one last thing, be sure to discuss your evacuation duffle bag scheme with your insurance representative. Understandably, an insurance claims agent might suspect arson if everything in a home is destroyed except irreplaceable items, such as family photos and videos.

Project: Store Your Family Photos Online

The Web is teeming with online photo processing services. These are the twenty-first century alternative to the drug store or supermarket film roll processing routine. Web-based outfits such as dotPhoto, Ofoto, and Snapfish are designed to sell digital photo print services. One way they attract customers is by offering free online album posting and sharing services. You can use the photo album feature of these services as a way to store and back up special family photos.

To take advantage of these services, you need to register for free and access your collection occasionally to keep your account active. Online albums are a good first step to protect and back up precious photos or prints digitized via a scanner. And as a bonus, you'll discover it's fun to use email notices to invite friends and family to view your albums online.

For this exercise, we use dotPhoto (http://www.dotphoto.com), which is a good representative example of a web-based photo album and print processing service. According to the dotPhoto tech support web page, you may upload and store as many photos or albums as you wish, so long as you remain active. *Active*, in this case, means you access and update your online photo collection regularly. I recommend accessing your account at least once a month to preserve your active status and storage space.

Materials

To complete this project you'll need

- Personal computer connected to the Internet
- Digital photos on your hard disk (from a digital camera, scanner, or photo CD)
- Online photo album service—This project uses the free http://www.dotphoto.com service.

Time

About one hour to set up a free account on dotPhoto, create your first album, and upload it to the service.

Name Your Picture Files

Millions of digital photos are sitting on hard disks around the world with really informative names such as IMG_101.JPG. Wow, that really tells me a lot! And to make matters worse, these mystery snaps are usually dumped en masse into the Windows XP My Pictures folder. It's time to get disciplined, for the sake of your sanity and posterity.

In Chapter 2, you saw how the Choose Pictures to Copy Wizard asks you to give a series of photos a base name before they are transferred from a digital camera into your PC. That's a start, but it's not enough. When I transfer photos from a scanner or camera, I create a unique folder under the My Pictures area of my hard disk. I give the folders dates and some kind of meaningful name, such as Easter in Medford 2004.

The really dedicated archivist goes one extra step by giving each photo a descriptive name. Remember, 100 years from now, IMP_101.JPG will mean nothing to your descendants.

Step 1: Register with dotPhoto

1. Fire up your PC, connect to the Internet, and point your browser to http://www.dotphoto.com.

2. When the opening page appears, look for the Join Now button.

3. Click it and follow the instructions to set up your free account and password.

Step 2: Create an Album

Log in to the dotPhoto service with your new account and password and click on My Albums at the top edge of the screen. On the next screen, scroll down until you see the toolbox area on the left and click Create New Album.

The next screen presents a fill-in-the-blanks form that helps organize and identify the album's content. Here you should give the album a name, assign a password for access, provide a brief text description, and enter start and stop dates for the subject matter. You can also assign it to one of the service's premade categories, from Art and Culture to Travel and Vacations.

After completing the form, the next screen announces that your album is empty. Look to the lower left of the empty notice, where you are prompted with the words Please Add Your Photos or Create New Subalbum. Click Add Your Photos and a new menu appears, as shown in Figure 3.1.

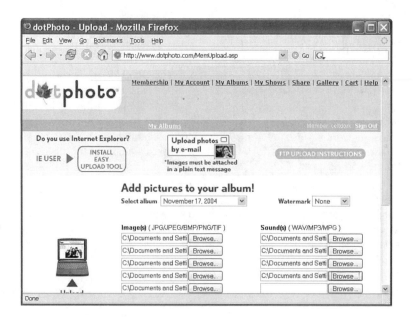

FIGURE 3.1

Hey, does this screen look familiar? It's a lot like the file attachment screen in Yahoo! mail we saw in Chapter 2.

Use the Browse feature to find and fill each photo box with an image to be uploaded to your dotPhoto online album. When you've targeted all your snaps, click the Start Upload button at the bottom of the screen. Sit back and relax. Depending on the resolution of your photos, the number of images in your album, and the speed of your Internet connection, it could be a few minutes or even an hour or more for the upload process to complete. At the end of the upload routine, a dialog box appears, announcing the process was successful.

After the upload is complete, you should review your album. Scroll to the top of the screen and click My Albums. The display refreshes to show your album(s) as clickable icons, as shown in Figure 3.2.

tip

If you are using Microsoft's Internet Explorer browser, you can speed up the selection and uploading of photos to a dotPhoto album by installing the Easy Upload tool. Click the Install Easy Upload Tool button at the upper-left area of the screen, as shown in Figure 3.1. Follow the onscreen instructions to download the program. After installation, a new Upload Files to dotPhoto dialog box appears with a Select button that allows you to highlight one or multiple photos to be uploaded. After selecting the photos, click the Upload button to transmit all the files to your new album.

FIGURE 3.2

The My Albums screen shows all of your online albums as clickable icons.

You now have your first online stored album! Repeat the process to create a collection of albums.

Step 3: Tour dotPhoto

Now that you have an album in place, let's take a quick tour of dotPhoto and learn about its various benefits and features.

1. Log in to your dotPhoto account and when you arrive at the page displaying the online stored album(s), explore the tool icons and features contained in the vertical box areas to the far left.

2. To start, learn how to add a text caption to a photo in one of your stored albums. Click the icon for your stored album. Select a photo from the album and click it. A larger image of the photo is now displayed. Look to the left for the toolbox and find the Edit Title icon. Click the Edit Title icon and the screen refreshes to display an Edit Photo Information worksheet. Follow the intuitive fill-in-the-blanks forms to add a caption.

3. If you have not already done so, you can edit your snaps by clicking the adjustable wrench Edit icon found in the toolbox or at the upper-right corner of a highlighted image. The small set of tools includes an auto adjust, a red eye fix, and a rotate set of buttons.

4. Don't miss the Edit Sound feature in the toolbox. Look for the icon with musical notes. Click this button and, after downloading a small utility application (prompts will guide you), you can record narrations for each photo in your album.

5. Sharing your albums via email greetings is a standard feature with online photo and print services such as dotPhoto. When you have the My Albums page displayed, showing your album, look to the far left for the Actions vertical box and find the Share Album icon. Click this icon and a very intuitive menu appears to guide you through the process of emailing a greeting to a friend. The email notice will contain a link to allow the recipient to see your album online.

6. The Actions and toolbox options contain a ton of fun things to try. Spend some time familiarizing yourself with all the goodies and project ideas.

tip Storing your special digital photos online is a good preservation move. But it's in your best interests to do more. Grab some blank CDs and copy your photos to them, using the CD recording software provided by your PC manufacturer. Make two copies of each disk and store the second set in your safe deposit box at the bank or give a set to a relative or neighbor for safe keeping.

Are You Hooked Yet?

Try out some of the other online services offering free album storage, including http://www.ofoto.com and http://www.snapfish.com.

For a deluxe experience, you might consider the full feature SmugMug service at http://smugmug.com. For an annual fee of $29.95, you can create and store albums with hundreds of high-resolution photos, upload sets of photos in one step, allow your friends to download and print images, and even create a special web address for access to your albums.

Project: Make Digital Reproductions of Your Existing Paper Photo Albums

It hit me in the head like a brick one Saturday morning as I was looking at the rows of three-ring binder photo albums my wife has meticulously created throughout the past 20 years. Page after page of precious photos carefully documented with hand written notes under each photo. What a disaster it would be if these albums were ever damaged by flood or lost in a fire!

Although it's true that nothing can truly replace the feel and sentimental value attached to those albums, that's no reason not to take some measures to protect their contents. You can do this by scanning each page with its photos and handwritten notes and creating a faithful digital reproduction of each album. Think of it as being a high-tech photocopy scheme.

tip The three-ring binder photo albums enhanced with handwritten notes under each photo led me to the scheme of scanning entire pages to preserve the total look and feel of the original. The downside to this approach is the size of the full-page scans. I've had to use a lot of disk space. If your hardcopy albums do not allow pages to be easily removed, I suggest removing and scanning each photo separately. You'll net better quality scans overall. Give each photo a meaningful name, such as photo 1 page 1, and store them in folders with names reflecting the source, such as Grandma Kate Album 1942.

I pulled down one of the binders off the bookcase, opened it, and placed the first page in my scanner. In a few seconds my PC screen filled with an exact duplication that could be saved as a digital file (see Figure 3.3).

FIGURE 3.3

It's not fancy, but it does the preservation job. Here's one scanned page from our family photo album for the year 1990.

This may be the least glamorous project in the book, but it's one of the most important preservation moves you can make before you go wild on the digital multimedia side of the street. And, as you can imagine, it's been an ongoing process that's consumed countless hours.

caution If the album you want to scan is old and delicate or will not lend itself to scanning, I suggest you try using a digital camera to take close-up snaps of the photos. Check to see if your camera has a close-up mode. It's not worth damaging a fragile album just to scan it.

Materials

For this project you'll need

- Personal computer connected to a scanner. (If you don't own a scanner, see the first project in Chapter 2 and look for the "Shopping for a Digital Camera or Scanner?" sidebar.)

- Existing paper photo albums with removable pages that can be laid flat against the scanner's glass plate. A permanently bound album can be used but it's a tricky process to scan pages when they can't lay completely flat. The good news is most scanners have lids that can easily be removed to accommodate an open book.

- Scanning software provided with your scanner, or the Windows XP Scanner and Camera Wizard program (which is what I prefer and used for this book).

Time

Less than 30 minutes to follow the steps to scan the first page of an existing paper photo album. After that, your time investment will vary depending on the number of albums to be scanned and digitally stored. After you get going, it shouldn't take more than a few minutes to scan each page.

Step 1: Prep Work

Grab a paper photo album, fire up your PC, and make sure your scanner is connected.

Next, create a folder under My Pictures and give it a name an archivist would love, such as Family Photo Album 1990.

Step 2: Scan Each Album Page

Start up the scanning software provided with your scanner or, as I'll do for this exercise, use the Windows XP Scanner and Camera Wizard and follow its instructions for scanning a page of your album to a file on your PC.

You'll find more detailed instructions in Chapter 2. Repeat the process for each page in your album. Give each file a meaningful name (for example, Page 1 Album 1990).

tip When you scan an entire page, you create a rather large file. I've found that setting your scanner to create a 200 dots per inch (dpi) image, which you can do from the Scanner and Camera Wizard, yields a good onscreen display that does not eat up huge amounts of space on your hard disk or backup CD.

Step 3: Back Up Your Digital Album

After you've scanned your album pages to your PC, you should burn a copy of them to a CD (or DVD). Label and store one set at home and another in your safe deposit box, or other trustworthy, offsite location.

Project: Restore Heirloom Photos

My sister and I wound up being the end of the line for several family trees. Like many families, between us we have no shortage of boxes of fascinating old photo prints. In my case I have photos on glass plates, tin-types, and old yellowed paper prints. Some are in astonishingly good shape. Others, which came from my grandparents who lived in Florida (not a photo-friendly climate) suffer from mold damage and water stains.

Are you in the same boat? Looking for a way to not only preserve photos but even digitally remove scratches and blotches? Then this project is for you. What you can do with a decent PC, scanner, and photo-editing software to remove scratches, wrinkles, and spots from a digitized photo is nothing short of astonishing!

In the previous chapter, you learned how to apply several special effects for the sake of pure creative fun. Here you will learn how to leverage some of the cool editing and repair tools found in programs such as Ulead's PhotoImpact to touch up and restore damaged photos.

Materials

To complete this project you'll need

- Scanner connected to your personal computer.
- Damaged, old, and faded print photos.
- Photo-editing software with a touchup or repair feature. To save time, we'll use the free trial version of Ulead's PhotoImpact you downloaded and installed to do the activities in Chapter 2.

Time

If you already downloaded, installed, and learned the basics for Ulead's PhotoImpact, the following project takes about one hour. If not, add another hour to download and install the PhotoImpact program. For instructions to complete this process, see the Turn Your Photo into a Color Charcoal Drawing, an Impressionist Style Painting, or an Antiqued Photo project in Chapter 2.

Step 1: Select and Scan a Damaged Photo

Select a damaged photo print. The photo I'll use for this exercise shows the farm buildings and corn field of my grandfather's farm in Illinois, as shown in Figure 3.4. As you can see, some bad blotches and horizontal surface streaks have marred the image. Look carefully at the extreme left edge of the photo at the large vertical blotch. It's that area we'll repair in this exercise.

Damage to photo

FIGURE 3.4

This is a small, badly worn, 1930s era photo of my father's childhood farm in Illinois. The photo is marred with streaks and discoloration that are ripe for digital repair.

Next, scan the photo to your PC using the steps outlined in the previous project. If necessary, refer to the Chapter 2 project, "Get a Digital Scan on Your PC." Again, if the photo is permanently affixed to an album that is not a good candidate for laying flat on a scanner surface, try using your digital camera. Make sure you create a special folder under the My Pictures area of your hard disk and name it Photo Repair Test.

Step 2: Open the Picture in PhotoImpact

Start up the PhotoImpact editing program by clicking Start, All Programs, Ulead PhotoImpact. Click File, Open on the top toolbar to navigate to the location of your damaged photo file.

After PhotoImpact opens and displays the photo, go to the top horizontal menu bar, and click Photo, ExpressFix (the first selection in the drop-down menu).

Step 3: Make Automatic Adjustments

Your first step is to allow PhotoImpact to automatically suggest adjustments to the basic settings such as contrast, sharpness, and so forth.

When you click ExpressFix, a new dialog box appears with your original scan on the top left and a view with various degrees of Overall Exposure adjustments applied, as shown in Figure 3.5.

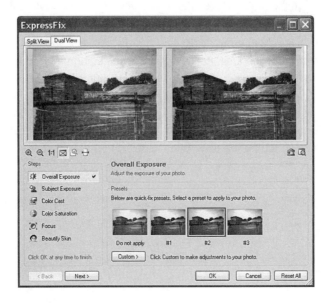

FIGURE 3.5

The ExpressFix feature presents the original digital image flanked by a version showing one of three optional automatic adjustments.

Note the three Overall Exposure auto adjustment options displayed in the lower area. Try all three and decide on the one you feel delivers the greatest overall improvement. Next look at the Steps toolbox to the left and try the remaining auto adjustment filters including Subject Exposure, Color Cast, Color Saturation, Focus and Beautify Skin (obviously for portraits). When you have applied the filters you like click OK and the changes are applied and the revised photo displayed.

Step 4: Touch Up the Photo

Now that you're back at PhotoImpact's main interface, look at the far left vertical strip filled with icons. Move your mouse pointer over the icon that looks like a flip-open compact case (the words *Touch-up tool* appear).

Click the Touch-up Tool icon and a Tool Settings—Brush dialog box appears with a variety of settings and adjustments you can play around with later. For now, just close out this dialog box and move your mouse over the surface of the digital image. You'll see your mouse pointer now looks like a cross-hair target.

Your next move relies on pure gut judgment. The idea is to use the target pattern mouse pointer to select an area on your photo you think would match the damaged area. In my case, I started with the largest damaged area to the far left edge and placed the target on a good area very close to the large blotch. With the target pattern in place over a good zone, I held the Shift key down and clicked the mouse. The target pattern started to blink and remained in place. As I moved the mouse pointer it transformed into a circle shape.

Ready for the magic? If you're following along using your own scanned photo, move your circle pattern mouse pointer to the damaged area, left-click your mouse, and start dragging the pointer over the area. Suddenly, you are painting the area with the color or pattern picked up by the cross-hair target. To repair a different area, hold the Shift key down and move your mouse pointer to a good spot next to a zone to be repaired. Left-click your mouse and it once again turns into a circle pattern. Although not always perfect, the effect can be remarkable, and in my case I was able to all but eliminate the visible damage on the far left edge (see Figure 3.6).

Touch-up tool icon

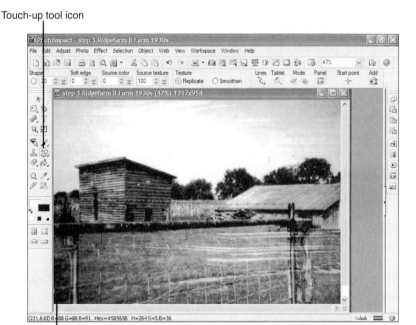

Damaged area with applied touch-up

FIGURE 3.6

The virtual repair I pulled off with the Touch-up tool created a remarkable fool-the-eye result.

Keep painting the area until you are satisfied with the results. Repeat the process to repair other areas. Save the file under a new name so as to preserve the original scan.

Hey, you just learned a trick photo restoration professionals charge big bucks to do!

tip

As you'll soon discover, this can be a delicate operation. Note, however, that you can use the zoom feature on your photo editor to improve your fill-in painting accuracy.

Project: Create an Animated, Music-Enhanced Digital Album

This project starts your introduction to the second of two digital album-making software packages we cover in this chapter. The digital album we made using dotPhoto was a good entry-level experience, but the end result was limited to online delivery. Now it's time to graduate to the next level. In this exercise we'll use the free Photo Story 3 program from Microsoft to make an animated, music-enhanced album you can playback on your PC, share via email, or burn to CD disc as a movie file.

Photo Story 3 is not a time-limited trial shareware product. You may use this free program indefinitely to build compelling slide-show albums. Simple wizard screen displays walk you through the process of gathering your photos, creating an album, editing images, and adding text, titles, background music, and recorded narrations. The program even supports special effects, such as pan and zoom.

Materials

For this project you'll need

- Personal computer connected to the Internet
- Set of digital photos on your hard disk
- Microsoft's free Photo Story 3 program
- A microphone connected to your PC or a webcam with a built-in microphone if you want to use the recorded narration feature

Time

With a DSL or cable high-speed link to the Internet, figure on 20 minutes to download and install the program. With its remarkably easy-to-follow onscreen menus, you can have a basic Photo Story 3 album with 10 images up and running in less than 15 minutes. Add an hour to fully explore the program's features.

Step 1: Download and Install Photo Story 3

Follow these steps to download and install Microsoft's Photo Story 3:

1. With your PC turned on and connected to the Internet, navigate your web browser http://www.microsoft.com. Key in the words **Photo Story 3** in the search bar in the upper-right area of the opening screen display, and then click the link for Photo Story 3 for Windows.

> **note** During the installation process and when you first run the program, you might encounter requests for you to load ActiveX control, update your Media Player to revision 10, and/or enter your Windows XP operating system's product code. Simple onscreen wizard displays guide you through all of the operations, if needed.

2. On the page dedicated to Photo Story 3, look for the Download Photo Story 3 link and click it. When the File Download dialog box appears, click Save and use the Save As dialog box to place the file in your downloads folder under My Documents.

3. When the Download Complete dialog box appears, you can close out all other windows to clear the deck (optional) and then click the Open button. The Windows installer kicks in and fires up the Setup Wizard. Follow the onscreen prompts to accept the license and default directory. When the installation process ends, click the Finish button in the Wizard Completed dialog box.

Once downloaded and installed, you can launch the programs by opening the Windows Start menu and selecting, All Programs, Photo Story 3. The following steps show you how to build a slideshow album, enhance it with special effects transitions, add background music, and play it back on your PC.

Step 2: Gather Your Photos and Build an Album

When you first start up Photo Story 3, you are presented with an initial splash screen that offers three choices: Begin a New Story, Edit a Project, and Play a Story. Select Begin a New Story and click Next to get started building an album.

1. The first action is to import the pictures you need to build your album presentation. Click the Import Pictures button and use the File Browser dialog box to find the folder holding the pictures you want to add.

2. When the images in your target folder are displayed, select them and click OK. Your selected photos will be displayed in a horizontal band at the bottom of the Import and Arrange Your Pictures dialog box, as shown in Figure 3.7.

3. Want to rearrange the order of your imported photos? No sweat. Just use your mouse pointer to highlight and then drag and drop an image to any position in the horizontal work area. When you have all your photos lined up, click Next.

FIGURE 3.7

The Import and Arrange Your Pictures dialog box guides you through the process of inserting and organizing the photos for your slideshow album.

Step 3: Add Text Captions, Record Narration, and Apply Special Effects Transitions

Now it's time to add some special effects and other cool gimmicks to your album:

1. The next screen to appear after you select the photos for your album is the Add a Title to Your Pictures dialog box. A work area to the right of each highlighted photo provides a place to key in text. Note the buttons along the top of the text entry box to customize and position the text. To change a font, click the button with the letter *A* and a comprehensive Font Adjustment dialog box appears. Highlight each photo and add text as you like. Click the Next button when you have completed this step.

2. The Narrate Your Pictures and Customize Motion dialog box offers wizards that help you record narration for each image and determine the special effects transitions you'd like. The recording tool to the right of a highlighted image uses simple Record and Stop buttons. Be sure your PC microphone or webcam with built-in microphone is plugged in and installed properly to use this feature.

3. Under each highlighted photo you'll find a Customize Motion button. Click it and the Customize Motion dialog box appears with the Motion and Duration tab in the foreground. You can accept the defaults or use the Specify Start and End Position of Motion tool to determine where a close-up of your photo starts. You can also set the number of seconds each image is displayed.

4. Click the Transition tab on the Customize Motion dialog box and a series of special effects transitions are offered in a scrolling box, as shown in Figure 3.8. Highlight an effect icon and an animated simulation is applied to the image above. When you find a transition you like, click the Save button to apply it to the image. Repeat these steps to apply the same or different transitions to each image.

tip

Another nifty tool on the Transition tab is the Preview button. Click it to see a reproduction of how the transition will appear in the final production, using the picture you've selected.

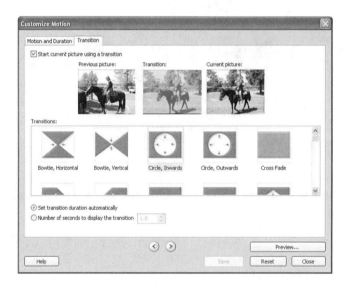

FIGURE 3.8

The Transition tab presents a library of special effects transitions you can apply to each photo.

5. When you're done with the Customize Motion dialog box, click the Close button.

6. At this point I suggest you click the Save Project button at the bottom of the Narrate Your Pictures and Customize Motion dialog box. Change the default file name of PhotoStory1 to something meaningful to you and note that the production will be saved in the My Videos folder under My Documents. When you have finished, click Next.

Step 4: Select Background Music

With pictures selected and an effect added, it's time to wrap up the creative process by adding some background music.

1. When the Add Background Music dialog box appears, note the three main buttons: Select Music, Create Music, and Delete Music. If you have some music files on your CD in the .wma, .wav, or .mp3 format, you can use the Select Music button to browse and select a compatible music file.

2. For our exercise, let's use some of the canned music provided with the program. Click the Create Music button and the Create Music dialog box appears. Simple drop-down menus at the top allow you to select a genre, style, bands, and moods. For my horse riding album, I selected a banjo country style tune and clicked the Low Intensity button to keep the music subtle, as shown in Figure 3.9. Click OK when you're done.

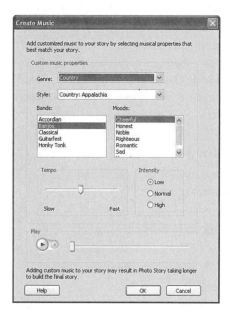

FIGURE 3.9

The Create Music dialog box offers the choice of using a music file already on your hard disk or one of numerous canned tunes provided with the program.

3. Click the Preview button on the Add Background Music dialog box to test drive your album slide show in all its special effects transitions and music glory. When you are happy with your overall composition, click Next.

Step 5: Save and Share Your Album Slide Show

Follow the steps below to save your album (story) for playback on a PC:

1. With the Save Your Story dialog box now onscreen, select the Save for Computer Playback option. Note that this is one of several save options Photo Story 3 offers. In the future you may, for example, also save an album in a video file format suitable as an email attachment or for playback on a handheld computer.

2. Click the Save Your Story for Playback on Your Computer option and move to the File Name area in the center of the dialog box. Note the white box with the default `My Videos\PhotoStory1.wmv` as the default directory and file name. Change the file name to something meaningful to you.

3. Next check out the Quality Settings area at the bottom of the dialog box. Click the Settings button to view, via a Preview drop-down menu on the Settings dialog box, a host of quality settings designed for different purposes and playback devices. For this exercise, select Profile for Computers—3 (800×600). This setting creates a playback video window 800×600 pixels in size.

   Note that there are plenty of other format choices available, useful in specific situations. For example, there are settings ideal for email attachments, DVDs and Video CDs, and handheld computers or cell phones. Click OK to return to the Save Your Story dialog box. Click Next and a progress bar reports on the status of your video file's production.

Step 6: Enjoy the Show!

Follow the steps below to view your completed video album production and save it.

1. When the video file combining your images, transitions, titles, and music is completed, the Completing Photo Story 3 for Windows dialog box offers two choices: View Your Story and Create Another Story.

2. Click View Your Story to see how the final cut looks and sounds. The Windows Media 10 player automatically loads and plays the file.

3. When you're finished, exit Media Player 10 and return to the Completing Photo Story 3 dialog box. Be sure to click the Save Project button and use the Save As dialog box to ensure your creative work is preserved on hard disk.

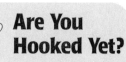

Are You Hooked Yet?

If you like Photo Story 3, you might enjoy experimenting with PhotoJam from Shockwave, which is available at http://www.shockwave.com. The current version, PhotoJam 4, is a fun program that offers some hilarious special effects including one that applies an old black-and-white movie effect to your album slideshow. While the demo is only good for two hours of use, the purchase price of less than $30 is quite reasonable for all the features it offers.

Your completed Photo Story 3 production takes the form of a video file that you may burn to a CD and share with friends. Be sure to tell the recipient to update her Windows XP Media Player to the latest version before trying to playback your album video file. Also, if when playing back the file using Media Player, the recipient complains that it looks grainy or blurry, tell her to place the mouse pointer over the video, right click, select Video Size, and ensure that the Fit Player to Video on Start feature is checked. Close down Media Player and try again.

Project: Crank the Digital Album-Making Creativity Dial to Full Blast

In the previous project we used Photo Story 3 to create a simple, slide show-like presentation. Now it's time to fully tap the 3D graphics and multimedia capabilities of a modern PC to create an animated, multimedia-enhanced photo album. In this project you'll make a digital photo album with simulated 3D turning pages, sound effects, music, captions, the whole nine yards! And you'll learn how to publish your album as a CD that can play on a PC or a DVD player connected to a TV.

Materials

For this project you'll need

- Digital photos on your PC's hard disk.
- Advanced multimedia album-maker software. We'll use FlipAlbum 6 Suite.
- MP3 digital music file(s) for background music.
- CD burner to create an album disc for playback on a PC or DVD player connected to a TV.

Time

Budget about three to four hours for this baby. You'll need to download and install the free trial version of FlipAlbum 6 Suite and spend some quality time learning the ropes. Following that, you'll gather and insert a series of photos and then add text captions and a background music file. The final steps include making a disc for PC playback and a version you can play in a DVD player connected to a TV.

Step 1: Plan Your Project

This one requires a little planning, even more so than the projects we've done so far. Although you can obviously select any topic under the sun, let's start with something simple. How about an album to preserve your vacation memories? Use Windows Explorer to make a new subfolder under the My Pictures area on your hard disk and name it `Vacation Photos 2004`. Find and copy your digital photo files to this new folder. Again, I strongly recommended you make copies of all photo files to be included in this test album. Keep the original snaps intact. If you have prints as your source, follow the steps in Chapter 2 to scan and create digital photo files.

Step 2: Download and Install FlipAlbum 6 Suite

Follow the steps below to find and download the 30-day free trial version of FlipAlbum Suite 6.

1. Turn on your PC, connect to the Internet, and point your browser to http://www.flipalbum.com.

2. On the opening page, look for the listing of PC products. Find and click the Try button to begin downloading a free trial version of FlipAlbum 6 Suite. I've been using various versions of the product for the past few years and it gives you a solid introduction to the world of sophisticated multimedia album-making software.

3. An initial screen gives you the option of providing your email if you want notifications from the manufacturer. Click the Go button to begin the download process. A File Download—Security Warning dialog box appears. Click Save and use the Save As dialog box to place the file in your downloads folder. Click Save and a progress bar appears, indicating the status of the transfer of data to the folder you selected or created.

4. When the Download complete dialog box appears you may, if you wish, clean your desktop by closing all other open windows before clicking the Run button. Click the Run button and follow the onscreen menus and dialog boxes to complete the installation. You might encounter a Security Warning dialog box asking if you want to run the software. If you do, click the Run button.

5. Follow the onscreen menus and dialog boxes to complete the installation. When the installation completes, the last Download Status dialog box remains on screen. Close this window, and then click Start, All Programs, E-Book Systems, FlipAlbum Suite Eval, and then the FlipAlbum Suite icon.

6. When you place your mouse pointer over the FlipAlbum 6 Suite Eval selection, a new mini menu appears listing FlipAlbum Help, FlipAlbum Sample, FlipAlbum Suite and Uninstall FlipAlbum Suite. Select and run Sample for a taste of what this program can do. You'll see a message indicating you have 30 days to try the software. Click OK and the sample tutorial album kicks into gear.

Play around with the mouse pointer. The lifelike 3D look and feel, combined with the turning page sound effect, gives digital photo albums made with this product show-stopping appeal.

Step 3: Create an Album

Now it's time to create an album, which we'll do using the FlipAlbum's QuickStart Wizard.

1. Look at the upper-left toolbar area and click the large Start button to bring up the QuickStart Wizard. It shows a very clear three-step process for creating your first animated album, as shown in Figure 3.10.

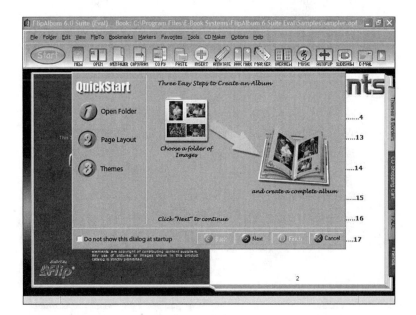

FIGURE 3.10

Flip Album 6's QuickStart menu presents three easy steps to create a basic animated album.

3. Click Next at the bottom of the QuickStart window and scroll up to the top of the file tree display. Click the My Documents folder icon and then go to My Pictures and find the folder you made to hold the set of photos for your first FlipAlbum experiment. With the folder you want highlighted, click the Next button.

4. Now it's time for step two, page layout. Select Single Image per Page and click Next to move to the third step.

5. Next it's time to pick a theme for the album. The trial version shows only one choice, a charming but retro Mother Goose–like theme. The full version includes loads of themes. For now, go ahead and use this theme. It gives you a taste for the potential effect. Later I'll show you how to create your own custom theme.

Note the artwork for all the album elements this theme provides, from front and back covers to decorative page separators. Click Finish and sit back for a few seconds as the program assembles all the elements to make your first FlipAlbum. In a few seconds your album should appear on the screen.

Step 4: Navigating Your FlipAlbum

Now it's time to learn how to navigate your FlipAlbum and explore its structure. Place your mouse pointer over the surface of the album cover. The pointer should look like a hand. Now move to the upper edge of a page opposite of the center binding. The hand pointer turns into the image of a dog-eared page. Left click your mouse and voilà, the page turns, accompanied by a convincing sound effect (see Figure 3.11).

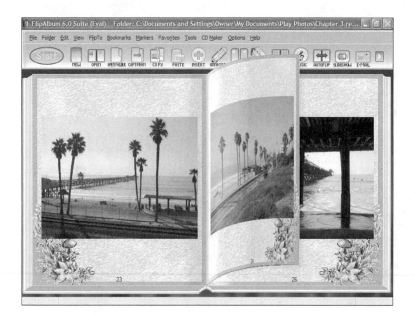

FIGURE 3.11

Following the steps in the QuickStart routine automatically generates a 3D album with animated turning pages you can control.

That's cool, but you can take even more complete control of the page turning. Move your mouse pointer to the lower outer edge of a page and the pointer symbol changes to look like a hand holding a page with text lines across it. Left click and suddenly you are in control of the page turning speed and position. Slowly move your mouse pointer left and right and the page dutifully follows. The images even bend with the shape of the page.

Time for a tour of the layout and organization of your album. The first page turn reveals a gallery of thumbnail reproductions of each photo in the album. The number of pages in the gallery will vary as determined by the volume of photos in your collection.

Click through the gallery page(s) to find the Contents page. You'll see a list of all the photos by

> **tip** FlipAlbum's controls also allow you to jump to the front cover, back cover, table of contents, first page, or index with a few mouse clicks. Place your mouse pointer in a border area of any page (not on the surface of a photo) and right-click your mouse, Flip To, and then select the location you want.

name with a page number assigned. Move your mouse pointer over the table of contents and each photo is highlighted, one after the other. Highlight and left click an entry and, bingo, the album instantly jumps to the page where the image is displayed.

Click through all the pages and you'll discover at the end of the album an index page(s) that performs the same function as the table of contents.

Step 5: Basic Editing

Follow the steps below to control photo positioning and to create text captions.

Let's look at some of the basic FlipAlbum editing functions:

- To better position your photo (vertically) on a page, place your mouse pointer over the area of a photo. Click the mouse and dashed lines and little boxes appear at each corner of the image. Hold the left mouse button down and move the mouse pointer up and down to reposition the photo.

- You can also add a simple text caption. Find the Pencil tool on the top horizontal toolbar. Note that it's split down the middle. Click the left side of the Pencil to insert a text caption for the left page, or the right side for the opposite page. When you click either side of the Pencil icon, a blank box appears. Type in a short caption. Note the wide range of text font, color, type size, positioning commands, and other choices available, as shown in Figure 3.12.

Enter caption text here

FIGURE 3.12

Clicking the Pencil icon brings up a text box to create your caption.

Step 6: Add a Musical Background

Follow the steps below to add a running musical background.

1. Find the musical note icon on the top menu. Click it and an Information dialog box appears stating No Book Background Music Is Defined, Do You Want to Select One Now? Click Yes and a new Set Book Options dialog box appears with the Audio tab on top. Leave the Enable Flipping Sound and Enable Audio boxes checked. You'll see the background music box is empty. To do the next step, you must have a WAV, MIDI, or MP3 format music file on your PC.

2. Don't worry if you are not familiar with these music and sound file formats. Click Start, My Music and then use the search tool to for files with a `.wav`, `.mp3`, or `.mid` ending (the geeks call this an *extension*). The search operation will present any files it finds in your My Music folder that FlipAlbum accepts.

3. With a music file identified or ripped, placed on your hard disk, and with the Audio tab of the Set Book Options dialog box again displayed, find the Add button and click it. This brings up an Open dialog box displaying the folders under your Windows XP My Documents area.

4. Scroll through the horizontal panning display and go to the My Music folder and open it. If the files in My Music are in one of the three formats the program recognizes, you'll see the files listed, as shown in Figure 3.13. Highlight a file and click Open.

> **note** At the very least your My Music folder should have a subfolder called Sample Music with two files in it that use the Microsoft `.wma` format. Unfortunately, FlipAlbum will not use these files. If you weren't able to find any other digital music that FlipAlbum can use in your My Music folder, grab one of your commercial music CDs and use the built-in Windows Media Player 10 software (click Start, All Programs, Windows Media Player) to *rip* (transfer) a track to your PC as an MP3 music file. See the CD-ripping project in Chapter 6, "Turn Your PC into the Ultimate Music Jukebox," to learn how to do this. (Note that by default Windows Media Player rips music using the WMA file format. You'll need to configure it to rip to MP3 files instead.)

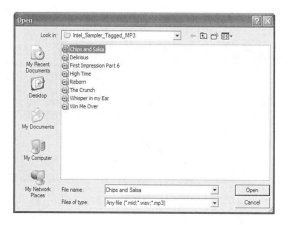

FIGURE 3.13

If your My Music folder contains files FlipAlbum 6 recognizes, a list of eligible candidates is displayed.

5. You are now returned to the Audio tab with the information FlipAlbum needs to find the file displayed in the Background Music List box. Click OK on the lower right of the Audio tab. Your album appears in all its glory, playing the background music you selected.

Step 6: Customize Your FlipAlbum's Looks

Although the Mother Goose theme default we've been using here is cute, it's not going to be ideal for most albums, including the vacation album I've been using as an example here. Follow these steps to create your own theme using digital pictures from any folder on your hard disk.

1. With your test album on display, go to the top menu bar, click Tools, Create Theme.

2. The Create Theme dialog box appears. At the top, give your custom theme a name. I keyed in Vacation 2004. Look at the bottom of the dialog box and click the Add/Edit button to begin the process of replacing the default artwork for each album element with a photo you select.

3. You'll discover the first time you click Add/Edit, an Open dialog box appears that allows you to navigate to a folder on your hard drive containing the photos you want to use to build a custom theme set. Find the photo folder you want and then highlight and click the image you want to serve as the front cover. Repeat the process for all the elements. You may also double-click any album element frame box shown in the Create Theme dialog box and then highlight the photo you want to insert. I used digital snaps from my vacation 2004 photo folder as shown in Figure 3.14.

FIGURE 3.14

The Create Theme dialog box allows you to select digital photos as cover art, page backgrounds, and so forth.

4. Click OK and a dialog box announces the new theme has been created.

5. Return to the top toolbar and click Options, Set Theme. The Themes dialog box appears, listing choices that now include the theme you just created. Highlight your theme and click OK. In a few moments, your album gets a makeover based on your custom theme.

6. At this point, be sure you save your masterpiece because we're going to burn it to a CD.

Step 7: Put Your Album on CD

To make a CD album disc for playback on a PC, open FlipAlbum 6 (making sure to close the QuickStart Wizard) and follow these steps:

1. Go to the upper toolbar and click Open. The Open a Book dialog box displays with an empty horizontal box. Click the down-arrow button on the far right of the box and a list should drop down with your album cited. Highlight your album and click OK.

2. With your album now onscreen, go to the top horizontal menu bar and click CD Maker, Make Album CD. The Create Album CD menu displays with the default buttons Create a New Album CD/Single Album on CD already selected. We're going to make a single album CD, so click OK.

3. In a few seconds, a Create a New Album CD Folder dialog box appears. Look for the Album CD Folder Name horizontal box at the top with the default name AlbumCD. Change that to a custom name, such as `Vacation 2004 Album CD`, and then click Create. A new folder under the My Documents area of your hard disk is created to contain the files needed to make a disc that can playback on a PC.

4. After the files needed are copied to the new folder, an Album CD Options dialog box appears with three items: Set Album Options, Set Album CD Title, and Preview Album CD (see Figure 3.15).

FIGURE 3.15

The Album CD Options dialog box allows you to set playback controls, provide a name for the production, and test drive how it will play back on a PC.

5. Click Set Album Options and note the various features available, such as manual or auto flipping controls. Leave the default settings in place and click OK. Next click the Set Album CD Title and key in the name you want, click OK, and move to the Preview CD Album button for a preview of your composition.

6. To end the preview, click File, Exit. Now it's time to make your CD.

7. When you return to the Album CD Options dialog box after exiting the preview, click Next and the Burn CD Information menu appears. Follow the very simple instructions to burn a CD with all of the files listed. Insert a blank CD disc in your CD drive and click the Burn to CD button.

tip
If your PC does not automatically run your Flip Album, open My Computer (click Start, My Computer) and double-click the icon for the CD drive that contains the CD. Search for a file called startCD and double-click it.

caution
Although most DVD players have no trouble playing a video CD, there are some out there that do. If you're unsure, check your DVD player's manual. Many DVD players also highlight video CD compatibility with a logo or text on the front of the player.

8. Sit back and relax as the files are burned on the CD disc. The time it takes this process to complete varies with the speed of your CD recorder. It should take less than 15 minutes on most modern drives.

9. When the burn process completes, you'll have a CD disc that should automatically start when you insert it into a CD drive on a PC running Windows XP.

Step 8: See Your Album on TV

Did you know that commercial DVD movies you buy or rent are not the only form of video disc a modern DVD player can handle? Most of these marvels of technology can also play something called *video CDs (VCDs)*. In this exercise we're going to transform your FlipAlbum into a VCD you can pop into your DVD player and enjoy on your TV screen!

1. First use Windows Explorer to create a new folder under the My Documents area and name it VCD Album Test.

2. If you already have FlipAlbum 6 up and running with your album displayed, that's great. If not, follow the steps you learned in the previous exercise to find and open your album.

3. Click the CD Maker drop-down menu found on the upper horizontal toolbar. Select Export Album for TV Viewing.

4. An Export Album for TV Viewing dialog box appears with three choices: MPEG Format, AVI Format, and Slide Show. The first two refer to specific video formats you'll learn about in Chapter 4. For now, let's go for the Slide Show option, which creates a single album presentation on a regular CD disc that can be played back using a DVD player.

About MPEG and AVI

The option to create an MPEG or AVI video file version of your album is a powerful feature.

The MPEG option takes your album and transforms it to the MPEG-1 video format needed to create a VCD. This option is designed to be used as an intermediate step in the creation of a VCD containing multiple FlipAlbums. However, you need a separate video-production software package designed to make VCDs and DVDs to do this. The Slide Show option in this version of FlipAlbum only creates a single album VCD.

The AVI option converts your FlipAlbum into a high-quality video format that can be used with a separate video-editing program to create input files needed for menu-driven SVCDs (higher resolution VCDs) and even DVDs.

Keep this in mind as you travel through Chapter 4. There you'll learn how to make your own VCDs, SVCDs, and DVDs.

5. Click the Slide Show button, but before you click OK at the bottom of the menu, we need to tell the program to put the production in the VCD Album Test folder I asked you to create earlier. Note the text Select the Location and Name of Export Folder. A default directory and folder is provided, but I'm a big fan of making folders with descriptive names so it will be easy to find your work in the future.

6. Click the little rectangle button to the right of the white box holding the default folder path information. A Create a New Folder dialog box appears, which you can use to tell FlipAlbum 6 where to store the VCD files. First find your VCD Test Album folder and highlight it. Notice that at the top of the Create a New Folder dialog box, there is a field labeled Folder Name. The default is Album Still. Change that to something meaningful, such as Vacation 2004. Click Create and the program builds a subfolder under the VCD Test Album folder named Vacation 2004. The files needed to create the VCD are placed in the new subfolder.

7. You are now sent back to the main Export Album for TV Viewing dialog box. Click OK. Wait a few seconds and a Saving dialog box appears showing a progress bar. The photos and other associated files are being prepared for the VCD recording process.

8. When the saving process is complete, a Capture Album Pages dialog box appears (see Figure 3.16). Skip over the Export Location field and focus on the Flipping Interval slider. You can move the slider bar to the left or right to adjust the amount of time a two-page spread of your album is displayed on your TV screen. My preference is to go with eight seconds, but ultimately your selection here will vary based on personal tastes.

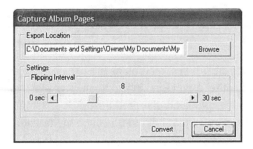

FIGURE 3.16

The interval slider bar makes it easy to select the amount of time a page will display when played back on a DVD.

9. Okay, it's time to burn the CD. Insert a blank CD into your PC's CD burner. Make sure the Burn to CD-R/RW check box is checked on the Capture Album Pages dialog box and then click the Start button. You might see a prompting message stating Please Make Sure That an Empty CD-R/RW Disc Has Been Put in CD-writer.

10. A Capture Album Pages dialog box now displays a progress bar and the message Exporting *Your Album Name*. When this completes, a Burning Files to CD dialog box shows a progress bar gauging the burning process. You will hear your CD drive come to life as the files are burned on the disc.

11. If all goes according to plan, an Information dialog box appears, announcing This Album Has Been Successfully Burned to CD.

12. Okay, it's the moment you've been waiting for—time to play your disc using a DVD player connected to a TV. Remove the disc, label it with a permanent marker, and insert the disc into your DVD player.

13. Playing a VCD on your DVD is a different ball game than playing a commercial DVD. It might take a few seconds for your player to analyze the disc. In a few moments the DVD player's screen should display VCD. But wait, nothing is happening. No worries! Just press the Play button on your DVD player and in a few seconds your album is presented on your TV screen.

Seeing your Flip Album displayed on the TV is a rush. The VCD format discs you make are a great option for sharing your albums with a friend or relative who does not own a PC. VCDs are nifty, but there are a few limitations. First, your slide show VCD does not deliver the eye-catching 3D page turning. Likewise, because TV resolution is considerably lower than that of your PC display, text captions may be unreadable on your TV screen. If a VCD is your output goal, be sure the text captions are made using a large font size and a short message.

Using FlipAlbum to Preserve and Share Family History

Are you a genealogy nut? If yes, read on as my personal project story may inspire you to use FlipAlbum or another album-making software package to save and share your precious family history. Recognizing that programs such as FlipAlbum 6 can be powerful family history tools, here's what I did to transform my father's WWII photo album into a digital heirloom.

Ever see the 1990 movie about the crew of the Memphis Belle bomber? The film dramatically portrayed the harrowing experiences of a B-17 bomber crew flying missions over Germany. My father lived that story as he served as a top turret gunner and master mechanic on his Flying Fortress.

When not rattling off rounds from his double barrel machine gun in pitched battles in the sky, he'd pull out a small camera and capture shots of combat, life on the plane, and his R and R trips throughout Europe (see Figure 3.17).

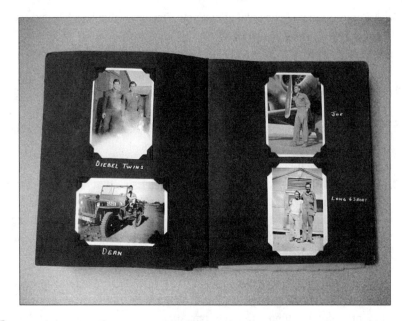

FIGURE 3.17

My father's WWII album is full of tiny photos measuring a mere 2.5 by 3.5 inches.

Like so many war heroes, my father never talked much about his experiences before he died in 1966. When my mom passed in 1981, I inherited his now frail and aging little album. Because it's such an important piece of family history, I wanted to create a special, enhanced digital version my sister Carol and my dad's sister Virginia could hold, cherish, and pass down to future generations.

Enter FlipAlbum 6 and a variation on the idea of having a musical MP3 audio file background. Instead of using music, I recorded my Aunt Virginia's voiced recollections of Dad's war stories and used them as a running audio narration. (See Chapter 7, "Turn Your PC into a Recording Studio," on how to record audio using your PC.) To complement my aunt's voiceover, I added informative text captions to each image in the album. The result was very rewarding, as shown in Figure 3.18.

This is a perfect example of how the power of your PC can preserve the kinds of memories many families have collected through the years. I can tell you the reaction of my sister and aunt was worth all the hours of work it took to put this together!

Are You Hooked Yet?

The kinds of exercises I've covered here just barely scratched the surface of all the things a photo album-making program such as FlipAlbum 6 Suite can do. Other popular PC photo album-making programs include

- Adobe PhotoShop Album ($49.99, http://www.adobe.com)
- Magix Photo Story on CD and DVD ($39.99, http://site.magix.net/index.php?411)
- Paint Shop Photo Album ($49, http://www.jasc.com)
- Ulead CD and DVD PictureShow 3 Deluxe ($49.99, http://www.ulead.com)
- Creating Keepsakes Scrapbook Designer Deluxe ($29.99, http://www.broderbund.com)

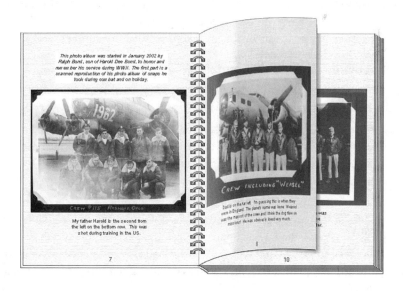

FIGURE 3.18

Using FlipAlbum 6, I created an annotated 3D album narrated by my Aunt Virginia.

Project: Create Paperback or Hardbound Albums

So far, our projects have all resulted in purely digital output. This time the goal is a paperback or hardbound photo album made using your digital snaps. Digital albums are wonderful and they have their place. But the good old tangible album you can hold in your hands is far from obsolete in most families. In this exercise you'll learn how to use one of the many online album-making services to create a composition on your PC and upload it to a photo album web service for production.

Materials

To complete this project you'll need

- Personal computer connected to the Internet (high speed DSL or cable link strongly recommended).
- Digital photos on your PC's hard disk.
- Album-making software provided from one of the online photo album-making services. For this exercise we'll use MyPublisher.
- A wallet with at least $9.95 to spend for a paperback album from MyPublisher, plus a small shipping fee.

Time

About two to three hours to download and install the MyPublisher album-making software, set up an account with the service, insert your photos, arrange your page layouts, provide text captions, and upload your final project via the Internet.

Step 1: Get the MyPublisher Software

As with most of the projects so far, you need to first download and install the necessary album-making software from MyPublisher.

1. With your PC turned on and connected to the Internet, point your browser to http://www.mypublisher.com. Look for the Get Started tab which brings up an initial introductory page describing and illustrating the MyPublisher BookMaker program you'll download and use to make your album.

2. Look to the upper right and click the Next button to start the download process. Look for the large Download Now button. Click it and the standard Windows XP File Download dialog box appears. Click the Save button and then use the Save As menu to locate and open your downloads folder under My Documents. When you are ready, click Save. It's a very small program that should download quickly.

3. Use Windows Explorer again to find and open your downloads folder. Double-click the `bmsetup.exe` file. Accept the license agreement and click OK when a polite message appears thanking you for downloading the program. When the installation is complete, the program automatically opens.

Before we jump to the next step, I want to call your attention to the online help guide MyPublisher provides. When you first start up the BookMaker program, a Quick Start Guide page should appear. Read through the outline of steps and tips this page provides. You can always get to the program's help resources by clicking on the Help button on the far right at the top of the program interface.

Although the Quick Start Guide is good, I want to personally walk you through the essential steps needed to make and order your first album.

Step 2: Create an Album and Load Photos

1. Go to the top of the program and click File, New Book. The screen now displays a Windows Explorer-like tree listing of your hard disk's folders in a vertical box on the left.

2. Return to the File menu and click Save As. Type in a meaningful name for your album in the small pop-up menu and click OK.

3. Use the folder tree display on the far left to navigate to the folder containing the photos you want to insert into your album. When you open a folder containing digital photos the images are displayed as thumbnails on the right side of the screen.

4. To select photos from any folder, and in any order you like, simply highlight and drag the photo you select down to the lower horizontal area at the bottom of the screen, as shown in Figure 3.19. Another option for adding photos is to highlight the photo you want and then click the Add Photos button at the bottom. You may also highlight more than one photo at a time (by holding down the Ctrl key when clicking each photo) and then click the Add Photos button.

Step 3: Get Organized and Enhance Images

After you have your photos selected, it's time to get organized.

1. Look at the bottom horizontal toolbar with these choices: Get Photos, Organize, Enhance, Book, Purchase, and Help. Click Organize and the screen changes to a display of all the photos you have selected in a box with a scroll bar on the far left. Not happy with the order of the photos? No problemo! Just drag and drop each image into the order you want.

2. Next click the Enhance button and a new screen appears with your selected photos now displayed in a scrolling vertical zone to the far left.

3. In the main work screen area, the photo you selected is displayed. Check out all the editing tools at the bottom, as shown in Figure 3.20. Play around with each. You can always undo any applied effect using the Undo tool on the far right.

Drag and drop photo

FIGURE 3.19

Finding and selecting images for an album is easy with BookMaker Add Photos screen.

Drag and drop photo

FIGURE 3.20

The BookMaker program offers a solid set of basic editing tools, including one to transform your snaps into black-and-white images for an old-time look.

Step 4: Design the Layout

BookMaker gives you complete control over the layout of the album you're creating. From the number of pictures to put on a page to the use of double-sided printing, the choice is yours.

1. With all your photos now edited, click the Book button on the bottom toolbar to begin the page layout and text caption entry process.

2. Explore the various page layout options, including one image or multiple photos per page and single- or double-sided printing. Note that in the lower-right corner of the screen, two tools are displayed—Theme and Template. Click the down arrow button associated with Template and a listing of options appears, from a single photo per page to mixtures of multiple images per page. Select the setting you want.

3. To determine the number of images per page, use your mouse to drag layout templates from the far left and drop it on the photo displayed in the main work area. The template is applied with the photo now inserted, as shown in Figure 3.21. Repeat this process for all the pages of your album.

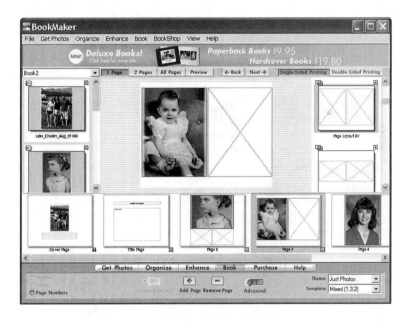

FIGURE 3.21

Scroll through the page layout options displayed on the far right vertical box and use your mouse to drag and drop the desired template on the page displayed in the center area.

Step 5: Add Text

Now it's time to add some text captions so that you can give the pictures in your album some context. (This is an option I really like.)

1. Return to the lower-right area of the screen and click the down-arrow button associated with the Theme box. I suggest selecting the Traditional theme. This theme provides a compact text box area for each photo.

2. Next, let's set up your cover page and enter text. In the bottom horizontal area showing the photos in your album, the left-most image is labeled as the cover page. Highlight this page to bring it to the center work area. The program takes the first photo in your group and automatically places it as the cover image. To change the image, drag and drop an alternative from the lower horizontal lineup of the photos in your album.

3. Note the three horizontal empty boxes below the cover image. Clicking on any of these boxes brings up a large horizontal work area into which you may type a title or caption, as shown in Figure 3.22. You may also use the tools provided to change the font size and style.

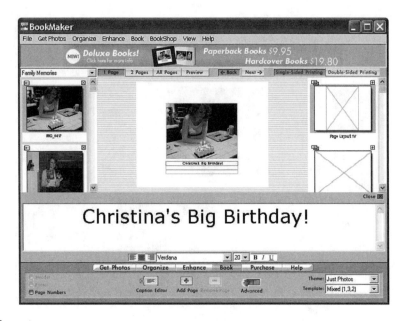

FIGURE 3.22

Adding a text caption to a photo is a breeze. Click an outline box below or next to a photo and a work area opens, ready for you to key in text.

4. When you are finished with the cover page, add text using the same steps for all the pages of your album.

Step 6: Test Drive Before You Buy

Drum roll please; it's time for a test drive. Notice the 1 Page, 2 Pages, All Pages, and Preview buttons above the main photo displayed in the central area of the screen. The 2 Pages button displays two pages of your album at once. And don't miss the buttons in the upper-right area where you decide if you want double- or single-side printing.

Are You Hooked Yet?

MyPublisher is just one of many equally rewarding online album making services available today. I encourage you to explore what Ofoto, Shutterfly, Snapfish, SmugMug and others have to offer.

When you are finished with your design, click the Preview button to dry run the layout before you plunk down your hard-earned cash to order the production and shipping of a paperback or hardbound album.

Step 7: Upload Your Album

If you're happy with what you saw in the preview, the next phase is to register with MyPublisher, place your order, and upload the album.

1. Move from the Book screen by clicking the Purchase button. From the general greeting page, move to the lower-right corner and click Continue. As a new customer, you'll be directed to enter your email address. Once that's entered, click the I'm a New Customer button.

2. Click the Sign in Using Our Secure Server button and the Create or Edit a Customer Account screen displays. Fill in the information boxes and click Continue. Fill in the billing information address screen and click Continue.

3. From here wizard pages guide you through the process of ordering a paperbound or hardbound album and the steps to upload your album to the MyPublisher service.

4. Congratulations! In about two weeks your album will arrive in the mail, just like the one I made of our summer vacation photos, shown in Figure 3.23.

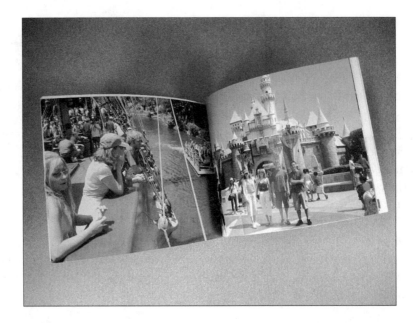

FIGURE 3.23

The photos I took of our vacation using a standard 3.2 megapixel digital camera looked great in my first MyPublisher album.

What's next? Now that you have your sea legs when it comes to digital photo restoration, preservation, online sharing, and album making in various forms it's time to explore the world of digital video. Chapter 4 will give you the tools and skills to digitize and preserve your home video tape movies. You'll even learn how to make DVDs you can play on the big screen TV!

Lights, Camera, Action!

The incredible, morphing PC never ceases to amaze me. Clever software programmers and hardware engineers just keep finding new and exciting roles for it to fill. In this chapter you'll discover how video gear you might already own, combined with editing software, a CD or DVD burner, and some attachments, can transform your home PC into a movie-making studio.

All the magic starts by getting your home videos off tape and onto your PC's hard disk. After mastering the basic skills needed to accomplish this, you'll learn how to

- Edit video clips
- Stitch clips together to create compositions
- Add titles and transitions
- Make a variety of enhanced video files and discs designed to play on a PC or DVD player

Here's a roadmap of what lies ahead:

- Learn how to capture video using a digital camcorder or analog VHS/Hi8 gear and store it on your PC's hard disk
- Learn how to transfer old analog video tapes to a digital camera
- Learn how to edit digital video clips using a program called MyDVD (free trial version available)
- Create a Video CD (VCD) or DVD using MyDVD with menus that will play on a DVD player

Skills and Gear Check

If you know how to operate a PC, digital camcorder, Hi8 analog camcorder, or VHS player, you're ready to go.

Materials

For the projects in this chapter you'll need

- A modern Windows XP personal computer. Video editing and production is a power-hungry task for your PC. The more power you have, the less time it takes to apply edits and special effects. Ideally, you should have a Pentium 4 processor operating at 3GHz or higher or a laptop with a Pentium M processor running at 1.8GHz or higher.
- High-speed connection to the Internet to download the trial MyDVD software.
- A standard USB 2.0 high-speed port (this applies to VHS or Hi8 tape users who will be directed to purchase a video recording adapter).
- A standard high-speed FireWire (also called 1394 or i.Link) port for digital camcorder users.

Open Wallet Alert

This chapter contains projects that require the purchase of gear needed to link a digital camcorder, VHS player, or Hi8 camcorder to a PC.

Digital video camcorder owners are looking at an investment of around $40 if their PC is not already equipped with a FireWire port. Add about $20 if your digital camcorder did not include a FireWire cable (you'll learn all about this later).

VHS or Hi8 analog tape users are looking at a potential investment of around $30 for a USB 2.0 adapter (if their desktop PC does not have this built in). Analog tape users will also need around $100 to $200 for a video-capture device (which can be an external box or an internal adapter card).

That said, analog tape users who purchase or own a digital camcorder can use patch cables costing less than $10 to transfer all their VHS and Hi8 tapes to digital tapes and then pursue the digital camcorder projects in this chapter.

In either case, to go for the ultimate home movie and to produce DVD discs, you must have a DVD burner installed in or connected to your PC. Check your desktop or laptop; if it's brand new, you might have one already built in. If not, get ready to spend from $100 to $200 to add this feature.

There's no way to avoid these investments, but I've made every effort to select modestly priced sample products.

- Built-in or externally connected CD and/or DVD burner to create final productions that can be played on a PC or DVD player.
- Blank CD and/or DVD discs.

Analog Versus Digital Video

If you boil it down to the roots, the world of video is divided into two camps—analog and digital. (Beyond that, you have multiple standard and high-definition video standards and plenty of digital video file formats.)

Analog camcorders and VCRs record video and audio input in a form that differs from the codes used in digital video. I could launch into a science lesson, but let's cut to what you need to know right now: Each time you make a copy of an analog tape, you lose quality. And time, moisture, sunlight, and so on gradually deteriorate analog tapes. That's why going digital rocks. You can convert analog video to a format based on a digital code and, in effect, stop the march of time. And tapes made with a digital camcorder, of course, are digital from the get go.

Some digital camcorders use the same tapes as those needed for a Hi8 analog camcorder. New digital tape camcorders typically use the mini-cartridge format. But here's the kicker—whatever size tape your digital camcorder employs, images and sound are recorded using a digital code.

Digital video offers lots of advantages, including

- Video and sound can be duplicated without loss of quality
- Better overall image quality
- Ability to quickly capture and transfer from a digital video camcorder to your PC where you can edit it easily

What's the downside? Whether your source tapes are analog or digital, when you capture them to your PC, they create very large files. For example, it can take more than 4GB to store one hour of DV-AVI-quality video (the highest recording setting

note If your family video memories are on VHS or Hi8 tapes, you're in trouble! Imagine discovering one day that your baby's first steps, your wedding, your son or daughter's first T-ball home run are lost forever. Experts tell us that traditional analog video tapes (VHS, Super VHS, VHS-C, and Hi-8) may deteriorate to the point of being unwatchable in as little as 10 years.

The tools and techniques in this chapter can be applied to help preserve your old VHS or Hi8 camcorder video treasures and create new digital heirlooms stored on CDs or DVD discs.

note Today, digital video camcorders use three ways to save movies. Until very recently the world of digital video camcorders included models that recorded movies directly to either tapes or miniature DVD discs. Most models today record to either MiniDV or Digital8 cassette tapes. New models that write video files to onboard hard disks are also now coming to market. These cutting-edge models make it even more convenient to quickly transfer digital video files to a PC.

used today with PC video recording software, and the format recommended if you plan to edit your video files). File sizes vary by format. For example, the MPEG-2 format delivers high quality video with much smaller file sizes. However, DV-AVI is the preferred format for PC-based video editing.

Project: Use FireWire to Connect a Digital Camcorder to a PC

There's a lot to love about the technology we call FireWire. First, it makes it super easy to patch your digital camera and PC together. Next, the digital information stored on your camcorder's tape can move to your PC's hard disk at a fast clip using this link. And last, software designed to take advantage of a FireWire connection allows your PC and mouse to remote control your digital camcorder (more about this later).

In this project digital camcorder users will learn how to

- Identify a FireWire (also called 1394 or i.Link) port
- Purchase and install a FireWire adapter card into a desktop PC or laptop (if not already factory installed)
- Use a FireWire cable to link a digital camcorder to a PC

Time

If you own a PC with a factory-installed FireWire port, it will take less than a minute to patch your digital camcorder to your PC. If you need to purchase an adapter card for your desktop or laptop PC, figure about one hour for desktop users (after you go to the store and buy the adapter card) to install the card and about 30 minutes for laptop users to install a PC card on their systems.

Step 1: Check Your PC for FireWire

Follow these steps to determine if your PC has a FireWire port.

1. Before you do anything, grab the owner's manual that came with your PC and see if it lists a FireWire, 1394, or i.Link port on your PC. If it does, great. Move on to the next section. If not, you'll need to inspect your PC first hand.

note FireWire was developed by Apple Computer as a way to transfer digital information between a computer and peripherals at high speeds. One of its key advantages is that it's designed so the computer can instantly recognize when a device is connected to it ("auto detect" and "plug-and-play").

note I know it's goofy, but this port goes by one of three names. The Apple crowd prefers FireWire, with the international engineering community defaulting to the 1394 name selected by the Institute of Electrical and Electronics Engineers (IEEE) standards group. Sony uses the i.Link name to identify this port on their PCs and digital camcorders. For simplicity, I'll stick to the FireWire name (it sounds cooler, and the folks at computer stores all know what this means).

2. Look over the front and back of your PC and see if you find a rectangular port with one curved end at the top. A laptop FireWire port takes a mini form. Both of these ports are shown in Figure 4.1. If you have a FireWire port on your PC, jump to Step 3: Find or Buy a FireWire Cable. If not, proceed to Step 2: Purchase and Install a FireWire Adapter.

FIGURE 4.1

A standard desktop PC FireWire port (left) looks like a rectangle with one of the short sides taking a somewhat curved shape (note the symbol that identifies the port). Due to size limitations, many laptop designs use mini FireWire ports (right).

Step 2: Purchase and Install a FireWire Adapter

If your PC doesn't already have a FireWire port, don't fret. Modestly priced FireWire adapter cards can be found in your local computer or office supply store. Prices for desktop cards run around $30, with PC card adapters for laptops going for about $60. Examples of desktop and laptop FireWire adapters are shown in Figure 4.2.

Desktop users can add a FireWire adapter card in two ways—have one professionally installed or install it manually. Either way, you'll need to purchase the card. If you're not sure what to look for, take this book to your local computer or office supply store and show the sales clerk Figure 4.3. Lots of choices are available from companies such as Adaptec, Belkin, IOGear, Startech, and Orange Micro.

FIGURE 4.2

On the right is an ADS Technologies PYRO 1394 Port PC card adapter for a laptop. On the left is a CompUSA PCI card designed for desktop PCs that adds three FireWire plugs.

If the notion of fiddling with your PC's innards makes your heart race and your face go pale, take your PC to a computer repair shop and pay them to do it (many mainstream retailers, such as Best Buy and CompUSA, can do this job in a flash). If you're willing and able to be your own mechanic, installing an internal adapter card is fairly quick work, but the details of doing so are beyond the scope of this book.

In a nutshell, you must cut off all power to your PC, remove the case, and insert the new FireWire card into an open PCI slot (if your PC has one available). Generally, the only tool required is a Phillips screwdriver, which may be needed to open the case and to remove the metal plate that covers an empty expansion slot. After installation, you'll need to restart Windows and provide it with the *drivers* it needs to recognize your card. The instructions that came with your adapter card should provide the necessary details for all parts of this process.

If you own a laptop, the job is much simpler. Obviously, if you have a FireWire port already, you're good to go (refer to Figure 4.1). If not, don't feel bad. It's not a feature found on most laptops.

The good news is your laptop should have one or two PC card slots (thin credit card-sized slots that can accept expansion cards). Consult your user's manual to confirm where your slots are located on the laptop. PC card slots can be used to hold lots of goodies, from wireless network adapters to cards that add functions such as USB and FireWire ports.

If you need to purchase a FireWire PC card, take this book to your local computer or office supply store and show the sales clerk Figure 4.2 and point to the PC card example. Companies that make FireWire PC cards include Adaptec, ADS Technologies, CompUSA, IOGear, Star Tech, and SIIG.

Follow the manufacturer's instructions to the letter when installing the card. You might be asked to install driver software before you insert the card.

caution **Wait!** Be sure to check your manufacturer's warranty statement to ensure that opening the case and installing a card does not void your warranty.

Step 3: Find or Buy a FireWire Cable

A FireWire cable is required to link your digital camcorder to your PC or laptop's FireWire port. The first logical step is to see if your digital camcorder or FireWire adapter card came with a FireWire cable. For desktop users, your cable should look like the one on the left in Figure 4.3, with the laptop version having a mini-plug at each end, as exhibited in the cable on the right.

FIGURE 4.3

Two forms of the FireWire cables are shown in this photo. The one on the left is designed for desktop PCs, with the one on the right for laptops. If one didn't come with your PC, laptop, or digital camcorder, expect to pay around $20 for a quality cable.

FireWire cables are not hard to find, but it's important to get the right one for your situation. Most desktop PC FireWire cables have a large connector at one end designed to be inserted on the PC side, with a mini-plug at the other end for insertion into the digital video camcorder. Most PC laptop card adapters opt for the mini-port, so you'll need a mini-to-mini style FireWire cable. Do your homework before you hop in the car and spend your money at the computer or office supply store.

tip
If you're shopping for a new video camcorder, make sure it has a FireWire port. It's a good time to buy because digital video camcorders are readily available for $300 and more.

caution
FireWire technology transfers a lot of data at very high speeds. The quality of the cable you use has a bearing on the quality of the signal. Cheap cables might diminish signal quality. Go for a high-quality cable from makers such as Belkin and Dynex and expect to pay around $30 and more.

Project: Recording Your Analog Videos to Digital Cassette Tapes

If you have a digital camcorder and also have old analog video cassette tapes you want digitized to your PC, you can put your digital camcorder to work as a middleman.

At first glance, this might seem like jumping through an extra hoop. You might be thinking, "Why not just buy an external USB-connected adapter box to work with my old analog tapes?" The motive for this project is clear—transferring your analog tapes to a digital camcorder enables you to take advantage of the benefits of the FireWire link.

Time

This is open ended, depending on the number of tapes you have to convert and how much video is on each tape.

caution Before you get started, it's important to understand that there will be a slight loss of quality from the original analog video tape when transferring to your digital camcorder. I think the upside of digitizing the material and having the benefits of the PC-to-digital camcorder link make the tradeoff and sometimes lengthy time investment acceptable.

tip If your videos are on Hi8 analog tapes that are the same size as the ones your digital camcorder uses, you might be in luck. Some digital camcorders, my Sony model for example, can identify and play back an older Hi8 analog tape. With this feature you can take advantage of the FireWire link to transfer your analog videos directly to your PC without the need for a capture device like the one used in the next project, "Capturing Analog Video to Your PC."

Step 1: Locate the Adapter Cable for Your Digital Camcorder

Before you begin, check the operating guide that came with your digital camcorder. In most cases your digital video camcorder came with an adapter cable with red, white, and yellow standard composite plugs at one end. The red and white connectors correspond to left and right stereo sound. These are the same standard plugs used for a stereo system. The yellow plug is what the engineers call a *composite video line*. At the other end of the cable is some form of connector designed for your specific camcorder, as shown in Figure 4.4.

After you've got this cable, you're set to get started. (If for some reason this cable has come up missing, check with you camera's manufacturer about ordering a replacement.)

Step 2: Connect Your Analog Source to Your Digital Camcorder

With your adapter cable in hand it's time to connect your analog source (VHS player, Hi8 analog camcorder, and so forth) to your digital camera.

Set your VHS player or Hi8 analog camcorder next to your digital video camcorder. Use the factory-supplied adapter cable to attach the audio and video plugs in the back or front of a VHS player (look for the set of plugs labeled Video Out and Audio Out). Connect the yellow composite video plug to the Video Out connector on the back of your VHS player. If a Hi8 camcorder is the source, consult its operating guide and attach the plugs accordingly.

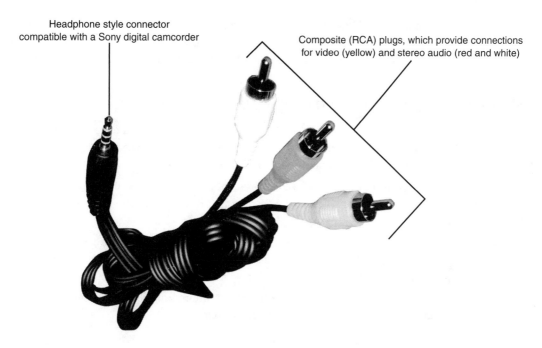

Headphone style connector compatible with a Sony digital camcorder

Composite (RCA) plugs, which provide connections for video (yellow) and stereo audio (red and white)

FIGURE 4.4

This cable connects a Sony digital video camcorder to a VHS player or Hi8 camcorder.

Step 3: Record Your Videos

Now it's time to move your analog video to its new digital home.

1. After the patch cable link is established between your VHS player or Hi8 analog camcorder and a digital camcorder, turn on both.

2. Place the old analog tape in the VHS or Hi8 unit, and a blank tape in the digital camcorder.

3. Make sure your digital camcorder is set to record video not from its lens but from the cable link you've established. (Consult your camcorder's manual, if necessary.)

4. Press play on the VHS or Hi8 side. When the camcorder's viewfinder displays the video you want to record, press its Record button.

5. At this point, you can kick back and wait for the recording to finish. This is a "real-time" process, so if you have a half hour of video to record, it will take a half hour. (Make sure you have enough tape.)

6. When you're done, stop both analog playback and digital recording.

note Some VHS and Hi8 camcorders offer *S-Video connectors* (they are round in shape). If your digital camcorder has an S-Video jack, use a standard S-Video cable to link the VHS or Hi8 player/ camcorder to the digital camera, and the red/white audio cable for the audio side. Why bother? S-Video (short for Super Video) technology will send a higher quality video stream to your digital camcorder.

When you finish, you'll have a digital tape reproduction of your old analog tape(s), and that's a great preservation step in and of itself. This new digital duplicate tape may now be used for the various digital camcorder projects in this chapter.

Project: Capturing Analog Video to Your PC

Not ready to buy a digital camcorder? No worries, mate! This portion of the chapter walks you through some of the easiest and least expensive solutions I've discovered to date to meet your needs and produce enjoyable digital video.

This section opens with an exercise to decide what approach you will use to link your analog VHS/Hi8 tape sources to a PC. Based on that decision you will do one of the following activities:

- Determine if your PC has a USB 2.0 port, and purchase an adapter card if needed (PC Card USB 2.0 adapter for laptops). Use the USB 2.0 port to link to an external analog video recording box (that you may also have to purchase).

- Purchase and install an internal PCI video recording card and follow the product's instructions for linking to an analog video source.

 ## Time

If you opt to manually install a PCI video recording card figure on about 30 to 40 minutes. For those who intend to use an external video capture box (via a USB 2.0 connection) figure about the same amount of time (more if you need to install a USB 2.0 adapter card).

Step 1: Pick a Video Capture Device

Your first challenge is deciding how you want to connect a VHS tape player or Hi8 analog camcorder to your PC or laptop. For desktop users, it all boils down to two choices:

- Buy and install a PCI video recording card designed to accept analog video and audio patch cables/connectors.

- Or go for an external USB 2.0-connected recording box designed to accept analog video and audio patch cables that, in turn, connect to a VHS player or Hi8 analog tape camcorder. If your PC does not have USB 2.0 ports, you'll also need to buy a USB 2.0 PCI card.

Based on my experience, I recommend that desktop *and* laptop users go for the USB external video recording box option. It's easier to work with and video capture quality is good. Another nice benefit is the external box may be easily moved around and used on multiple PCs.

Although plenty of quality competing products are out there, you should select the one that works best for your needs. I have selected Adaptec's VideOh! DVD external recording box for this project (see Figure 4.5). It's a product that has received good reviews and does the job as well as any in its price range. Competing products worth checking out come from companies such as ADS Technologies, AVerMedia, Belkin, Canopus, Pinnacle, Plextor, and TDK.

If, however, you decide to go with an internal PCI Video recording card solution, jump to Step 4: Install a Internal PCI Video Recording Card.

note As an added bonus, whether you opt for an internal card or external box, most video capture products come bundled with video-editing software that enables you to make VCDs and SVCDs (using a standard CD burner) and DVDs (assuming you own a DVD/CD combo burner). What a deal!

FIGURE 4.5

Adaptec's VideOh! DVD external video recording solution is one of many on the market today. It connects an analog video source, such as a VCR, to a USB port on your PC.

Priced just under $100, this solution is designed to capture and convert any analog video source into digital video files. To speed delivery of the digitized video to your PC's hard disk, this product exploits the speed of USB 2.0 technology.

The VideOh! DVD package also includes a full version of Sonic's MyDVD, which is the very consumer–friendly, step-by-step oriented software program that will be used in this chapter to record, edit, and produce home videos on Video CDs and DVDs.

Step 2: Locate a USB 2.0 Port on Your PC

This step assumes you've made the decision, as I suggest, to go with an external USB 2.0 connected recording box solution. Follow the steps below to determine if your PC has USB 2.0 ports.

Determining whether your PC has USB 2.0 ports on it can be a little tricky. Although your PC, if it's less than five years old, certainly has USB ports, the older USB 1.0 ports are identical in appearance to the second generation USB 2.0 versions (see Figure 4.6).

FIGURE 4.6

USB 1.0 and USB 2.0 ports are physically identical.

Because any modern PC will have at least two ports that look like this, the first step is to consult the documentation that came with your system to make sure they are of the USB 2.0 variety. If they're not, you'll need to purchase and install a USB 2.0 PCI expansion card for a desktop PC or a PC card product for a laptop, as discussed in the next step.

What Is USB?

USB stands for *universal serial bus* and is a feature found on most PCs made after 1995. USB *ports* (openings into which you plug a USB cable connected to a USB-compatible product such as a printer or digital camera) are usually found on the back of a PC, though many modern PCs include them on the front as well.

To make matters a little more confusing, there are now two versions of USB. USB 1.0 transfers data at 12 million bits per second. USB 2.0 boosts the speed to 480 million bits per second (that's 60 megabytes per second). Although the standards are compatible and use the same ports, connecting a USB 2.0 device to a USB 1.0 port forces it to use the slower speed, which might impact its performance. To obtain the best video results you *must* use the fast USB 2.0 technology (especially if you plan to record captured video to DVD).

Step 3: Install USB 2.0 Card (If Needed)

If your PC only has USB 1.0 ports and you find yourself faced with installing a USB 2.0 PCI card, don't fret. It's a simple procedure many can do themselves (especially with the help of a tech-head friend or family member). The process is almost exactly the same as installing a FireWire card, which I covered in the section, "Purchase and Install a

FireWire Adapter," earlier in this chapter. If, however, you have no interest in mucking with your PC's innards, most retail electronics chains that sell these cards can install them. Just bring in your copy of this book and show their PC salesperson Figure 4.7.

FIGURE 4.7

Desktop owners can add USB 2.0 ports using a PCI card, such as the SIIG model shown on the right. For laptop PCs, the Adaptec brand PC card shown on the left combines two USB ports with two FireWire ports.

Step 4: Connect the Adaptec VideOh! DVD USB Box to Your PC

Whether you had to buy a USB 2.0 adapter card or have a PC with the ports already built-in, the next step is to connect your capture device (Adaptec's VideOh! in this case) to one of the available ports. After that, we'll establish a link to your analog tape source (VHS player or Hi8 camcorder). If you use a USB 2.0 capture box other than the VideOh!, don't worry. You should find that the procedure I describe here is consistent with your device.

I'm not going to duplicate the information provided in the installation manual for the VideOh! DVD box. Instead, here's a run down of the basic steps you can expect with products like the VideOh! DVD box:

1. **Software installation**—Some USB products (and internal cards for that matter) require software to be installed before you connect the hardware to a PC. VideOh! DVD's installation calls for the insertion of the program disc containing a driver (a software program that helps Windows XP recognize and work with the product) in the PC's CD drive before making any physical hardware links.

tip For laptop owners, it's a breeze to purchase and then slip a PC card into the side of your laptop. Go to a computer or office supply store and ask for a PC card USB 2.0 adapter for your laptop. Purchase one and follow the instructions provided with the product.

note If you use an internal (PCI) video capture card (see Step 4 of this project), the only real difference from the text I've provided here is that you'll connect your VHS or Hi8 player directly to the card (or to a special adapter cable that connects to it).

2. **Power**—Connect electrical power to the capture device using the provided adapter.

3. **Patch the VHS/Hi8 player to the external recording box**—Carefully study Figure 4.8. VideOh!, and other like products, provide an audio/video patch cable to connect it to a VHS or Hi8 analog source and, in turn, to the PC or laptop's USB 2.0 port. While it may look tricky, it's actually a very simple setup.

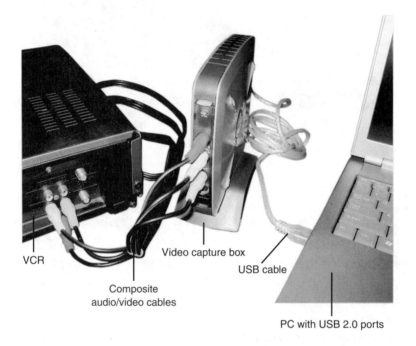

VCR

Video capture box

USB cable

Composite
audio/video cables

PC with USB 2.0 ports

FIGURE 4.8

Connecting a VCR to a PC-connected video capture device allows you to transfer old VHS or Hi8 tapes to your PC.

4. **Making the USB link**—Connect the VideOh! DVD box to the PC. Insert the USB cable supplied with the product in the back of the recording box and the other end in an empty USB 2.0 port on the PC.

After these connections are made and you turn on both your PC and the VideOh! DVD box, Windows XP automatically detects it as a new device. If the manufacturer dictated that you install the included software prior to this point you should be set to go. If not, use the product's documentation to install any necessary software or drivers.

If all goes well, the process ends with a small dialog box on the Windows XP desktop announcing that the product is installed and ready to use.

Step 4: Install a PCI Video Recording Card

Those of you opting to use an external capture box can skip this step and move on to the video capture projects in this chapter. If want to go with an internal adapter card, it's a relatively straightforward process.

Installing a PCI video capture card involves the same process discussed previously relative to adding a FireWire card to a desktop PC. If you need to go this route, refer to the step "Purchase and Install a FireWire Adapter Card," in this chapter. Follow the installation instructions for the card you select.

Good general purpose PCI video capture cards for desktop PCs include products from ADS Technologies and Pinnacle Systems.

Project: Install Sonic MyDVD

Whew! However you reached this point in the chapter, you should now be set to capture some video (analog or digital) to your PC and really start having some fun. The remaining projects in this chapter use the MyDVD video capture, editing, and disc production software package from Sonic.

If you purchased the Adaptec VideOh! external capture box, MyDVD is included. Follow the instructions provided in the product's installation guide to install MyDVD. The same applies to those who purchased an internal PCI video capture card bundled with MyDVD. After you install MyDVD, jump to the next project.

If you are a digital camcorder user or you installed a PCI analog video capture card that did not include MyDVD, follow the steps below to download and install the free 14 day trial version of MyDVD.

Time

Budget about one hour to download and install the free trial version of MyDVD. Your time initially will vary based on the speed of your Internet connection because the MyDVD trial software download is about 150 megabytes.

Step 1: Download MyDVD

Follow the steps here to visit the Sonic website, find the free trial download link, and download the program's Zip folder to your PC's hard disk.

1. Connect to the Internet and point your browser to http://www.sonic.com. When the main page opens, go to the top area and click the Support link. On the Support page, find the Quick Links area and click the Downloads link.

2. A small Get Support for Your Sonic Products dialog box appears. Use the Choose Your Product drop-down menu and select MyDVD.

3. The Downloads screen appears with a quick registration fill-in-the-blank set of boxes for your name and email address. Enter your information and click the big red Submit button to begin the download.

4. A progress dialog box displays, showing the estimated time to download the 147MB file.

note Zip folders are digital packages containing one or more compressed files. Many software manufacturers offer downloads of their products compressed into Zip files/folders so they can be more quickly transmitted via the Internet to your PC. It's a great technology that's been around for years, and is supported in Windows XP.

Step 2: Install the Trial Version of MyDVD

When the download completes, use Windows Explorer to navigate to find a folder named MyDVD_Trial-1. This is a Zip folder containing compressed files.

1. The icon for the Zip folder might appear as a folder with a cute little zipper on it. Highlight the folder with your mouse and right-click.

2. When the drop-down menu appears, search for the Extract All option and click it, as shown in Figure 4.9. This initiates the Extraction Wizard. Click the Next button and the Select a Destination dialog box appears.

FIGURE 4.9

When you find the MyDVD_Trial-1 Zip folder, right-click its icon and select Extract All from the drop-down menu.

3. Use the Browse button to navigate to your downloads folder and click the Next button to start the extraction process. Note the Extracting progress bar displayed at the bottom of the Select a Destination Wizard window.

4. When this step completes, an Extraction Complete dialog box appears with the default of Show Extracted Files checked. Click the Finish button and the screen refreshes to show the Windows Explorer utility and a MyDVD_Trial-1 folder (now without the zipper). Double-click the folder and the set of now decompressed files appears.

5. Find and click the Setup file to start the full installation of MyDVD.

6. Follow all onscreen menus and prompts to complete the installation.

7. The first time the program runs, a prompt screen appears asking you to register online. Follow the steps to register for support and updates.

note After downloaded and installed, you may use the MyDVD trial version for 14 days or up to 50 uses, whichever comes first.

Step 3: Get to Know MyDVD

With Sonic MyDVD installed it's time to get acquainted with what I've found to be one of the most intuitive video capture, edit, and production software packages for consumers I've experienced to date. Using MyDVD (free trial or full version bundled with the Adaptec VideOh! box) and a CD or DVD burner, you have a wide range of output options, including the production of VCDs and DVDs.

What the Heck Are VCDs and SVCDs?

Your home DVD player has a lot of tricks up its sleeve you might not know about, including the ability to play video files burned on to CD. These hidden talents are due to the fact that nearly all DVD players sold in North America are made in Asia. In that part of the world, rental movies for years before the advent of DVDs were burned on CDs using the VideoCD (VCD) and Super VideoCD (SVCD) formats.

As a PC owner with a CD burner, you can take cheap CD blanks, video editing software, and a standard CD burner and make your own VCDs. The video is closest in quality to a VHS tape, so it won't look as good as a DVD, but it's still a great way to make an inexpensive disc you can play on most family DVD players.

Discs burned in the SVCD format bump up the resolution to deliver quality closer to a DVD, but not all DVD players support them, so check your owner's manual.

The MyDVD software selected for this chapter can create VCDs or DVDs.

Follow these steps to become familiar with the basic working menus and features of MyDVD:

1. Go to the Windows XP desktop and look for the MyDVD icon and double-click it. (You can also open the Start menu and select All Programs, Sonic, MyDVD, Start MyDVD.) A clear and simple-to-understand Welcome to Sonic MyDVD! splash page appears, as shown in Figure 4.10.

2. Move your mouse to the upper-right area of the welcome window and *mouse over* (highlight without clicking) the DVD-Video option and then the Video CD selection. As you do, the information displayed in the main part of the window changes to reflect the differences between a VCD and a DVD. Take a few minutes to read the information for each option.

FIGURE 4.10

MyDVD's welcome screen serves as the launch pad for VCD or DVD projects.

3. MyDVD offers three major activities: Create or Modify a DVD/Video CD Project, Record Direct-to-VCD/DVD, and Edit an Existing VCD/DVD Disc. In this chapter we will work exclusively with the Create or Modify feature. After you've mastered the exercises below, I encourage you to return and learn about the other two main project areas, especially the very convenient Record Direct-to-VCD/DVD that allows you to dump the contents of a video tape directly to a blank CD or DVD.

4. For some extra homework, I also recommend examining the Tutorial resource, which can teach you a lot about MyDVD that I don't get into in these pages.

Project: Record Digital Video Clips Using MyDVD

This project shows digital camcorder users how to capture and edit video clips using MyDVD. This is a key step leading to the production of a VCD or DVD.

 Time

Figure one hour to familiarize yourself with the Capture dialog box functions and to record and edit three segments of about five to eight minutes each.

Step 1: Get Set Up

I've already covered the basics for hooking up your digital camcorder to your PC, but there are a couple of extra nuggets you'll need to do to kick things off.

1. Before you do anything, make sure you've connected your digital camera to your PC via its FireWire cable.

2. Turn the camera on and place it in playback mode. If this is the first time you have ever connected your digital camcorder to your PC, allow Windows XP a few moments to detect the camera. The end of that process results in a dialog box announcing the product is ready to use.

3. With your digital camcorder turned on and linked to the PC, start up Sonic MyDVD (refer to the previous project if you don't remember how).

> **note** The steps in this project touch the surface of what a program like MyDVD, and other comparable consumer video-editing packages, can do. The purpose here is to whet your appetite as to the possibilities of recording and editing video on a PC. If you enjoy the experience, I strongly encourage you to spend a lot of quality time experimenting with MyDVD's range of editing, special effects, and menu building features.

Step 2: Start a New MyDVD Project

When you reach the opening Welcome screen of MyDVD, move to the upper-right area and highlight the Video CD selection. Next, click the Create or Modify a Video CD Project link. The main project screen now appears, as shown in Figure 4.11.

FIGURE 4.11

MyDVD's main project screen opens with a default menu and text. The left channel holds the key commands to record video, import videos previously recorded, add a slideshow, and add submenus.

Take a moment to look over the layout. The largest area holds the background and text elements making up the onscreen menu you'll build for your VCD. Below that is a toolbar area with a Preview play arrow and a large red Burn button. Note the series of numbered buttons that look like a telephone keypad (we'll see later what they do). On the far left edge are the key command icons to record/capture video, get videos, add a slideshow of photos, and add submenus.

Step 3: Capture a Video Clip

At this stage your digital video camcorder should be turned on. Move your mouse to the Capture icon showing a video camcorder and click it to display the Capture dialog box. The Capture dialog box contains a set of controls and settings buttons that will define your recording session, as shown in Figure 4.12.

FIGURE 4.12

MyDVD's digital camcorder Capture dialog box offers VCR-like buttons to remote control a digital video camcorder and a large red Start Capturing button.

Here's a run down of the key elements:

- A large preview window with VCR-like control buttons directly below. As a digital camcorder owner using a FireWire link, you have the advantage of being able to use these controls to remotely operate your camcorder.

- A Grab Frame camera icon you may click to capture a still image from a single frame of video. These still images can be saved as JPEG photos and inserted into video clips (an editing feature not covered in this chapter, but one you may pursue at a later date). To grab a frame, just play your video. When you see a spot you want to capture as a still image, click the Grab Frame icon and use the Save As dialog box to name and save the file in a folder. This function is disabled when you are capturing video to your PC.

- A details pane at the bottom edge of the dialog box contains lots of very helpful information. A running clock of the capture time and file size being created is displayed. My favorite features are the Record Time Available and Drive Space Available readouts that dynamically report on the amount of hard disk space available for your video files. This feature enables you to monitor how much video your hard drive can accommodate (remember, video files are large).

Follow these steps to capture a video clip:

tip
Before you click the Start button to begin the capture process use the play, fast forward, and/or rewind onscreen remote controls to position your digital camcorder's tape to the exact spot where you want to start recording.

1. Before clicking the red Start Capturing button, click the Record Settings button that brings up the Settings dialog box. Go to the Record Settings area and click the Quality drop-down menu and select DV format. This records video at the highest quality setting and is a good move if you plan to edit your clips or produce a DVD. Also ensure that the Record drop-down menu is set for Video and Audio. Click the OK button to return to the Capture dialog box.

tip
As you add clips to build the structure for a VCD or DVD, be sure to consistently stop and save your work. Click the File drop-down menu at the top toolbar and select Save As. Use the Save Project As dialog box to give the project a name and save it to an existing or new folder.

2. When you find the spot in your video at which you want to begin recording, click the red Start Capturing button and your digital video camcorder should spring to life. For test purposes, record a five to eight minute sample video clip and then click the red Stop Capturing button.

3. A Save As dialog box appears asking you to give your clip a name and store it. Use the New Folder icon (find the symbol of a file folder at the top with a starburst pattern on the edge) and create a folder to hold the clips for this project. Give the folder an applicable name, such as VCD Test Videos. Then give the clip a name and save the file.

4. When the Capture Complete dialog box appears announcing that the file has been saved, click the OK button, which returns you to the Capture dialog box.

5. Before we record another clip for our test, click and drag the Capture dialog box to the side and look at the main menu template. You'll see an icon in the center of the menu with the file name shown below it (see Figure 4.13). Cool! You are beginning to build a multi-clip menu-driven VCD. Later, when you insert your finished VCD into a DVD player, this opening menu will be displayed on your TV screen (more about this later).

6. Now return to the Capture dialog box and record one or two more clips, giving each a meaningful name and storing them in the VCD Test Videos folder. When you finish capturing/recording video clips, click the Finish button on the lower-right corner of the Capture dialog box.

Video clip

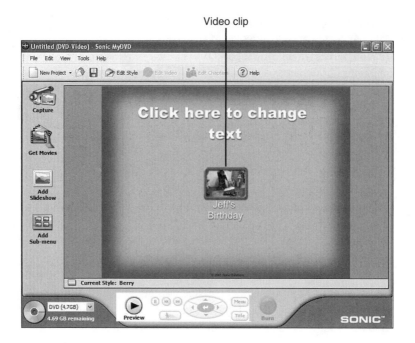

FIGURE 4.13

After saving a recorded video clip, MyDVD automatically inserts an icon on the menu for your VCD project.

With video clips captured to your PC, you're ready to really put MyDVD to work. The next project focuses on capturing video from an analog source (like a VHS tape). If that's not a something you intend to do, skip ahead to the project, "Edit Video Clips Using MyDVD."

Project: Record Analog Video Clips Using MyDVD

In the previous project I walked your digital camcorder cousins through the steps to record several video clips and set the stage for the creation of a VCD. This project will guide you through the same steps using the MyDVD program to capture video from a PCI analog video card or the VideOh! USB-connected recording box.

 Time

Figure one hour to familiarize yourself with the Capture dialog box functions and to record and edit three segments of about five to eight minutes each.

Step 1: Get Set Up

Follow these steps to prepare for the recording of an analog video clip using a PCI analog video capture card or the VideOh! external box:

1. PCI analog video card users should follow their product's instructions, and use the cables provided, to connect an analog tape source to the card. VideOh! users can refer to Step 4 of the project "Capturing Analog Video to Your PC" in this chapter. Consult the product's guide, if necessary.

2. With your analog tape source (VHS or Hi8 camcorder) turned on and linked to the PC, go to the Windows XP desktop and double-click the MyDVD icon, or click Start, All Programs, Sonic, MyDVD, Start MyDVD.

Step 2: Start a New MyDVD Project

When you reach the opening Welcome screen, move to the upper-right area and highlight the Video CD selection. Next, click the Create or Modify a Video CD Project link. The main project screen now appears (refer to Figure 4.11 in the previous project).

At this point many of the steps necessary to capture a clip with MyDVD are similar to those in Step 2 of the project "Record Digital Video Clips Using MyDVD" in this chapter. I have provided the basics (especially the differences) here, but you should refer to that section if you want more detail on the MyDVD interface and features, such as Grab Frame.

Step 3: Capture a Video Clip

Now that you're ready to capture some video, move your mouse to the Capture icon showing a video camcorder and click it to display the Capture dialog box (refer to Figure 4.12). Note that the VCR-controls on this screen are disabled when capturing from an analog source. Then follow these steps to capture some video clips:

1. Press the Play button on your analog tape source. Don't worry about recording at this stage. Do you see video playing back in the preview window? If not, click the Record Settings button and look closely at the Video section of the Record Settings

Are You Hooked Yet?

Digital camcorder owners interested in a free alternative to Sonic MyDVD can take advantage of Windows XP's built-in Windows Movie Maker program. It's a remarkable video production program, considering it comes bundled with the Windows XP operating system at no additional charge. While it lacks the ability to burn VCDs, SVCDs, and DVDs that can be played on your DVD player and it does not work with external USB-connected video recording solutions such as the VideOh! Product, Windows Movie Maker is a great tool for capturing digital video, editing it, and burning video files to a disc (playable on any PC). It can even compress capture video to a point where you can send it to friends and family over the Internet via email. (In my experience, the program also works quite well with most internal PCI video capture cards.)

To use Windows Movie Maker, click Start, All Programs, Accessories, Entertainment, Windows Movie Maker. Spend some time with the Help tutorials to learn how to use this program with your FireWire connected digital camcorder.

tab (see Figure 4.14). The Source drop-down menu offers two choices for analog tape users—Video Composite or Video S-Video. If your selection matches the cable type you are using, you should see the video playing in the preview window.

2. With the Record Settings tab still displayed, make sure the Record drop-down menu is set to Video and Audio and the Quality drop-down menu is set to Good (1 hour)—which, by the way, is your only option. If you like, but I don't recommend it, you can disable the preview during recording. You would only do this if your PC is too weak to record and display a preview at the same time.

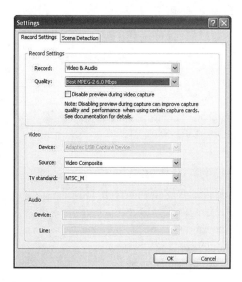

FIGURE 4.14

The Record Settings dialog box allows you to choose your capture source and the quality with which MyDVD should record the video.

3. Stop your VHS or Hi8 source and, using the manual controls on the VHS or Hi8 analog camcorder, position the tape to the spot where you want to start recording.

4. When you are set to go, press the Play button on your analog tape source and quickly click the large red Start Capturing button on the Capture dialog box. The button now changes to a Stop Capturing mode as the video is being recorded and saved to your PC's hard disk. When you have captured the desired amount, click the Stop Capturing button, followed by manually stopping your tape source.

5. Follow the onscreen dialog boxes to give the captured video clip a name and save it in a directory. Close the Capture dialog box and the main MyDVD screen appears, showing your video clip automatically inserted into the menu work area (refer to Figure 4.13).

6. Repeat the video clip capture process to create two or more clips in preparation for the VCD disc project.

At this point you are ready to join with your digital camcorder cousins to work on the "Edit Video Clips Using MyDVD" project.

> **tip** As you add clips to build the structure for a VCD or DVD, be sure to consistently stop and save your work. Click the File drop-down menu at the top toolbar and select Save As. Use the Save Project As dialog box to give the project a name and save it to an existing or new folder.

Project: Edit Video Clips Using MyDVD

In this project we'll use a handful of MyDVD's key video-clip editing tools to add a transition to the front and back of each clip and add a text title.

Time

Figure about 30 minutes to edit three clips.

Step 1: Open the Edit Window

With your main project menu displayed (per the previous video capture projects), double-click one of the captured video clip icons and a MyDVD dialog box double-checks to ensure you want to enter the scene window where you can automatically or manually detect scenes. Click Yes and the Mark Scenes for Editing dialog box appears. For our exercise to create a simple VCD, I'm going to ask you to skip this step. You may always return at a later time and learn what this dialog box can do. For now, click the Cancel button to enter the Edit window.

Step 2: Add Transitions and Other Effects

The Edit window, as shown in Figure 4.15, is packed with tools and features to explore fully at a later date.

The key elements shown here include

- A filmstrip–like horizontal box at the bottom displaying the first frame of the video clip to be edited.
- Three special effects enhancement tabs at the upper right: Fades and Dissolves; an image adjustment tab (lightning bolt icon) offering a drop-down menu with numerous choices, including a handy image brightness and contrast wizard; and a text overlay wizard tap that makes it easy to insert floating text.
- On the far left vertical toolbar area are two tools worth noting for future editing sessions: Get Media (which allows you to insert other video clips or still images in the filmstrip tray) and the Add Audio icon (which facilitates inserting background music files in formats such as .mp3.)

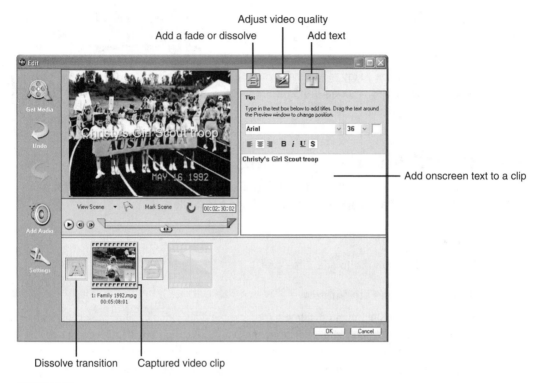

Adjust video quality

Add a fade or dissolve

Add text

Add onscreen text to a clip

Dissolve transition   Captured video clip

FIGURE 4.15

MyDVD's Edit window uses wizards to help place transitions before and after a clip, add text, and adjust brightness and contrast.

For our simple exercise, follow the onscreen instructions to place a fade or dissolve at the front and back of your clip and add a floating text title. Click OK and the edits are applied to the video clip. Repeat the process for the other captured clips. Each time you complete the cycle, you are returned to the main menu screen (refer to Figure 4.13). At this stage you are ready to create your first VCD.

Project: Create a VCD Using MyDVD

Now it's time to take all of your work from the previous two projects and burn a VCD that will play in a DVD player. When the finished disc is inserted into a DVD player, the TV screen will present the menu with video icons you designed earlier.

Materials

To complete this project you'll need

- CD or DVD burner installed in your PC or externally connected
- MyDVD program installed
- DVD player that accepts VCDs

> **note** The default opening menu background will vary based on the version of MyDVD you use. The screen images in this chapter are based on the MyDVD 5.2 program bundled with the Adapter VideOh! At the time of this writing, the free trial download offered by Sonic was MyDVD 5.0.

Time

If you followed the instructions above and recorded two or more clips of five to eight minutes in length, budget about one hour to edit the VCD menu screen and text, burn a VCD disc, and test in your DVD player.

Step 1: Edit the VCD Menu

Just like any DVD, when you play a finished VCD in a DVD player, the first thing that appears is a menu. In this case, the menu is the default background that appeared as you built your sample project to this point. The default background may be acceptable, but the title text needs to be added.

Follow these steps to change the opening menu's background and the text:

1. Move your mouse to the menu bar at the top of the screen and click the Edit Style icon. This brings up the rich and powerful Edit Style dialog box (see Figure 4.16).

2. Check out the far left vertical channel populated with a series of background templates. Use the scroll bar to see the entire set. Find one you like, click on it, and the new background is automatically applied, as shown here. For my menu I changed the background from a solid tone to the Birthday Kid template that automatically changed the title and video clip text.

3. Don't be shy. Click around and see what all the functions can do. For example, find the Menu Options area on the left and click the Animated buttons checkbox. When your disc is played on a DVD player the video icons will play a few seconds of the video—it's a great special effect.

4. When you have finished exploring the Edit Style dialog box, click the OK button to return to the main menu work screen. All of your changes are now implemented and displayed.

5. To change the main title text move your mouse pointer over any part of the top text and it automatically highlights and is bounded by a box. Position your mouse pointer on a letter and click. A blinking cursor now appears. Delete the default text and replace it with your title.

FIGURE 4.16

The Edit Style dialog box is a sight to behold! You can select templates for menu backgrounds, change text styles at will, and apply other special effects.

6. With the cursor still blinking and the main title framed in a box, click the Edit Style link at the top of the screen to once again bring up the Edit Style dialog box (refer to Figure 4.16). Move to the Change Text area and click the font drop-down menu showing Arial Black as the default.

7. Keep exploring other features, and don't miss the Select custom music track option. This feature allows you to add background music from digital MP3 music files on your PC's hard disk.

8. After you play with the Edit Style dialog box, click the OK button at the bottom and you are returned to the main work screen.

If you're happy with the look of your main menu, you're ready to burn a VCD.

Step 2: Preview and Burn a VCD

Before we burn a menu-driven VCD, be sure to save all your hard work. Follow these actions to preview and then burn your first VCD disc.

1. Move to the bottom horizontal toolbar area and click the large black Preview arrow button. Depending on the nature of your menu, an Information dialog box might appear. For example, if you use animated video clip icons, this dialog box informs you that in preview mode, the animations will not be reproduced. Click the OK button.

2. The keypad at the bottom is now activated to simulate what will happen when you insert a VCD into your DVD player (see Figure 4.17). Click the Number 1 button and the first clip plays. Click the numbers for your other video clips to test drive the final composition.

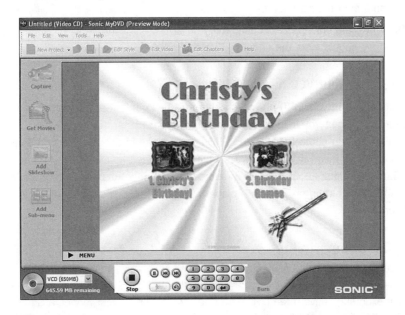

FIGURE 4.17

The VCD Preview Mode presents a numeric keypad to simulate how each video clip will be played when the finished VCD is played in a DVD player.

3. At last it's time to burn a VCD. Click the large black square Stop button to end the preview mode.

4. Pop a blank standard recordable CD-R into your PC's CD burner. Be sure to use a CD-R and not a CD-RW blank, which are often less-compatible with set-top DVD players.

5. Before you click the Burn button, look at the bottom far left corner of the screen where an icon for a disc is presented. Notice that the drop-down menu there tells the program if you are using a 650 or 700MB blank CD. Make sure you've selected the correct disc type. Today the majority of CDs offer 700MB of storage, but the CD's label usually indicates its capacity.

6. Okay, here we go! Click the big red Burn button and a Safety dialog box appears telling you that the project must be saved before burning. Click the Yes button and in a flash the Make Disc Setup dialog box appears. The settings shown should correspond to your burner. Leave the default settings unchanged and click the OK button.

note Moments after inserting a blank CD-R in your burner, Windows XP might present a generic dialog box asking what program you want to use to burn the disc. If this happens, click the Cancel button and return to the MyDVD screen.

7. Loading and Checking Media dialog boxes flash by quickly and the burning process should start. On the main menu, a burn progress horizontal bar is presented at the bottom of the screen area.

8. When the burn process completes, the CD drive should eject the disc.

> **note** The time it takes to burn your VCD (and this applies to DVD production as well) depends on the size of the source video files, the speed of the CD or DVD burner, and the power of the PC's brain to manage the whole process.

Step 3: Play Your VCD in a DVD Player

Playing a VCD in your DVD player is a different ball game than playing a commercial movie DVD. When you load a commercial DVD, your player quickly presents a menu of clickable chapter choices. Later, the DVDs you'll make in this chapter will do just that, too. When you insert a VCD into a DVD player designed to accept this format, the machine will think about it for a few moments and might display VCD on its LCD screen. Press the Play button on your DVD player and you should see the menu appear on the TV screen.

VCD Compatibility

I can't guarantee the VCD you just made will play in every DVD machine on the planet. The key is to look at your DVD player's documentation to see if it supports VCD discs.

For example, I have three DVD players at home. Our newest model, a Samsung, plays everything under the sun, except my VCDs. Our older Pioneer and inexpensive Audiovox DVD players, on the other hand, love our VCDs. If the VCD you just made fails in your DVD player, try it on other systems. For a comprehensive compatibility listing see http://www.videohelp.com/dvdplayers.php.

If your player does not play VCDs, it might support the higher resolution SVCD format discs. Unfortunately, MyDVD does not create SVCDs, so you'll need to look for a video editing and disc production software package that does. See the "Are You Hooked Yet?" sidebar at the end of the chapter to find a listing of other products to investigate.

Remember the telephone keypad numbers bit as we composed our VCD and took it for a preview test drive? Here's why that was important. Instead of using the arrow controls on the DVD player's remote control to highlight and then click a chapter icon (as you would with a DVD), you must enter the number corresponding to the clip you want to view. Look at your DVD's remote control and press the number corresponding to the clip you want to view and then press Enter.

VCDs are fun, but the video quality might disappoint you. For me, VCDs are great as rainy day projects for kids or to make low-cost souvenirs. For video discs you'll really want to watch and keep, you need to step up to the world of homemade DVDs.

Project: Make a Homemade DVD Using MyDVD

To use MyDVD to create and burn a DVD disc, you must have a DVD burner and blank DVD discs, making this one of the few projects in this book where it's very possible you won't have the necessary hardware.

If you have a modern PC, there's at least a fair chance it came with a DVD burner already installed. If so, or if you've already upgraded your PC to include one, you are in great shape! If not, find your wallet. To play in this sandbox you'll need around $100 to $200 dollars, which is actually considerably cheaper than just a year or two ago when a good PC DVD burner could cost more than $400.

> **note** When it comes to CD burners, it's a simple world of one universal recordable (CD-R) and rewritable (CD-RW) format. Unfortunately, DVD blanks come in one of two formats: DVD+ and DVD- (with the usual "R" or "RW" separating recordable from rewritable discs).
>
> Although early DVD burners usually only supported one of the two formats, most recent drives can handle either "+" or "-" discs. That said, although most set-top DVD players can read both, check your player's manual to see if it favors one recordable DVD format over the other.

After you're set with a DVD burner and blank discs, you'll find that recording a DVD isn't much different from the steps we just followed to create a VCD.

Materials

For this project you'll need

- MyDVD software installed
- Built-in DVD burner or external USB 2.0 or FireWire-connected alternative
- Blank DVD discs
- Recorded video clips and a DVD menu project created via MyDVD's DVD project wizards

Time

Budget about two hours to repeat the same steps used to create and burn a VCD disc. Obviously, you'll start by selecting a DVD project instead of a VCD project at the opening of the MyDVD program. Your burning time will vary depending on the length of your video clips. For your first DVD production, I strongly suggest you work with a collection of short video clips, ideally about five minutes each. The key at this stage of your training is to quickly learn and experience the overall process.

Step 1: Open a DVD Project with MyDVD

Click the MyDVD icon on your desktop, or click Start, All Programs, Sonic, MyDVD to open the program. On the main menu, select the Create or Modify a DVD-Video Project option.

The sequence of steps is essentially the same as with a VCD, so you should refer to the previous project if you need a refresh on any of the steps. That said, here are some key points I want you to know at the outset:

- When you record video clips from your digital video camcorder for a DVD project, use the highest quality setting available to you. Digital camcorder users should select the DV format. Analog tape source users should select Best MPEG-2 6.0 Mbps (refer to Figure 4.14).

- Your homemade DVD's menu, I'm happy to report, should behave in the same way as a commercial DVD. When the finished product is played on a DVD player, the TV screen will show chapter buttons you may highlight and click using your player's remote control.

- You will be able to store a full hour of the highest quality video your PC can produce on a single-layer DVD disc, with up to two hours on a dual-layer disc. It may be possible to program MyDVD and other editing programs to double the time on both single- and dual-layer DVD blanks, but I don't recommend it. Trust me, go for the top video quality settings.

With these exceptions noted, the experiences you gained making a VCD will make following MyDVD's steps for making a DVD disc easy to tackle.

Step 2: Play Your DVD in a DVD Player

This step assumes you have successfully produced a DVD using MyDVD. When you insert your homemade DVD into a DVD player, a menu should appear with chapter buttons you can click with the remote control to start playback. That's great, but the real thrill is the video quality. Depending on the original source of the video and the settings you used to capture it, your homemade DVDs should look much better than your VCDs. In fact, I like to say that my DVDs pass the wife test—when my wife saw the first homemade DVD I made nearly three years ago, she did not ask why the video looked funny. Instead, she directed me to start transforming all our old VHS and Hi8 tapes to DVDs ASAP.

note Until recently, single-layer, single-sided DVD discs ruled the world of DVD recording on a PC. This technology offers discs with a capacity of 4.7GB of storage that can be made to hold one hour of video recorded at the highest quality.

The new kid on the block is the dual-layer DVD (burners and discs) that effectively double the fun with a whopping capacity of 8.54GB when recording to DVD+R DL discs. You can create up to two hours of home brew video at the highest quality level on a single dual-layer disc.

Buying a DVD Burner

There are two ways to add a DVD burner to an existing desktop PC. You can install a DVD burner in a desktop PC or pay a computer repair shop to take care of this for you. If neither of these options sound appealing, a really convenient alternative (that's also ideal for laptop users), is to go for an external USB 2.0- or FireWire-connected model. Although a little pricier, its much easier to connect an external burner to your PC's USB 2.0 or FireWire port than it is to install an internal drive. Plus, they're portable and can be taken from PC to PC.

As I mentioned earlier in this project, the latest technology for DVD burners at the time of this writing is the dual-layer DVD format. If you're going to buy a drive today, it's a good idea to make sure the one you choose supports this feature. A host of products are available from $100 and up from HP, Memorex, Lacie, Benq, NEC, Samsung, and Pioneer.

Taking the Next Step

For me, making homemade video discs is one of the most rewarding personal computer experiences I've had yet. Take it from me, it's easy to become an addict! You can have hours of fun making VCDs or DVDs using old home movies, or get your kids in the act by creating music videos or sophisticated homework presentations.

At the beginning of the chapter, I touched on the theme of home movie preservation. Let me share a family story that might inspire you to apply the skills learned in this chapter. About 18 years ago, my wife Carolyn took a box of her father's family vacation 8mm reel films from the 1950s and early 1960s to a service bureau that transferred them to VHS tapes (then the state of the art). About two years ago I digitized the whole lot and burned a set of DVDs which we distributed to her brother and mother. What an experience! Movies that for years sat in a box collecting dust are now modern DVD big-screen productions our family can enjoy for decades to come.

Breathing new life into old family videos is just the tip of the PC video fun iceberg! Home digital movie making does much more than just preserve the past. My son Jeff has produced sophisticated skateboard DVDs and productions documenting his band's live concerts. And you should see the looks on the faces of his friends and their parents when we hand them souvenir DVDs of each performance.

note After word gets around that you know how to make DVDs, your popularity will expand rapidly! My wife told a friend at work about our home PC video studio. Her son is serving in Iraq and his girlfriend wanted to send home videos he could play on the platoon's DVD player. What a joy it was for us to take her VHS tapes and turn them into DVD discs. She mailed the discs to the soldier and his entire platoon could watch them on their DVD player.

What's next? A moment ago I mentioned my wife's friend and her son serving in Iraq. Thousands of remotely stationed military folks are staying in touch with the home front using laptop computers and video/audio web cameras. It's all part of an amazing array of products and services available today that can leverage the power of your PC and the vast reach of the Internet to bring loved ones and friends closer together. Get ready to dive into the world of webcams and Internet phone services!

Are You Hooked Yet?

To discover other great video-editing software, go to the Featured Software section of the Personal Computing area of the Intel website. You'll find listings and links to great programs the Intel home personal computing team suggests for average consumers to try.

To find this resource, turn on your PC, connect to the Internet, and go to http://www.intel.com. On the opening page, look for the Personal Computing selection and click that button. Now look for the Featured Software button and click it. You'll see a page with categories, such as gaming, video, photography, and more. Click the Video link and then the link for Video Editing to view the current list of suggested software.

Melt the Miles That Separate You from Loved Ones

When our daughter Christina headed off to the University of Oregon, her car was loaded with boxes, bags, and suitcases packed with clothes, school supplies, a small TV, DVD player, stereo, and her trusty laptop. As we looked over the final checklist, there was one item I made sure was not left behind. It was a *webcam*, a tiny digital video camera that would enable us, via the Internet, to see her face and hear her voice between school breaks.

This chapter looks at fun and affordable ways an Internet-connected PC can melt the miles that separate you from friends and family. We'll kick off with an introduction to web cameras (or webcams). You'll learn how these remarkable little workhorses offer great bang for your buck when it comes to personal communications via the Internet.

After mastering webcams and basic Internet audio/video conferencing, the focus shifts to audio-only communications based on something engineers call *VoIP (Voice over Internet Protocol)*. You'll learn all about using a PC and a high-speed link to the Internet to make long distance PC-to-PC or PC-to-regular phone line audio calls. First, you'll test drive a free PC-to-PC VoIP service called Skype and then learn about a more sophisticated subscription solution called Vonage. Vonage, and similar services that are popping up like weeds these days, allows you to use a normal phone handset and a broadband Internet connection to make and receive calls from any traditional phone number.

In the opening section dedicated to webcams, you'll learn how to

- Buy, install, and explore the functions of a USB-connected webcam
- Use a free instant messaging service (MSN Messenger) to enjoy full video/audio conferencing
- Boost the quality of PC-to-PC web audio/video conferencing using a low-cost subscription service called SightSpeed

In the second portion dealing with VoIP audio calls, you'll learn

- What free and subscription VoIP services have to offer
- How to install and test drive the free PC-to-PC Skype VoIP service
- What more sophisticated subscription-based VoIP services, such as Vonage, have to offer

Skills and Gear Check

Before you jump into the projects, take a quick look below at the list of assumptions I'm making about your skills and gear.

Key assumptions:

- Your personal computer has a high-speed DSL or cable link to the Internet. If you use a high-speed satellite service, the two-way communications projects in this chapter will most likely not yield happy results. Although information does flow from the satellite to your PC at a fast clip, the data going the other direction travels much slower and can be delayed. Unfortunately, the result can be choppy exchanges.

Open Wallet Alert

This chapter contains projects that recommend the purchase of gear such as a webcam and a handheld microphone or headphone/microphone combo product.

General purpose webcams are available for well under $50, with specialty clip-on webcams for laptops priced from $50 to around $100. If you plan to communicate with a remote contact who also needs a webcam, consider buying a startup kit containing two units. Logitech's BuddyCam kit, for example, goes for just under $80 (see http://www.logitech.com).

To illustrate the enhancements a dedicated PC-to-PC web audio/video conferencing service brings to the table, I'll use SightSpeed. This service offers a free package for up to 15 minutes of daily use and an unlimited web conferencing plan for a modest $4.95 per month subscription.

If you elect to graduate to the Vonage VoIP subscription service discussed at the end of the chapter, you'll need an adapter box that goes for about $50 and one of two monthly packages—$14.99 for 500 long-distance minutes a month or $24.99 for unlimited monthly calling within the USA and Canada.

- You are using Microsoft Windows XP and know how to run the Internet Explorer browser. All onscreen illustrations, dialog boxes, and pop-up menu samples are based on Windows XP.

- Your PC is equipped with USB ports (preferably USB 2.0) and you know how to identify them.

- You have speakers connected to your PC or you have a headphone/microphone combo set.

> **note** For more information on USB 2.0, see the project, "Capturing Analog Video to Your PC," in Chapter 4, "Lights, Camera, Action!," of this book. Specifically, refer to the "What Is USB?" sidebar and Step 2 of the project.

Project: Buy and Install a Webcam

Years ago, one of the research scientists at the Intel Architecture Labs in Oregon told me his team's motto was "Choices equal stress." Well, get ready to stress out! Webcams come in a bewildering array of styles, sizes, and shapes. This project opens with shopping tips for finding the right webcam for your family and budget. The second portion covers how to install a webcam.

Materials

In addition to the items listed in the key assumptions above, you'll need a wallet with about $50 for a good desktop webcam with a built-in microphone. Expect to pay from $50 to $100 for a laptop clip-on model.

Time

About one hour to do the web shopping homework and read the buying tips.

Step 1: Picking a Webcam

With all the different brands and models, it can be difficult to figure out which webcam best suits your needs and fits within your budget. Figure 5.1 shows two versions of a USB-connected webcam aimed at desktop PC users. Figure 5.2 shows two examples of clip-on webcams designed for laptops.

If cost is a factor and you are new to webcams and plan to install one on a desktop PC, go for a small ball-type model with a built-in microphone, such as the QuickCam Messenger. The long-stem QuickCam Orbit is an example of a sophisticated desktop webcam. This baby offers higher resolution digital still images, a built-in microphone, and the ability to automatically follow your face as you move in front of it!

FIGURE 5.1

The QuickCam Messenger from Logitech (left) offers a built-in microphone, while the more expensive ($129.95) Logitech QuickCam Orbit (right) features a high resolution camera, automatic face-tracking, and a built-in microphone.

FIGURE 5.2

The Veo Mobile Connect on the left and the Creative WebCam Notebook on the right are examples of small webcams designed to clamp to the edge of a laptop's LCD display.

Laptop users have even more options. You can buy a standard ball-type webcam and connect it to your laptop with no problem. Or, if you plan to use a webcam on the road, go with a clip-on product such as the Veo Mobile Connect, Creative WebCam Notebook, or the Logitech QuickCam for Notebooks Pro. These small devices sport clever clamps designed to leverage your laptop's screen to serve as an armature.

Now, before you hop in the car and head to the store, tour some of the websites listed here to get a feel for the range of webcam products available today:

- Logitech at http://www.logitech.com
- Creative at http://www.creative.com
- D-Link at http://www.d-link.com
- Veo at http://www.veo.com

Study their features, factor in their costs, and consider what you really need. Is it worth an extra $80 to get a high-resolution camera and face tracking? After you have an idea of what the players are, it's time to go shopping.

> **tip**
> A webcam can be a great tool for banging out quick personal video greetings, such as capturing a few minutes of your kids performing for the grandparents. Use your imagination and lots of fun uses will become apparent. For example, high school kids today often have the option to turn in homework reports on CD. How about adding a video element tapping the utility of your webcam and Windows Movie Maker?

Keep these tips in mind as you shop for a webcam:

- **Get a model with a built-in microphone**—Bargain basement webcams offer a camera function only. For full audio and video conferencing, purchase a webcam with a built-in microphone, such as the ones shown in Figure 5.1. Although you can use a separately attached microphone, you'll also need a stand or the use of one hand to hold it. Webcams with built-in microphones are readily available for less than $50 from Logitech, Creative, D-Link, Veo, and others.

  That said, although a webcam with a built-in microphone is a great choice if more than one person will be on your side of the conversation, if you plan to fly solo, a headset with a built-in microphone is a smart accessory (see Figure 5.3). These combo microphone/headsets make it easy to position the microphone near your mouth to improve voice pickup. Look for a model that features *noise cancellation* to help block out ambient room sounds that could interfere with your voice input.

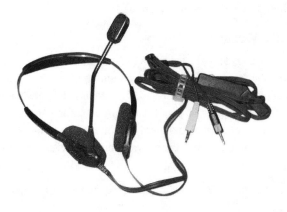

FIGURE 5.3

Andrea Electronics makes this microphone/headset model, which has noise cancellation and sells for around $80 (see http://www.andreaelectronics.com).

- **Check out the video and still-image resolution**—As with digital cameras, webcams are available at various resolutions. The high-end QuickCam Orbit, for example, can take digital snaps at up to 1280×960 pixels and record video at 640×480 pixels. The less expensive desktop models noted above capture video and still images at 640×480 pixels. For comparison purposes (relative to a digital camera), 640×480 resolution equals 1.3 megapixels, which is very low. Even cheap digital cameras these days usually support at least 3 megapixels. Still, for general purpose video conferencing, a webcam offering 640×480 pixels does the job just fine.

- **Review the bundled software**—Software bundled with webcams varies by manufacturer and models. The Logitech QuickCam Messenger, for example, comes with a suite of software for video email, setting up your own live-broadcast webcam, and creating a web-based album of images and videos.

> **tip**
>
> As you did your homework and checked out the websites above, you might have discovered PC-Cams. A *PC camera (PC-Cam)* is a hybrid webcam and free-standing digital camera. When connected to a PC, they function as a webcam. Disconnect the USB cable and you can run around taking digital snaps and even record short (low-quality) videos. These are a great choice if you want to have a webcam and, at the same time, give a child an entry-level digital camera.
>
> For representative examples, see the Creative PC-CAM line of products. The model PC-CAM 750, for example, sells for just over $100 and can take 2.1 megapixel digital still images or record up to 75 seconds of 352×288 pixel resolution video.

- **Get a long leash**—A desktop or laptop webcam uses a USB cable and port to link to your personal computer. Clip-on laptop webcams come with fairly short USB cables because the distance from the display and the USB port is small. However, when selecting a webcam for a desktop, check the length of the USB cable and go for a model with a generous leash. The webcam connected to our downstairs family PC has a seven-foot line, allowing us to pan the room and hold the webcam away from the PC to take group snaps.

Step 2: Install a Webcam

I'm off the hook here because it's your task to faithfully follow the instructions that come with the webcam you purchase. Avoid the temptation to rip open the box and immediately connect the webcam to your PC. Most USB products require the installation of a software driver before you connect the product to your PC. Be sure to consult your installation instructions. Plan on about one hour to install and learn the ropes of operating a webcam. Add another hour to fully explore and test drive the software bundled with the product you select.

Generally, installing a webcam entails

- Installation of the USB software (or *driver*) needed for Windows XP to recognize and work with the web camera typically comes first.

- If the webcam has a built-in microphone, you may also need to install a separate audio driver.

- The final step typically involves installing any bundled software programs followed by plugging the webcam's USB cable into the PC.

With this accomplished most webcam installation routines conclude with the testing of the camera's video and microphone to ensure it's ready for web conferencing.

Project: Use a Webcam with My Pictures and Windows Movie Maker

In addition to video web conferencing, you might be able to use your new webcam to take snapshots via the My Pictures program and record video clips through the Windows Movie Maker application. This project walks you through the steps to test your webcam and have fun with these two built-in programs.

Materials

A webcam installed on your Windows XP personal computer.

Time

About one hour to explore how to use your webcam with My Pictures and Windows Movie Maker.

Step 1: Test Your Webcam with the My Pictures Folder

Take these steps to see if My Pictures recognizes your webcam:

1. Open the Windows Start menu and click the My Pictures link.

2. When the My Pictures screen appears, wait a few moments and look at the Picture Tasks box at the upper-left corner. Click the camera icon labeled Get Pictures from Camera or Scanner.

3. If you have a scanner or another device My Pictures recognizes as a valid image input source, you are presented with a Select Device dialog box as shown in Figure 5.4. If this is the case, highlight the icon for your webcam and click the OK button.

note If My Pictures did not recognize your webcam, consult the product's installation guide. You might need to re-install the product's software.

This test works with most webcams, but not all. My Creative WebCam Notebook clip-on model, for example, fails this test but works just fine with MSN Messenger video conferencing and other video programs. And although my D-Link webcam doesn't work with My Pictures, Windows Movie Maker detects it immediately.

FIGURE 5.4

To determine if Windows XP recognizes your installed webcam, see if the Select Devices window shows your webcam as a valid image input device.

After you select your webcam (or if your webcam is the only image input device attached to your PC), a window showing an active video view appears along with options to take and store a digital snapshot. If you get this window then you know your webcam is hooked up properly and functioning.

Step 2: Using a Webcam with Windows Movie Maker

In Chapter 4 we looked at how to use Windows Movie Maker to record movies to your PC's hard disk using a digital camcorder. You can also use Movie Maker to record the video feed from your webcam.

To ensure that Windows Movie Maker can use your webcam, do the following:

1. Assuming your webcam is installed properly, open Windows Movie Maker (click Start, All Programs, Accessories, Entertainment, Windows Movie Maker) and on the opening screen look at the upper left Capture Video task list.

2. Click Capture from Video Device and a Video Capture Wizard dialog box appears listing available video input devices (see Figure 5.5).

3. The Wizard also notes the active audio source, which in this case is the webcam's built-in microphone. Click Next and a Captured Video File dialog box appears asking you to name the video clip you are about to make and determine the folder where it will be stored.

At this point click the Help drop-down menu and study the tutorials to learn how to record, edit, and publish video clips using Windows Movie Maker.

> **tip** Another compelling use for a webcam can be to monitor your family's home while you're away. Consult your webcam's documentation to see if the software bundled provided with the camera supports using it as a live broadcast webcam. If yes, you may be able to access your webcam via the Internet to tune in on what it sees in real time!

FIGURE 5.5

The Video Capture Wizard shows currently connected video input sources. If Windows XP recognizes your webcam, it's listed here.

See the World via Live Webcams

Speaking of live webcam broadcasts, the Internet is teeming with live webcam sites you can access via your web browser to see everything from waves breaking on a Hawaiian shore to the hustle and bustle of New York's Times Square.

Here are the addresses for two of my all-time favorite webcam directories that can offer hours of family discovery fun:

- **http://www.earthcam.com**—A huge collection of links to live webcams in categories from arts and entertainment to scenic and traffic cams.
- **http://www.webcambiglook.com**—This site offers links to live USA webcams by state.

It's a kick to tap webcams thousands of miles away, but don't forget to see if live webcams are part of your local scene. Use a search engine, such as www.google.com, and key in terms such as live webcams *name of your town or city*.

Warning—Unfortunately, webcams are also popular with the adult content crowd. If you plan to visit live webcams with the kiddies, take a solo tour of a site first.

Project: Install an IM Service

Email for the masses really kicked off in the mid 1990s. The ability to use the Internet instead of paper, envelopes, and stamps to send text messages across the street or around the world proved to be a monster hit. As great as email is, however, the recipient must be online and logged into his email account to know a message is waiting. And, on top of that, he must take the step of opening an inbox and actually finding your message.

This project guides you through a very quick and easy way to establish an IM account and conduct a web conference. The steps below, which use the MSN Messenger IM service, provide a model for installing and using any one of the other popular services such as AIM (America Online's IM service), Yahoo! Messenger, and ICQ.

tip If you use multiple IM services check out a utility called Trillian. This program, after installation, allows you to access multiple IM accounts, such as AIM, ICQ, MSN, and Yahoo Messenger, through one interface. To try out the free basic version, go to http://www.ceruleanstudios.com/. Click the Download Trillian Basic 3 button and follow the download instructions that follow.

If you're already an IM ace, feel free to jump to the next project, "Use Your Webcam to Conduct a Video Conference." There I'll show you how to set up a video conference using MSN Messenger as a model. If you're starting with a clean slate, contact the person with whom you wish to conduct a video conference and see if she already has an IM account in place that supports webcams. If she does, download and install the same service on your PC.

How to Download an IM Program

The most popular, free IM services are America Online's Instant Messaging (AIM), Microsoft MSN Messenger, ICQ, and Yahoo! Messenger. Each supports video conferencing using webcams. Here's how to find and download these services:

- **AIM**—Point your browser to http://www.aol.com and when the opening page displays, look at the left edge. Directly below the Screen Name and Password boxes, you should see a list of items in a box with a scroll bar. Find the entry Downloads and click it. Find the Download AOL Instant Messenger entry and click the Get It Now button. On the next page click the Download Now button and follow the onscreen instructions to install the program.
- **MSN Messenger**—Go to http://msn.messenger.com (see the instructions later in this project to download and install this free service).
- **Yahoo! Messenger**—Go to http://www.yahoo.com and on the opening screen, look at the upper-right corner. Find and click the yellow smiley face icon labeled Messenger. Follow the onscreen instructions to download and install the program.
- **ICQ**—Go to http://www.icq.com and on the opening screen, look for the large Download ICQ 5 button. Follow the onscreen instructions to download and install the program.

While these instructions were accurate at the time of this writing, do keep in mind that the specifics could change as these sites are updated.

If your contact does not have an IM service in place and each of you is starting fresh, I suggest learning the ropes by adopting the Microsoft MSN Messenger IM service. MSN Messenger is no better than the others noted above, but it does offer a clean and easy-to-understand interface along with good onscreen wizards to help set up webcams and microphones. And later you may always add other services.

The activities in this project will

- Guide you through the steps to install MSN Messenger

- Create an email address and password

- Send a test text message to your friend

- Highlight key features of the service

- Set up your webcam to work with MSN Messenger

tip If you use Microsoft's MSN as your email service, follow the installation steps to download the MSN Messenger but skip the actions to establish an email address and password. You use your existing account information when you log in to the MSN IM service for the first time.

Materials

In addition to the items noted in the key assumptions at the beginning of this chapter, you need a USB webcam product (desktop or laptop version) with built-in microphone or a combo headset/microphone.

Time

About one hour to download, install, and learn the ropes of the MSN instant messenger service, including setting it up to work with your webcam.

Step 1: Download MSN Messenger and Log In

Follow these steps below to download MSN Messenger, install the program, set up an account with screen name and password, and log in for the first time.

1. Turn on your PC and connect to the Internet. Point your browser to http://messenger.msn.com (note that in this case you do not enter "www"). On the opening page of the website, find and click the large Download Now! button.

2. If you use MSN as your email service, click the Go button associated with the Registered MSN User box. As the program downloads, study the tutorial page that explains the program's basic operation and features.

caution When you reach the http://messenger.msn.com site, be sure to go for the main Download Now button and not the Be the First to Use MSN Messenger Beta button. Microsoft usually has *beta* (new, but yet to be officially released) versions of Messenger available for download. As a rule of thumb, beta versions of any program are designed for advanced computer users. Advanced users know how to climb out of a pit if a beta version of a program damages files or corrupts the operating system. My advice is to stay away from beta programs and stick with official releases.

3. For users who do not have an MSN account, click the Go button associated with the Sign Up for a Free Hotmail Email Account area within the New MSN User box. Follow the menu pages to enter your profile information (name, state, time zone, gender, birth date, and so forth). This is followed by a form to create an email address name and password.

> **tip** MSN Messenger starts automatically when you log in to your PC. If you also want to automatically log on to the MSN Messenger service, enable (click) the Sign Me in Automatically box on the .NET Messenger Service dialog box.

4. Click Agree at the bottom of the profile window and if the information is accepted, the MSN Messenger program downloads to your PC's hard disk.

5. When the program download completes, a setup dialog box automatically appears. Follow the onscreen instructions to install the program. Note: One of the steps asks if you want to install the MSN toolbar, make MSN your browser's home page, and use MSN Search as your default search engine. For now, keep it simple by deselecting all these choices.

6. The process concludes with an Installation Completed dialog box. Click the Finish button and in a few seconds you should see a small icon of two human figures in the lower-right area of the horizontal toolbar of your main Windows XP screen. A small red dot with a white *X* appears over the icon.

7. Double-click the icon to open the .NET Messenger Service dialog box, as shown in Figure 5.6. Enter the email address and password you associated with your MSN Messenger account. Click OK and the opening main page of your MSN Messenger program appears (also shown in Figure 5.6).

FIGURE 5.6

To start up MSN Messenger and other IM services, you must enter your email address and password (left). The opening window for MSN Messenger (right) provides quick access to all of its features.

Step 2: Test Your Connection with a Text Message Exchange

Obviously, for Messenger to work you have to have someone to talk to. So before you proceed, keep in mind that at this stage you should have an IM counterpart on another PC that has also installed and logged into MSN Messenger.

Before you go nuts with exploring MSN Messenger's video conference features, it's a good idea to test the link between you and your remote contact. To get ready for this test, either call or email your friend and jot down his MSN hotmail address. Then make sure he knows to log into his own MSN account. Now you're ready to get started:

1. Sign in to your MSN Messenger account. On the main page (refer to Figure 5.6), go to the top, click the Contacts drop-down menu, and click Add a Contact.

2. The Add a Contact dialog box appears and asks if you want to choose a contact from your address book or create a new contact. Select Create a New Contact and click the Next button.

3. In the dialog box that appears, key in the email address for your contact. Enter the complete email address and click the Next button.

4. If the MSN Messenger service recognizes the address you entered, a dialog box appears announcing that the email address has been added to your contacts list. If the remote contact is online, he will see a dialog box appear asking permission to allow you to see when he is online. If the remote contact accepts, the torso icon on your main MSN IM window will go from a red (offline) to green (online), as shown in Figure 5.6. If the remote contact is not online or did not accept your request to see when he is online, the torso icon will be red and labeled as offline.

5. Assuming your contact is active, double-click his green torso icon to open a Conversation dialog box. Look at the bottom horizontal white box and find the blinking cursor. Type in `Hello, send me a message` or other suitable greeting and click the Send button. At the other end, your friend should see the greeting displayed in his Conversation dialog box. In return, you should receive a text message from your counterpart (see Figure 5.7).

If you're able to successfully trade text messages with another user, you know you've succeeded in installing and logging in to MSN Messenger.

For millions of IM users, plain old text message exchanges are so rewarding they never think of boosting the experience to include video and audio exchanges. Have a blast exchanging text messages in real-time, and when you are ready to add your webcam to all the fun, move on to the next project.

note MSN Messenger offers lots of bonus features including links to Expedia.com travel, MSNBC news, online games, and free web radio station links. On the lower portion of the screen (under the I Want to... box) are links for Add a Contact, Send an Instant Message, Send a File or Photo, Play a Game, and Search for a Contact. If you decide to keep MSN Messenger as your IM service of choice, you should return and explore these options further. Other popular IM services offer similar extras, too.

FIGURE 5.7

If your remote contact is logged into his MSN IM account and is in front of his PC, you can exchange text messages. This is a good step before attempting to conduct a webcam video conference.

Project: Conduct a MSN Messenger Video Conference

At last the big moment has arrived! It's time to conduct an audio/video conference with your remote contact. First, you need to set up MSN Messenger to use your webcam's camera and microphone, and then you can leap into the deep end of the pool by inviting one of your contacts to conduct an audio/video web conference.

Materials

In addition to the items noted in the key assumptions at the beginning of this chapter, you need

- USB webcam product installed (desktop or laptop version) with built-in microphone or a combo headset/microphone
- Instant Message service installed (MSN Messenger will be used to illustrate)
- A remote contact who has installed a webcam, is using the same IM service, and is online

Time

About 10 minutes to set up your IM service to work with your webcam. Assuming your remote contact is online and logged into the IM service, less than five minutes to establish a two-way video conference (time depends on quality and speed of your Internet connection).

Step 1: Run the Audio/Video Tuning Wizard

Before you can use MSN Messenger to conduct a video conference, it needs to know about the camera and microphone you intend to use. Open your MSN Messenger program and log in to the service. When the main screen appears, open the Tools drop-down menu and click Audio/Video Tuning Wizard.

Follow the instructions on the opening Audio and Video Tuning Wizard dialog box to close all other programs and ensure that your speakers, microphone, and camera are plugged in and, if necessary, turned on. I'm going to assume you purchased a webcam with a built-in microphone. Click the Next button and make sure your webcam is shown and selected as the Camera in the next dialog box (see Figure 5.8).

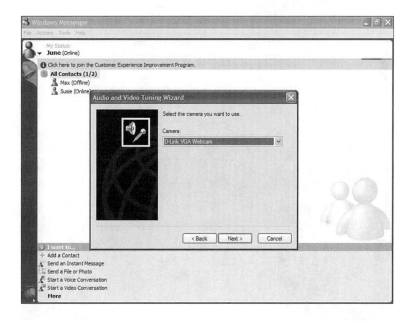

FIGURE 5.8

If your webcam is properly installed, the Select the Camera You Want to Use dialog box should list it in the Camera field.

The Audio and Video Tuning Wizard dialog box should now display a small, live video screen as shown in Figure 5.9. Click the Next button, read the instructions to prepare for a microphone test, and click the Next button again.

When the Microphone dialog box appears, check to ensure that your webcam's microphone is listed in the Microphone horizontal box (see Figure 5.10).

tip

Just before you start your first Internet conference, you can adjust your webcam's video properties. On the main MSN Messenger screen, open the Tools drop-down menu and click Web Camera Settings. On the Camera Settings dialog box that appears, play around with the brightness, contrast, white balance, saturation, and gamma settings to optimize your image quality.

Take note of the checkbox for headphone users. For now I suggest using your speakers. Click the Next button and the first of several audio test dialog boxes appears.

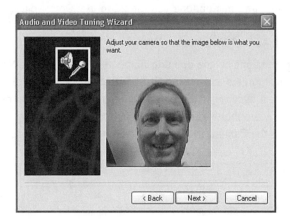

FIGURE 5.9

MSN Messenger's Audio and Tuning Wizard shows an active view of your webcam's video input.

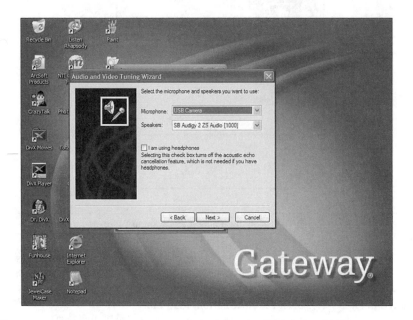

FIGURE 5.10

If your webcam's microphone has been properly installed, the Microphone field should list your webcam.

Click the Click to Test Speakers button and you should hear an audio track coming from your speakers. Use the slider bar to adjust the volume to an acceptable level. Click the Next button to move to the Microphone Test dialog box.

Read the instructions on the Microphone Test dialog box. Your goal is to see the horizontal loudness indicator register in the yellow zone (about three-fourths of the way across the horizontal bar), as shown in Figure 5.11. Use the microphone volume slider to adjust the input level as necessary. Click the Next button and then the Finish button. You are now ready for your first audio/video conference call.

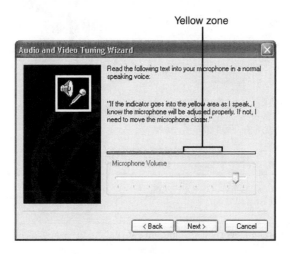

FIGURE 5.11

MSN Messenger's Audio and Tuning Wizard conducts a test to determine your microphone's input level.

Step 2: Make Sure Your Contact Is Ready

Double-check the main screen of your MSN Messenger program to confirm your contact is online and active. Send a text message asking if she is ready for a video conference. The assumption is that your counterpart has followed the same steps and is standing by, ready to go.

Step 3: Initiate a Web Conference

Go to the Actions drop-down menu on the main MSN Messenger screen and click the Start a Video Conference option. A Start a Video Conference dialog box appears, listing your currently active contacts. Highlight the icon for the person you want to contact and click the OK button.

In a few moments the Conversation window that we covered in the previous project appears. Now, however, it includes two video windows inserted to the right of your text message boxes. At this point, Messenger is asking your counterpart if she is interested in accepting your invitation for a video conference.

When the remote contact accepts the video invitation (by clicking Accept on the invite) you see your webcam's view on the bottom, with the remote webcam's view displayed in a larger screen above, as shown in Figure 5.12.

Remote webcam view

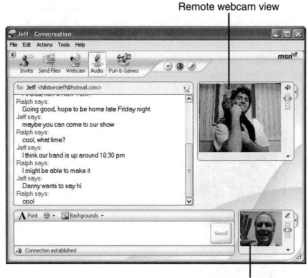

Local webcam view

FIGURE 5.12

When your remote contact accepts your video conference invitation, the video windows come alive to show each side's view.

At this point, you're free to chat away. You can see whatever is in front of your contact's camera (and hear what its microphone picks up), just as she can see and hear what's happening on your end. If necessary, you can adjust the incoming audio level of the remote webcam by using the vertical slider bar associated with it. Also note that there is a slider associated with your webcam window, allowing you to further adjust the input level of your microphone.

The first time you establish an audio/video web conference, it's a down–right kick! When my daughter's freshman dorm roommate saw her doing web conferences, she asked for help on setting up her family to do the same. It's a great way to keep in touch with distant friends and family. True, the video and audio quality is limited, but it's better than nothing!

Improving Your Web Conferencing Experience

If the video and audio quality of MSN Messenger's web conferencing left you less than satisfied, you might be a good candidate for a subscription service designed solely to host PC-to-PC audio/visual exchanges. A good example is the SightSpeed service (http://www.sightspeed.com).

For a taste of this experience, try the free SightSpeed basic package available on its website. It provides up to 15 minutes of PC-to-PC video conferences each day. The $4.95 per month subscription I use allows unlimited PC-to-PC video conferences daily and 15 minutes each day for multiparty calls involving up to four individuals.

Other enhanced web-conferencing services to explore include WiredRed (http://www.wiredred.com)and CUseeMe, managed by QuickNet (http://www.cuworld.com).

Project: Turn Your PC into a Telephone

IM services such as MSN Messenger are lots of fun, but you might have noticed the audio quality was not quite up to that of a regular phone call experience. This project uses a free VoIP service called Skype to boost the audio fidelity.

Skype facilitates secure, encrypted Internet audio calls worldwide using your PC and a high-speed DSL or cable link. The essential format for PC-to-PC calling is identical to the web conferencing you just tried with MSN Messenger. In fact, the audio portion of your MSN web conference is based on the same VoIP technology employed by the audio-only services I discuss later in this project.

To use the Skype service, you and your remote contact need to establish an account and download the program software. And, of course, both of you need to be online and logged in to the service to place and receive a Skype-hosted call.

As with a typical IM service, Skype does more than facilitate Internet phone conversations. It also offers file transfer services and instant chat.

Wait a minute! If this is so cool, why is it free? The Skype team uses the free basic PC-to-PC service to pique your interest and encourage you to try its fee-based service, which allows your PC to make (and receive) Internet phone calls to any regular phone number.

This project shows you how to

- Download and install Skype
- Set up a Skype account
- Test to ensure Skype can use your webcam's microphone or handheld/headset microphone alternative
- Call a registered Skype user

Materials

In addition to the items noted in the key assumptions at the beginning of this chapter, you need

- A microphone source. This could be a handheld PC microphone or a microphone built into a USB webcam product.
- Skype service downloaded, installed, and active on your PC
- A remote contact who has also installed and set up the Skype program on his PC

Time

About one hour to download and install Skype, set up an account, and test your webcam microphone (or handheld). Assuming your remote contact is online and logged into the Skype service, less than five minutes to establish a two-way audio call (time depends on quality of your high-speed link to the Internet).

Remember that you and your remote contact need to follow the steps below to place a Skype VoIP call.

Step 1: Download and Install Skype

Follow the steps below to access the Skype website, download the latest version of the program, and install it.

1. Turn on your PC, make sure you are connected to the Internet, and point your browser to http://www.skype.com. Spend some time exploring the tutorials, especially the pages that describe how encryption (scrambling) technology is used to facilitate secure communications. Skype can also support multipoint conference calls with three or more individuals. If this is of interest to you, check out the discussion on this feature. Return to the main opening page and find and click the large Download Skype Now button.

2. Internet Explorer displays a File Download—Security Warning dialog box alerting you to the pending download of a program file (for instance, the SkypeSetup.exe file). Click the Save button and use the Save As dialog box to place the file in the Downloads folder you created under My Documents. (This is optional; you may place the file in any folder or location). Click Save and the nearly 6MB file should transfer to the designated folder.

3. When the download completes, click the Run button and Internet Explorer displays another Security Warning dialog box, asking if you're sure that you want to run this software. Click the Run button and follow the onscreen dialog boxes to accept the agreement, default install folder location, options to place an icon on the desktop, and automatic startup whenever your PC is turned on.

4. The installation process concludes with a dialog box giving you the option to immediately launch the Skype program and/or launch an online tutorial. I suggest, as this is your first time using the program, that you click the View Online User Guide on Skype Homepage button. Click the Finish button and the Skype program fires up, while simultaneously opening the tutorial website in your web browser.

Step 2: Set Up a Skype Account

When the Skype program loads for the first time, a Create a New Skype Account dialog box appears. Note that there are two tabs—one for new members (the default) and a background tab for existing members. To start a new account (we're assuming you don't have one yet), fill out the New Users form by creating a user name and password. Decide if you want to have the program automatically start when you turn on your PC and if you want to receive email notices containing news and updates from the Skype team. Click the Next button and the window refreshes to display a progress bar.

note If you need to access the online tutorial in future sessions, click the Help drop-down menu at the top toolbar and select the Help option. The Skype Visual Guides for Windows web page automatically opens.

If your initial input information is accepted (for example, your user name is not already in use), a User Profile dialog box appears.

When you have completed the User Profile form, click Update.

Step 3: Open Skype and Set Up Your Microphone

When you complete the account creation phase, the full Skype VoIP calling program loads and is displayed, as shown in Figure 5.13. Click around and get familiar with the many features this program offers. Later we'll use the menus and icons to initiate a call with your remote contact.

Next, you need to make sure Skype recognized your microphone. For this exercise I'm going to assume you have a webcam with a built-in microphone. You may also use an alternative, such as a handheld or headset-attached microphone. The actions below show you how to tell Skype what audio input device to use:

note If you don't want Skype to load (in the background) whenever you log in to Windows, you should disable (uncheck) the automatic startup option when it appears during installation. If you elect to do this, you will need to manually start Skype by clicking Start, All Programs and then the Skype icon. You may also double-click the Skype icon on your desktop.

caution Read the text at the top of the User Profile dialog box carefully. Note that the information you provide is searchable via the Skype public directory. I use the service only with family and close friends, so I left all the boxes blank. The only thing I added was a snapshot of my mug that is displayed during calls.

1. Open the File drop-down menu found at the upper-left corner of the main Skype screen and click Options. In the Skype—Options window, select the Hand/Headsets tab (see Figure 5.14).

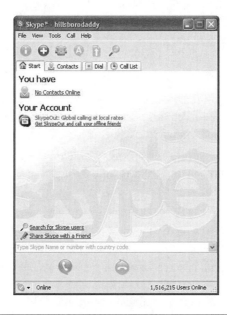

FIGURE 5.13

The main Skype program window contains tabs and tools to manage your account, add contacts, dial calls, and monitor your call list.

Micorphone to be used

FIGURE 5.14

Use the Hand/Headsets tab to tell Skype what device to use as the audio-in source. In my case I designated the microphone built-in to the Logitech webcam as the default input device.

2. Look at the entry shown in the long horizontal box labeled Audio In. The default is the default device for Windows. If your webcam's microphone has been set up as Windows XP's default audio input device, you're set. If not, click the down-arrow button and find the reference for your webcam's microphone. Leave the Audio Out and Ringing defaults set to the default and click the Save button. You may return to this tab at any time to adjust these defaults if you do not hear sound coming from your PC's speaker during a call.

Step 4: Add Your Friend As a Contact

Now that you and your remote contact have followed the same steps above, it's time to set the stage for a Skype VoIP call. Call, email, or IM your friend, to find out what his Skype username is. Jot it down and follow these actions:

1. Connect to the Internet and open Skype. Go to the upper horizontal toolbar and look for an icon of a green circle with a white plus sign. Click this button to open the Add a Contact dialog box.

2. Enter your contact's Skype username in the long blank horizontal box. Note the Allow the User to See When You Are Online box. Decide if you want this feature or not. I suggest you leave it checked. Click the Next button.

3. After a few seconds, Skype searches for your remote contact to determine if he is online. If so, a Request Authorization dialog box appears (see Figure 5.15). This dialog box sets the stage for sending a message to your remote contact. The default message is Please Allow Me to See When You Are Online. Note the button Request

Authorization to See His/Her Status and Allow This User to See When I Am Online. You might key in a personal text message, as I did with the greeting, "Hi Hillsboro Daddy." Click OK and your request is sent to the remote contact.

4. At this point, a dialog box now appears on the remote contact's screen asking if he wants to allow or block your contact request (also shown in Figure 5.15). Note the checkbox to add the requestor to the remote contact's My Contacts list. If the remote contact clicks the OK button, the two-way link is established.

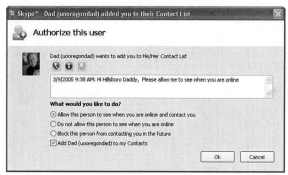

FIGURE 5.15

The Request Authorization dialog box (top) asks the recipient if he wants to allow you to see when he's online. The Authorize This User dialog box (bottom) lets the recipient decide whether you can add him as a contact.

Step 5: Place a Skype-Hosted VoIP Call

Now that you're set up with Skype and have added a contact, follow these actions to place a call:

1. Look at your Skype main screen and find the You Have area under the Start tab, which indicates if any contacts you have are online. Assuming the person you want to contact is awaiting your call, there should be a link indicating that you have (at least) one contact online. Click this link and the Contacts tab appears with

the name associated with the person listed. Click on the name and the entry expands to show the photo or icon the remote contact created for his account profile.

2. At the bottom of the Contacts tab, find the green cartoon-like balloon with an image of a telephone handset in white. Click this icon to initiate a Skype-hosted Internet audio call. On the receiving side, your contact hears a phone ringing sound effect and clicks the same icon (now displayed in a small dialog box) to answer your call. A full, two-way audio connection is now established with a special tab dedicated to your remote contact appearing (see Figure 5.16).

tip

If you liked using Skype but find using your webcam's microphone cumbersome, check out the USB-connected Internet phone sets available today. These amazing gadgets look and act like a regular telephone handset, but they are tailored for placing and receiving VoIP calls through your PC.

For more information on USB phones compatible with the Skype service, return to the website at http://www. skype.com and click on the Store link at the top of the page, and then click the Accessories link.

FIGURE 5.16

Each side of a two-way Skype Internet phone call sees a photo or icon representing the remote party.

3. To end the call, either party can simply click the red cartoon-like dialogue balloon with a phone handset image in the center (refer to Figure 5.16).

Skype offers a handy way to make free PC-to-PC VoIP audio calls. However, the world really opens up when you can use the Internet to also place calls to any regular phone number. Skype can do this using its optional fee-based service. To learn more, click the link under the Your Account section of the opening screen of the Skype program the next time you log on.

Taking the Next Step in VoIP (Internet Phones)

With the Skype experience under your belt, it's time to look deeper into what other full-feature subscription VoIP calling services offer. Many major telecommunications companies are leaping on the VoIP bandwagon, including the likes of Verizon, AT&T, and Quest. But they're coming late to the party, which means there are also a number of smaller VoIP startups that have gotten a foothold in this blossoming field. In particular, the features and services offered by Vonage, a pioneer in the world of VoIP public service, provide a good model for what's available to residential customers today.

Advantages of Internet Phone Service

Vonage offers two consumer subscription packages that support not only PC-to-PC but also phone-to-phone calling by leveraging your existing high-speed DSL or cable link to the Internet. Currently, its $24.99 monthly premium plan allows unlimited calling to anywhere in the USA and Canada. However, if you want to test VoIP for your primary phone service, I recommend that you consider the $14.99 basic plan that offers unlimited local calls and 500 minutes of long-distance calls per month. (If you go over, you're charged by the minute at rates competitive with the usual long distance companies.)

Not only are the calling plans far cheaper than traditional plain old telephone service (POTS), services like Vonage allow you to continue using the good old phone handsets you've known all your life. Just plug a standard phone handset into one of the approved digital phone adapters (which I explain shortly) and you hear a simulated dial tone. From there you may key in phone numbers as if the phone was connected to a traditional line.

Then there are the features. Vonage, and other subscription VoIP services in this class, provide a staggering array of control and performance features as part of its everyday service that you've traditionally had to pay extra for. Features such as voicemail, caller ID with name, call waiting, call forwarding, three-way calling, call transfer, called ID block,

note Although VoIP may be the hot "new" thing right now, in reality webcams and PC microphones have been facilitating VoIP exchanges for many years. So why the big fuss? Traditional dial-up Internet connections simply could not handle the volume of data needed to support good quality digital audio exchanges. In other words, VoIP sounded like you were communicating via tin cans and string.

Now that high-speed DSL or cable Internet connections have really broken through, VoIP with audio quality rivaling that of cell phones is not only possible, but is also cheaper than using traditional phone lines.

caution Although Vonage's many competitors (including AT&T, Verizon, Quest, and so on) offer similar calling plans, don't be surprised if the rates listed here change. VoIP is turning into a very hot, very cut-throat new business and the landscape will be ever-changing for the next few years.

multi-line support, and area code selection are included in most VoIP calling plans. In fact, there are also features not available at all on traditional phone service, such as having voice messages delivered to your email account.

That said, services like Vonage do require the purchase of a digital phone adapter box. For my home set up, I purchased a Linksys model PAP2 Vonage Internet Phone Service Start-Up Kit, shown in Figure 5.17. Other digital phone adapters are available from companies such as Cisco and Motorola. The Linksys kit I purchased at CompUSA has a suggested retail price of $59.99. Often, as was the case for me, special mail-in rebates might dramatically reduce the final cost. You can also purchase phone adapter hardware directly from the VoIP provider when you sign up.

FIGURE 5.17

The Vonage VoIP subscription service requires a digital phone adapter to use your existing phone handsets. Shown here is a Linksys model PAP2 that can support up to two lines.

Because VoIP services such as Vonage are designed for consumers using high-speed DSL or cable links to the Internet, it is assumed when you sign up that you have a DSL or cable modem.

Getting Hooked Up

The signup process for these services is generally straightforward, and I'll take you through my experience with Vonage. The first step is to set up an account by visiting http://www.vonage.com, selecting a plan, and registering online. You'll receive a confirmation email including the phone number assigned to your account.

The steps involved in connecting a phone handset to a digital phone adapter and, in turn, to a home network router are usually straightforward. However, they do tend to vary based on the service and type of phone adapter you've purchased. For a single PC setup, you need to

tip Depending on the service and where you're located, it's often possible to transfer your current telephone number to the new service (this can take a few weeks).

Better yet, services like Vonage even allow you to pick your area code regardless of your actual location. This can be quite a boon if you live in one area code but make and receive the majority of your calls from another.

1. Connect your existing phone handset to the digital phone adapter using a standard phone line. It is possible to connect multiple devices to this port using a splitter (which allows you to plug two or more phone cables into a single phone jack). Be sure to check the guide provided with your adapter to ensure this will not cause any problems with—or damage to—the unit.

2. Connect your PC to the digital phone adapter using an Ethernet cable. (In a single PC setup, this cable should originally have connected your PC to your cable or DSL modem.)

3. Connect the phone adapter to your cable or DSL modem. Most phone adapters include the second Ethernet cable you need to make this connection.

tip The Vonage site offers a comprehensive help section loaded with tutorials and step-by-step guides, along with contact information for tech support. It's a good idea to access and print out these tutorials (be sure to at least write down the tech support contact information) before you get started, just in case your PC is unable to access the Internet when you're done.

If your PC is part of a home network, your cable or DSL modem is probably connected to a router (also with an Ethernet cable). Your router, in turn, links to the PCs in your home using wires or with wireless links. These setups can vary depending on your VoIP service and personal preference, but generally you either

- Connect your cable/DSL modem to the phone adapter and then connect the phone adapter to the router's WAN/Internet ports.

- Leave your router connected to your cable/DSL modem and instead connect the phone adapter to one of the router's network ports.

Outside of making sure everything is plugged in, there's not much else to it. If all goes well, you may pick up the phone handset and dial away, but some setups may require additional work to properly set up and configure everything.

VoIP Pitfalls

Although moving up to a powerhouse service such as Vonage gives you the potential to drop your traditional phone line in favor of an all digital, Internet-based solution, this is definitely a technology where you need to look before you leap. Like any fledgling technology, it has its aggravations that you should consider before dumping your traditional phone line altogether.

- First of all, any electronic devices you have that make use of your phone line might not work with VoIP. These devices include some satellite boxes (for pay-per-view orders), TiVo, fax machines, and so forth. Some services support these devices better than others. Assume the worst before you sign up.

- You might have noticed the setup information I've provided didn't include your home's phone outlets. VoIP doesn't use them. This means most users are stuck using whichever handset is connected to the digital phone adapter. You can get around this by using an "expandable" cordless phone system, but that can get pricey.

tip If you own a Series 2 TiVo, you can buy an adapter that connects one of its USB ports to your home network. If you have a Series 1 TiVo and aren't afraid to open the box, you can purchase and install the TurboNet networking card from http://www.9thtee. com. Both options allow your TiVo to get its guide updates over the Internet instead of using a phone line.

caution Although it is possible to connect a digital phone adapter to your home's internal phone wiring, doing it incorrectly can destroy the adapter. Don't even think of attempting this unless you really know what you're doing.

- Usually the call quality on modern VoIP service is just as good as a traditional phone. However, Internet congestion and other obscure issues can cause temporary drops in voice quality. It's also not unusual to experience dropped calls or calls that won't go through at all.

- Because VoIP depends on the Internet, any disruption in your Internet service or electrical power in your home also kills your phone service. However, many services do allow you to automatically forward phone calls to a traditional phone line or cell phone when service is interrupted.

- 911 support also varies from service to service. Some services do not support 911 calls at all, although for others it depends on the area in which you live. This drawback is becoming less of an issue as time goes by.

If none of these factors have scared you off, you might be among those who are ready to jump on the VoIP bandwagon. My recommendation is to look initially at Vonage and other VoIP services as an augmentation to your existing traditional phone service. Try things out for a few months before you consider dropping your old phone line (though if you want to transfer your number, you're going to have to jump into the deep end). Just remember that VoIP calling is only as good and reliable as your high-speed Internet connection.

What's next? If you think music on your PC is limited to just burning CDs or downloading tunes, get ready to expand your ears! The next chapter covers the basics of making custom music mix CDs and buying and downloading tunes from the Internet, but also goes deeper into areas many consumers have yet to experience. Get ready to widen your horizons by tuning into a world of web radio and singing your heart out as you turn your PC into a karaoke machine.

Are You Hooked Yet?

If you're serious about VoIP, do your homework. Find out what's in your own backyard. Verizon, my local phone company, now offers a Vonage-like package called VoiceWing. Along with considering large outfits such as AT&T, check out smaller, independent VoIP services including

- Packet8 at http://www.packet8.com
- Lingo at http://www.lingo.com
- VoicePulse at http://www.voicepulse.com

Turn Your PC into the Ultimate Audio Entertainment Jukebox

Close your eyes and think of audio entertainment and personal computers. What comes to mind? Playing music CDs? Converting (or *ripping*) your commercial music CD collection to digital music files you can play on your PC? Transferring those digital music files from a PC to a handheld music player? How about all the controversy surrounding individuals downloading so-called illegal music files from the Internet?

Based on my experience, the list above covers about 99% of what most consumers think is the A to Z of audio entertainment on a modern home PC. If you fit this profile, get ready for a pleasant surprise!

In this chapter and the next, I'm going to open the door to the much wider audio entertainment and creativity experience a good PC with a fast link to the Internet can deliver.

In this chapter you'll learn how to

- Create custom party mix music CDs
- Buy music singles or entire albums online
- Turn your Internet-connected PC into a worldwide radio that can tune to live AM or FM talk, news, or music stations in your town or from around the world

- Access archives of digitally recorded AM or FM radio shows for listening at your convenience
- Tune in to a web-delivered version of a popular satellite radio service
- Use an online streaming music service to access vast libraries of music
- Turn your PC into a budget karaoke machine that can access free or commercial online sing-along tunes with synchronized lyrics

As with the previous chapter, free trial software downloaded from the Internet will be used whenever possible.

Skills and Gear Check

Before you jump into the projects, take a quick look at the following list of assumptions I'm making about your skills and gear.

Key assumptions:

- You know how to play a music CD on your PC.
- You've had some experience buying products on the Internet using a credit card.
- You know where to plug a microphone into your personal computer.

Materials

All of the projects in this chapter share a common need for a PC with speakers or headphones and a high-speed link to the Internet. The only other considerations are

- You have a CD or DVD disc recorder (also called a CD writer or burner) built into your PC.
- Your PC uses Microsoft's Windows XP operating system. All onscreen operating system illustrations, dialog boxes, and pop-up menu samples are based on Windows XP.
- You use the Windows Internet Explorer as your browser for these projects. All references to downloading steps and dialog boxes are based on the use of this browser.
- You have updated your Windows Media Player to the latest version. (If not, I'll show you how to do this.)
- Your wallet has about $3 in it to buy three songs from Wal-Mart's online music service, and about $6 to buy three karaoke tunes from PC Karaoke's online service.
- You own a PC microphone to record singing along with a karaoke tune.

Project: Rip Commercial Music Discs and Create a Custom Party Mix CD

In this project I'll show you the rock bottom basics of converting your collection of commercial music discs into digital files that can be used to create custom party mix CDs for personal use. You'll learn how to

- Use Windows XP's built-in Media Player software to rip the tracks of a commercial music CD into digital music files your PC or handheld music player can recognize.

- Use the Music CD creation feature of the Windows Media Player program to create a custom music mix CD.

Time

About one hour to check for the latest version of the Windows Media Player, rip three music albums, learn how to create a custom mix, and burn a CD.

Step 1: Check for Updates

Before we get started, you need to make sure you have the latest version of the Windows Media Player.

1. Because Windows Media Player performs the key tasks for this project, I want to first ensure you have the latest version. Go to the Windows desktop and click Start, All Programs, Accessories, Entertainment, Windows Media Player.

2. When the Media Player fully loads, look at the upper toolbar area and find the Help drop-down menu. Find and click Check for Player Updates.

3. If needed, follow the instructions to download and install the updated Media Player.

4. Stay connected to the Internet so the Windows Media Player, in the next step, can access a web-based database to gather information about your music CDs, such as album and track titles.

Step 2: Rip Music to Your PC

In this step I'm going to show you how to rip (copy, transfer, and so on) three commercial music CDs from your personal collection to your PC, which is

note I'm not a lawyer but here's what I understand the fair use law in the United States allows you to do with your personal collection of purchased commercial music. Basically, it's okay for you to make copies of material you purchased. But those copies can only be made for personal use or for a purpose related to education, journalism, or satire.

In other words, if you take a commercial music disc and use a PC to rip a copy and burn a backup to use in your car, that's acceptable. If, however, you use your home technology to knock off copies of CDs and start handing them out to friends or selling them, you are in clear violation of copyright law. And if you are so inclined, or in need of sleep inducement, do a Google search on the keywords Fair Use Law or Audio Home Recording Act 1992 and you can dig into this topic till the cows come home.

perfectly legal so long as you own the CDs. This is a preliminary step in creating your custom party mix CD.

The ripping process turns the music CD files into a digital format your PC can understand and play back. These digital music files stored on your PC's hard disk may also be legally used to create a backup of the original CD for your own personal use, or they may be mixed with files from multiple CDs to create new compilations for your personal use.

tip Media Player 10 uses Microsoft's WMA format as its default format for ripping tracks from a commercial music CD. The WMA format is great, but some programs, such as the FlipAlbum program highlighted in Chapter 3, "Share and Preserve Your Photos," can't use WMA music files. If you plan to incorporate a ripped track in a creativity program such as FlipAlbum, I suggest you direct Windows Media Player to rip tracks to the MP3 format. Refer to Step 3 of this project for more information on how to do this.

1. Select three commercial music CDs from your personal collection and insert one into the CD drive of your PC.

2. Wait a few moments and the Windows XP operating system detects the presence of an audio music CD. An Audio CD dialog box appears offering several choices, including Rip Music CD using Windows Media Player. Select this option and click OK.

3. The version of the Windows Media Player I used for this chapter (version 10) opened a Rip Options dialog box explaining the new digital formats the software now offers. If you encounter this message, click the Keep My Current Format Settings button, and click OK.

4. The Windows Media Player screen should now look like Figure 6.1 as the individual tracks are ripped and stored on the hard disk. A Rip Status progress bar appears as each track is read from the music CD, transformed into the digital format, and written to the hard disk. All of the tracks are placed in the My Music folder under My Documents.

5. When the ripping process is over, close down the Media Player and use Windows Explorer to navigate to the My Music folder. Make sure your Windows Explorer is set to Thumbnails view mode. You can do this by clicking the View drop-down menu and ensuring that the Thumbnails option is selected. When in Thumbnails view mode, you'll see a new folder created by the ripping process with the artist's name and an image of the album's cover art on the folder icon. Open the new folder and a list of the individual tracks is displayed.

6. Double-click any of the tracks in the new folder and Windows Media Player plays them.

7. Repeat this process for two more commercial music CDs in your personal collection.

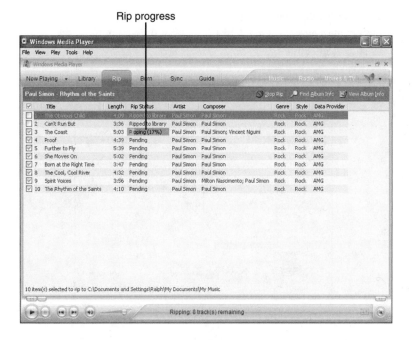

FIGURE 6.1

The Rip Status display's table shows the artist's name and title of the album, along with a list of your CD's individual tracks with titles, artist name, composer, genre, style, and data provider.

Step 3: Create a Mix CD

To create a party mix CD using tracks from the CDs you ripped:

1. Insert a blank CD disc into your CD or DVD recorder. A CD Drive dialog box appears asking if you want to Open Writable CD Folder, Burn a CD, or Take No Action. Highlight Burn a CD Using Windows Media Player and click OK.

2. A large area on the left side of the Windows Media Player screen holds the list of music tracks you can select to burn on the blank CD. Find and click the Edit Playlist button in the upper-right toolbar area. A playlist may hold tracks from any folder or album and in any combination you like.

3. The Edit Playlist dialog box appears divided into two parts—a View Library By: section on the left and a Burn List area on the right. Note the instructions at the top of the dialog box. The default shows the items currently in your My Music folder. The idea is to use the search tool, which operates similarly to the Windows Explorer program, to highlight an artist and then click the album name to reveal the list of individual tracks.

4. To begin building my custom mix, I selected a Paul Simon album I ripped. Then I highlighted, one at a time, four tracks from the album to be added to my burn list, as shown in Figure 6.2.

Drag and drop

FIGURE 6.2

The Edit Playlist tool gives you complete control to select individual tracks to add to your burn list. You may select tracks from any ripped album folder and in any order you wish.

5. Repeat this process with the two other albums you ripped to create a list of 10–12 songs.

6. Now let's really mix things up! As is necessary for your tastes, rearrange the order of tracks in the list. Place your mouse pointer over a single track and highlight it with a left click. Hold the left mouse button down and drag the track up or down to place it in a new position in the stack.

7. After you're happy with the arrangement, click OK at the bottom of the Edit Playlist dialog box. It disappears to reveal the final list of songs in the Burn List box.

8. It's time to burn, baby, burn! Look at the upper-right area of the screen and find and click an icon that looks like a CD disc with a small flame symbol and the words Start Burn.

9. The list of songs is first converted back into a format required by music CDs and then "burned" to the CD. Progress bars indicate by percentage the pace of each operation (see Figure 6.3). The burning process ends with a display showing the status of each item in your burn list as Complete and the door of your CD burner opens.

> **note** As you plan your mix CD, keep in mind today's blank CDs hold a maximum of 80 minutes of music. Keep an eye on the total minutes your mix represents before you start the burn process.

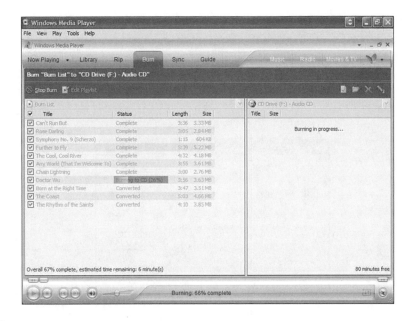

FIGURE 6.3

As Windows Media Player burns your party mix CD, progress bars indicate the state of the operation.

10. Remove the CD from the burner drive and try it out on your home or car stereo. Then label it using a permanent marker. I shy away from paper printed stick-on labels because I find they tend to wear, and wrinkles or bubbles on the paper surface wreak havoc when inserted into a car stereo slot-format CD player.

In this project I touched on just the most limited elements of what the Windows Media Player has to offer as a CD ripping and burning program. You can rip music tracks at varying quality levels and direct ripped files to be placed in folders outside of the My Music master area on your hard disk.

If you'd like to explore these features, open the Tools drop-down menu at the top of the screen and click Options. The Rip Music tab offers a wide range of controls and adjustments to try, as shown in Figure 6.4. You can direct ripped files to

caution Under most circumstances, when the burn process is complete, Media Player will automatically open the door of your CD burner. If you keep your case in an enclosed space or if your case has a door that covers your drive, make sure to open them so that the drive tray is not obstructed when it opens.

tip The default setting for ripping music with the Windows Media Player is the Microsoft Windows Media Audio (WMA) format set at 128Kbps. Don't worry if the 128Kbps means nothing to you—just pay attention to the adjustable slider. For the best sound quality, I always drag the slider all the way to the right. Music files created at this setting take more disk space to store but the improved audio fidelity is worth it to me.

any folder, change audio format from Microsoft's WMA to MP3 and even select recording quality settings within each format to either save hard disk space or deliver the best audio quality. Why use MP3? Why not always use the WMA format? The answer lies in the fact that all handheld digital music players I've used will accept MP3 files. Not all can read and play WMA format tracks, including the very popular iPod family.

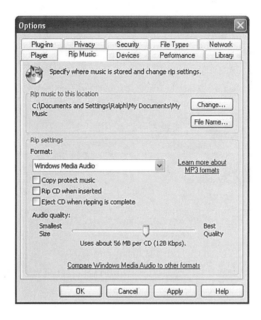

FIGURE 6.4

The Rip Music tab under the Options menu in the Windows Media Player allows you to use the WMA or MP3 format, control the quality settings, and direct the placement of ripped files on your hard disk.

Project: Buy Music Online

Welcome to the largest record store on Earth! It never closes and has nearly every track or album you can imagine in stock. I'm talking about the awesome shopping power of your PC connected to the Internet and a host of online music–buying services available today. Don't be confused. I'm not referring to online services where you buy real CDs and have them shipped to your home. Instead, I'm talking about buying and downloading music using an all-digital, all-cyberspace method.

Are You Hooked Yet?

I selected the Windows Media Player as the burner for this project because it is preloaded on modern PCs using the Windows XP operating system. Other rippers and CD-burning programs you might want to investigate include Easy Media Creator (http://www.roxio.com); Nero (http://www.nero.com); Musicmatch (http://www.musicmatch.com); Winamp Pro (http://www.winamp.com); and NTI CD & DVD Maker (http://www.ntius.com).

In this project you will learn how to

- Access an online music download and buying service
- Set up an account
- Search for music by artist
- Select and download three or more tracks
- Playback and use the downloaded tracks or albums

With so many online music buying and downloading services available today, it was tough to pick the one to serve as our sample. I chose the Wal-Mart online service because it uses extremely straightforward, step-by-step screen displays, offers individual tracks for just 88 cents, and does not require any kind of membership subscription.

Time

Allow at least one hour to access the Wal-Mart online music service, explore its search features, select several tracks to buy, set up a new account, and buy and download the tunes.

Step 1: Understand the Business of Digital Music

The Wal-Mart online music store, as with nearly all commercial download services I've used, imposes some restrictions based on licensing agreements with the artists and record companies. Wal-Mart's downloaded music files carry these conditions:

- You may download music tracks to one computer and back up music files to two additional computers.
- Burn up to 10 CD backup copies of a track or album.
- Make unlimited transfers to portable digital music players.

Step 2: Access the Wal-Mart Website

Although the Wal-Mart service I use as a tutorial for this project is a good representative for online music buying services, keep in mind that each service has its own unique features and methods

note If you are an Apple iPod digital music player owner, check out Apple's iTunes service to buy and download tracks to transfer to your player (http://www.apple.com/itunes/store/). The Wal-Mart online service, for example, uses the Microsoft WMA file format for its song downloads. Unfortunately, that's a format iPod players do not support. All digital handheld players I've used support the MP3 format, including iPods, and many also support WMA music files. If you are downloading music for playback on a portable player, make sure you know what formats your player supports and that any music service from which you buy music online uses a supported format.

note If you're interested in the Your Tunes, Your Way program, try downloading and installing it at a later date. After installing the program, an icon called Wal-Mart Music Downloads Store appears on your Windows desktop. Double-click it and your Windows Media Player fires up and goes to the MSN music online store (a resource shared with Wal-Mart).

for selecting, buying, and downloading tunes. What you are about to experience with the Wal-Mart service, however, will give you a feel for the basics that apply to all services.

Turn on your PC, connect to the Internet, and be sure to use Windows Explorer as your browser. The Wal-Mart music service works only with this browser. Point your browser to http://www.walmart.com/music.

Take note of the search tools and check out the highlighted music specials. Go to the far left vertical channel of the opening page and scroll down to the Music Categories section. Here you'll find the categories of music the site offers.

As you examine the front page, you'll notice the Wal-Mart music service prompts visitors to install its Your Tunes, Your Way program. This little program makes it easy to search or browse to find your favorite artist, listen to sample clips, and get suggestions for music you might like based on your artist searches. For now we'll skip this option to get right to the action.

caution Be very aware that the next steps will result in the purchase of tracks that, if you provide the necessary information, will be charged to your credit card. Be sure you're prepared to spend a few dollars before you continue and that you select an artist and tunes you really want to own.

tip Here's a suggestion for a twenty-first century allowance or reward for your teen. Set up an online music purchasing allowance she may use based on an account and credit card you set up. Using the Wal-Mart music store example, you could determine the award amount, log in to the service using your email and password, and then turn the PC over to your teen to select her weekly or monthly reward in the form of songs or albums to download and enjoy.

Step 3: Search for Tracks

Find the magnifying glass Search bar. Click the down arrow box to gain access to multiple search options, including search by album title, artist, and song title.

For this example, we'll search for an artist, so click Artist and in the horizontal box next to the Search icon, type in the name of a recording star or group. I typed in "Crow" (for Sheryl Crow).

Step 4: Select and Buy Music Tracks

Click the Find button and, in a few seconds, a page filled with a listing of all Sheryl Crow's albums fills the screen. In my exercise I scrolled down the screen and found the album art and section for her first CD, *Tuesday Night Music Club*. Whatever album and artist you select, find and click the See Music Downloads for This Album. This brings up a screen listing all the tracks on the album available for download, with the price and an option to listen to a short clip of the tune (see Figure 6.5). Click the Listen link and the Windows Media Player fires up and plays the sample. This is a great way to sample tracks before you buy, and is a feature common to all online music download services I've used.

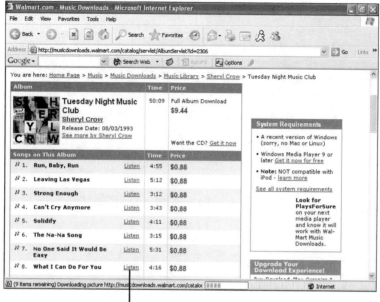

Click to preview

FIGURE 6.5

Music purchase and download sites such as the one offered by Wal-Mart provide short preview samples of the songs.

Let's say you want to buy and download three tunes from this album. Just click the blue Add to Music Cart associated with each song, one at a time. Each time, a screen appears to report the item has been added to your Music Cart. When you have all your songs selected, click the View Your Music Cart button and a summary screen listing the items and the total purchase appears, as shown in Figure 6.6.

Step 5: Register As a New Customer

When you are satisfied with your selections in the shopping cart, click the Proceed to Checkout blue button. Click OK if you get a Security Alert dialog box. Go to the New Online Customers box and click the Continue button. In the next screen you enter your name and email address and create a password. Decide if you want to subscribe to its newsletters and then click the Continue blue button. When the End User License Agreement page appears, scroll to the bottom of the page and click the blue I Agree button.

note Security dialog boxes such as the one mentioned here appear when you are about to be directed to a secure site to enter sensitive information, such as your name and credit card information.

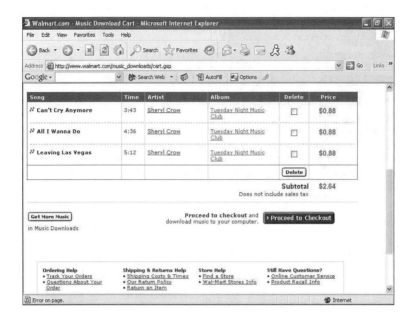

FIGURE 6.6

Music download and purchase sites maintain a running list of items you have selected to add to your checkout or shopping cart list.

A Select Payment Method page appears with a summary of your pending purchase. Wal-Mart music, as with most services, offers lots of payment options. I selected a standard credit card. Follow the onscreen instructions to enter your card data and click the Continue button. The Confirm and Place Order screen appears with instructions. You are allowed to download your music files after you complete this step. Review your order and click the Place Your Order button. A processing screen appears and the cycle concludes with a Download Your Music screen thanking you for the order.

Step 6: Downloading Your Music Tracks

Look carefully at the Downloading Your Songs instructions. Next click the Download All Songs Now blue button. A download program tool is installed to automatically place your purchased songs in the My Music folder under My Documents on your PC hard disk.

Follow the onscreen instructions and click the Yes button when a dialog box appears telling you the files will be saved to the My Music folder. The dialog box asks if you want the files saved to another directory. Click No and a Music Downloads dialog box appears that reports the progress of your song downloads, as shown in Figure 6.7.

note Did the download halt mid-stream on a given song? No problem, just click the Resume Download blue button to restart the process.

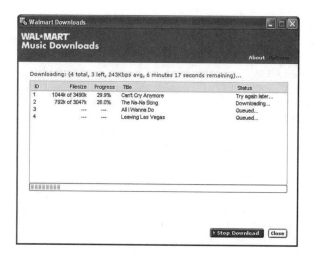

FIGURE 6.7

The Wal-Mart Music Downloads dialog box provides an accurate report noting the progress of the download and the estimated time remaining.

Step 7: Enjoy Your Downloaded Tunes

When the download of all your songs is completed, click the blue Open Music Folder button on the lower-left edge of the Music Download dialog box or, at a later time, click Start, All Programs, Accessories, Entertainment, Windows Media Player and use the top toolbar File drop-down menu to navigate to the album folder. Use your Windows Media Player (or another CD-burning program) to burn the files on a CD or transfer them to a handheld digital music player.

Congratulations! You are now a certified cyber music shopper, but remember your limitations. Although these limitations vary from service to service, in the case of Wal-Mart, you may listen to the songs on the PC used to download them, back them up on two other PCs, transfer them to handheld music players, and burn up to 10 CDs with the song(s) you purchase.

With access to thousands of songs, you can make some really fun and creative gifts. For example, for your child's next birthday (this really works when they are teens) find 10 or 12 hit songs from the year he was born. Download the set of tunes and using the party mix CD-burning skills you learned in the previous project, make a CD compilation. This can also be a great holiday stocking stuffer idea!

note The first time you double-click on a downloaded music file from the Wal-Mart service, a Windows Media Player dialog box might appear stating that you need a security upgrade to play the file. Click the Yes button. This engages a license-acquiring process giving you permission to use the file under the conditions noted at the beginning of this project. Also click Yes to any Back Up Your Licenses dialog boxes that might appear.

A Word About Internet File Swapping and Copyright Music

Show the project above to a group of teenagers and some of them might wrinkle their noses and tell you it's nuts to pay for music when you can get free tunes via file swapping on the Internet. They're talking about one of the file-swapping services that have caused such as stir in the past few years. These services, which have plenty of non-infringing uses, are under fire because they're consistently used to illegally trade copyrighted material. You can argue all day long about interpretations of the fair use laws on one side and the respect for copyrights on the other. I'm not a lawyer, but I do know that regardless of what you think about these free swapping schemes, some might put your PC's health at risk.

Here's a true story to illustrate my point. My daughter Christina is a student at the University of Oregon and about a year ago I went to her Kappa Delta sorority house for a visit. I was there to install a private wireless network for her room (which made her instantly the techno hippest kid in the house), and she asked me to help out a friend. Apparently her friend's laptop was so infested with random, uncontrollable pop-ups (including adult content) that she could no longer use her system at all. Before operating on the sick patient, I asked her if she was using one of the file-swapping services. Lo and behold, the one she was using is well known in the tech community as a carrier of spyware and other annoying parasites.

Free file-swapping schemes are sometimes hijacked by unsavory characters who attach junk to ride along with music files. In the case of my daughter's friend, the nasty pop-ups, spyware, and other nuisance entities had built up to the point of bringing her laptop to its knees.

I downloaded and ran a number of programs designed to clean up the mess, including Spybot and Ad-aware discussed in Chapter 1, "Is Your Home PC Ready for the Fun?" (and now Microsoft offers a spyware blocker, too). After removing 784 items clogging her laptop, she was finally up and running again. Before I put the repaired laptop back in her hands, I pleaded with her to stop using the file-sharing software she had installed.

The moral of this story is to avoid these free file-swapping schemes as a way to get free music from the Internet. Not only is it arguably illegal to download music you haven't purchased, it's just not worth risking your system's health. My 17-year-old son Jeff, for example, uses Rhapsody, MSN Radio, and other legal streaming services to get his online music fix.

Project: Listen to Live Radio

In your house sits the most powerful radio on the planet. I'm talking about the world of live web radio and access to a mind-boggling array of local, national, and international talk, news, and music resources that far exceeds any traditional radio gear.

This project introduces you to the many facets of Internet radio, from live AM and FM broadcasts of local and national outlets to cyberspace web-only stations.

In this project you'll

- Learn about the various forms of Internet radio
- Tune in to a live broadcast from a local or remote AM or FM radio station using the Internet
- Listen to a digitally archived broadcast from an on-air radio program
- Tune in to a cyberspace music or talk radio station

Time

The activities that make up this project require as little as 10 minutes to tune in to a local radio station's web broadcast and check out Windows XP's Media Player cyberspace radio channels to about one hour to download the RealPlayer software and explore its web radio offerings.

Step 1: Tune in to an AM or FM Station

The landscape of Internet radio is populated with many life forms including

- Websites for existing on-air AM or FM radio stations that offer live or archived web-delivered broadcasts of their programming.
- Web-only cyberspace radio stations.
- Subscription-based, online music listening services that include the broadcast of music collections grouped by genre. These music collections, in turn, are called radio stations (we'll look at this in the project dedicated to subscription web music services).

In this exercise we'll see if a local AM or FM station where you live offers web visitors a live or archived stream of its radio broadcasts.

1. Turn on your PC, connect to the Internet, and bring up your favorite web search engine, such as Google.
2. If you know the call letters or signal number for a local radio station, enter them in to the search engine. For example, in Colorado Springs there's a station with the call letters of kLite and its signal number is 106.3. Entering kLite or 106.3 in the Google search bar yields links to the station. If you don't recall the call letters or

Are You Hooked Yet?

Wal-Mart's online music store is just one of many available today. If you are using the latest version of Windows Media Player, look at the upper-right area of the toolbar zone where tabs for Music, Radio, and Movies and TV appear. Click the Music tab and Microsoft's online music service appears.

Other online music shopping resources to explore include

- Apple's iTunes at http://www.apple.com/itunes/
- Rhapsody at http://www.listen.com
- Napster at http://www.napster.com
- Musicmatch at http://www.musicmatch.com
- RealPlayer Music Store at http://www.real.com
- MSN Music at http://www.music.msn.com

signal number, enter these key words: `radio stations`, *name of your city*, and *name of your state*. And, of course, you can pick any city in the world and follow the exercise below.

3. Once you access a local station's website or, for that matter, a station anywhere in the world, look for a link usually labeled Listen Live, as shown in Figure 6.8. Click it and follow any onscreen instructions. You might be asked to download a small player application. In most cases your Windows Media Player is used to play the live stream.

Most radio station websites have some form of "Listen Live" link.

FIGURE 6.8

The Listen Live page for KXL Radio is a good example of how many of today's radio stations offer listeners the option to hear their shows live via the Internet.

Is it time to toss the old radio out the window? Of course not! Obviously, using a real radio to tune in to local broadcasts is still the most convenient way to go. But, as you become familiar with your super web radio options, new possibilities emerge. For example, I listen to live web radio broadcasts of local stations to keep in touch with the home front when I'm on the road.

caution If you work in an office with a broadband Internet connection, it might be tempting to use it to listen to the Internet radio while you work. Because any good IT staff will eventually notice this activity, you should make sure this is an acceptable practice before you connect.

Use your imagination, and the value of live web radio becomes even more apparent. Is your place of birth outside the USA? Tune to the old country with web radio. Learning to speak a foreign language? Exercise your ears by listening to stations in French, German, Italian, you name it!

Web Radio 101

The sound quality of an Internet-based radio broadcast might not be fabulous. Talk radio stations, for example, broadcast their web radio using *low bit rates* (that's techno babble for lower quality). Low bit rate streaming web audio (radio or any form of audio) is used to ensure the widest audience range can access the broadcast, from dial-up regular telephone links to high-speed broadband services. As we progress in this chapter, you'll hear the difference between low and high bit rate broadcasts.

Also, when it comes to listening to web radio, low bit rate or high, it really pays to have a high-speed DSL or cable link to the Internet. And that's not just for the ability to support higher bit rate broadcasts, but also to reliably sustain a link to the radio station's computer system that's dishing out the stream of broadcast data to your PC via the Internet. It's been my experience that using a slower dial-up link to live web radio often results in breakups of the audio stream or intermittent loss of the connection.

Step 2: Tune in to RealPlayer's Radio Stations

The first time you attempt to tune in to a radio station's live broadcast via the Web, you'll notice a few things. First, you might be asked, as I was for the KXL AM web broadcast, to download and install a plug-in program or special audio player program. Don't be surprised if you are asked to download the RealPlayer program (available at http://www.real.com/player). RealPlayer and the Windows Media Player are very popular playback vehicles for web radio. In this step we'll take a look at using Real Player to gain access to a host of different radio broadcasts.

1. If you were not prompted earlier by a radio station to download and install the RealPlayer program, go to http://www.real.com/player and look for the link/button to download the free program.

2. Be sure to look carefully at the web page and find the small underlined text Free RealPlayer. The other player is subscription based. Click the Free RealPlayer link and follow the instructions to download and install the program.

3. When you open the program, look to the upper-left area and find the Radio button in the View box (see Figure 6.9). Click it and have a ball. The intuitive interface makes it a breeze to surf for every kind of station imaginable.

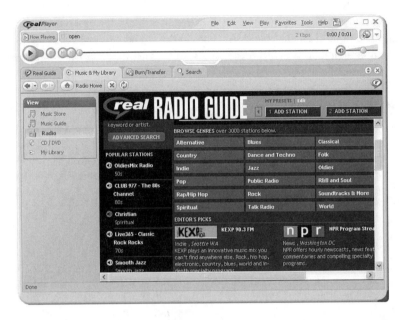

FIGURE 6.9

The free RealPlayer program offers lots of features, including an easy-to-use radio guide.

Step 3: Test Drive Radio-locator.com and Amfmstation.com

You can further expand the number of radio stations you'd like to listen to by using the popular search tools at radio-locator.com and amfmstation.com.

To get started, visit http://www.radio-locator.com and try searching for AM or FM radio stations by ZIP code, state, or call letters, as shown in Figure 6.10. The listings for AM or FM stations offer a lightning bolt code indicating if the station broadcasts its audio on the Internet. The site also has a search feature to specifically find Internet streaming radio stations. You can spend hours of happy hunting here!

Next, check out http://www.amfmstation.com. Much like radio-locator.com, you can search for web radio stations by state, city, frequency, and call letters.

Are You Hooked Yet?

Want more web radio adventures? Just for fun, consider adding a software program to record web radio so you may listen to programs at your convenience. Go to http://www.replay-radio.com and download the free trial version of Replay Radio. This nifty program allows you to record web radio programs and listen to the audio files at your convenience. Think of Replay Radio as being like a VCR for capturing web radio broadcasts.

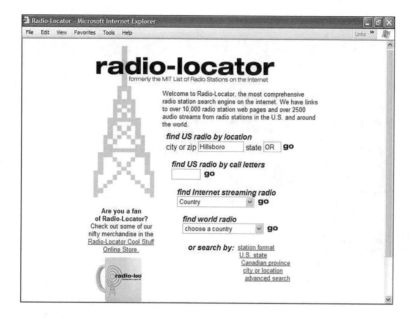

FIGURE 6.10

The search page for radio-locator.com makes it a snap to find a station in your back yard or anywhere in the world that offers live web broadcasts.

Step 4: Listen to Web-Archived Radio

Here's something the good old traditional radio can't do—replay shows. Okay, a few specialty radios are available with built-in recorders. And, of course, if your stereo deck includes a cassette tape player/recorder, you can record radio broadcasts. But here's the catch—recording radio using these methods works great only for capturing live content in real time. As you'll see through the exercises in the activity that follows, knowing how to find and access online digital archives of past AM or FM radio shows is a great convenience tool, especially for loyal talk radio fans.

Many radio shows, especially the nationally broadcast talk programs, offer archives of past shows. In this exercise we'll visit the Computer America Radio Show, access its archive of past shows, and discover two ways to enjoy the archived content.

1. Turn on your PC, connect to the Internet, and point your browser to
http://www.computeramerica.com.

2. When the opening page displays, find and click the Listen button. The Listen to Computer America web page offers lots of options, from listening to the show live from 10 p.m. to midnight nightly (EST) to an option to access the past two weeks of the show.

3. Find and click the Listen to Daily MP3 Archives button to bring up the archives page (see Figure 6.11). Select a show, click it, and in a few seconds your Windows Media player kicks into gear and starts to play the streaming audio file.

Click a link to hear a show

FIGURE 6.11

Computer America's archive page is a good example of how many talk shows offer listeners the option to hear past programs.

4. Some radio show web archives, such as Computer America, also offer the option to download a stored show as an audio file you may copy to your PC hard disk and listen to at your convenience. Try this out by right-clicking one of the archived Computer America shows and selecting the Save Target As option in the menu that appears. Save the file to your hard disk (preferably in a folder you created for it). Now you can find and click the saved file at any time and your Windows Media Player will fire up and play it back. Not all radio online archives, however, offer a file download option. You'll have to experiment with the sites you visit.

tip

Each radio show uses different terms to find archived content. For example, the Into Tomorrow radio show (http://www.intotomorrow.com) opening web page has an icon called Shows. As you search for other radio show archives on the Internet, you'll discover that some radio shows require visitors to register to gain access to stored programs. In most cases it's free to register, but double-check the privacy statements to ensure your email address will not be shared or sold to a third party.

Project: Stream High-Fidelity Music via the Web

My hands down, all-time favorite web-based audio experience involves enjoying the vast libraries of high-fidelity music offered by today's online subscription listening services. In this project I'll introduce you to the Rhapsody service as a representative of this genre of web audio entertainment. It's one of many web outfits that for a modest subscription fee (about $10 a month) will fill your PC's speakers with music from vast libraries containing a half million tracks or more. Rhapsody, for example, at the time of this writing, offered a library of more than 800,000 songs and instant access to more than 50,000 albums representing more than 40,000 artists.

Our family has been using Rhapsody and several other services for more than a year. The experience has changed the way my 17-year-old son, 21-year-old daughter, my wife, and I think about music entertainment. Instead of buying lots of CDs, we now rent access to music via the web. My son and I have even rigged up a way to transmit our streaming web music to our family room stereo (you'll learn more about the various ways to link your PC you your stereo in Chapter 8, "Digital Show and Tell").

In this project you'll

- Download, install, and take a free test drive of the Rhapsody online music service
- Learn how Rhapsody organizes its libraries of content
- Enjoy this service's virtual radio stations and create your own custom broadcast

Time

The activities that make up this project require about two hours to download and install the Rhapsody program, set up an account, and conduct a full tour of the various services.

Step 1: Download and Install Rhapsody

The first step in streaming music through Rhapsody is to visit the Rhapsody website and set up your trial account. The Rhapsody service offers a free seven-day trial, and two monthly subscription plans. The $4.95-per-month Rhapsody Radio Plus plan allows access to more than 50 commercial-free virtual radio stations organized by genre. The $9.95-per-month All Access plan provides access to the service's entire collection of more than 20,000 albums, as well as all the virtual radio stations. With this plan, which is what I'm going to have you test drive, you can conduct searches by album title, artist, and/or track title.

1. Turn on your PC, connect to the Internet, and point your browser to http://www.listen.com. Find the Get the 7-Day Free Trial box and click the Get It Now button.

2. Select the All Access premier plan option. I want your experience to go beyond just listening to prepackaged radio streams by genre that the basic plan offers. The premier plan adds the ability to search for and play individual artists and full albums. Leave the $9.95/month button clicked and then click the green Select button.

caution Completing the registration process with the Rhapsody service begins a seven-day free trial period. If you like the service and want to continue, do nothing. After seven days your card will be charged $9.95 each month for the service. If you don't want to continue, you *must* call a toll-free number (listed on the Rhapsody account pages) and request a cancellation to avoid charges.

3. On the next screen, fill in the blank boxes to create a username and password and provide an email address and other information. Decide if you want product updates and the newsletter and then click the Continue button.

4. On the next screen, enter your credit card information and click the Continue button at the bottom of the page.

5. Now it's time to review the purchase information screen and read the terms. Click the I Agree button and then click Submit.

6. A congratulations page now displays indicating that all of the credit card information checked out okay. Click the large Download button to get the program delivered to your PC's hard disk.

7. When the Windows File Download dialog box appears, click the Save button and then use the Save As dialog box to navigate to (or create) a folder where you want to store the program.

8. Go to the folder where you put the file and double-click it. The Rhapsody installation program now begins. Follow the onscreen instructions to accept the terms of use and choose the folder where the program will be stored.

9. Next, a screen display appears, asking if you connect to a proxy server. As a home user, this generally does not apply to you, but if it does, you or the techie in your family will know what to do. Leave the Enable check box blank and click Next and Next again to install the program.

10. An Install Progress dialog box appears, followed by a dialog box asking if you want to launch the program, create a shortcut on the desktop, and create a shortcut in the Quick Launch toolbar. Accept or reject these programs as you see fit.

Step 2: Log into Rhapsody

When the installation process completes, the Rhapsody service program automatically starts. If you need to start the program manually, click Start, All Programs, Listen Rhapsody.

> **caution** Rhapsody does not filter out explicit language in some of the pop tunes and comedy tracks. They do, however, flag content as explicit. So use judgment on how to handle this with your family. For younger children, I recommend supervised use of the service.

1. The first thing to greet you is a Login Form dialog box with your username already entered and a password box below, awaiting your input.

2. Enter your password and decide if you want to bypass entering it each time you log on by clicking the Remember Me check box.

3. Note the Select Your Bandwidth box. As discussed at the beginning of this chapter, you should be a broadband user and the default assumes this accordingly. Make sure the box shows Broadband/DSL/Cable.

4. Now click the Log In button.

5. In moments the full Rhapsody home screen page appears on your screen, as shown in Figure 6.12. Take a moment to let it all sink in, as there's a lot to explore.

FIGURE 6.12

Clear, simple control icons and section titles make Rhapsody's opening page one of the most attractive and intuitive interfaces of its kind.

Step 3: Navigate Rhapsody

The Rhapsody service is loaded with fun zones to explore, including Album Spotlight, Radio Spotlight, Featured Mix, Browse Genres, My Library, Playlist, and a Radio button for access to tons of virtual stations. In the following exercises we'll explore each one.

tip One of my favorite features is the Album Info button located beneath the album art for the current track. Click the Album Info button and you are automatically transported to a page dedicated to the album. This feature has introduced me to hundreds of artists I might otherwise never have experienced.

- **Album Spotlight**—For instant gratification, find the Album Spotlight box on the right side and click the underlined text associated with the album highlighted. The screen refreshes to show a section dedicated exclusively to the album. Look immediately to the right of the album artwork and click the Play Now green speaker icon. The first track of the album begins to play and is displayed in the top horizontal control area. At this point you could sit back, relax, and allow Rhapsody to play the entire album, or use the controls in the upper-left area to skip to the next track, stop the music, and so forth.

- **Radio Spotlight**—Find and click the Home button (near the center of the screen). Now move to the right side of the display and down to the Radio Spotlight zone. The team at Rhapsody constantly rotates highlights of the virtual radio stations offered. Click the Play Now green speaker icon and hear what's in store for you. The first track is loaded and displayed in the upper horizontal control bar area.

- **Featured Mix**—Click the Home button and note the Featured Mix area just beneath the Radio Spotlight box. Every week the editors of the service put together fun mixes for you to enjoy.

- **Browse Genres**—Click the Home button and then look directly below it for the Browse Genres long vertical box. Scroll down the list and click a category to access albums and artists allocated to the each genre. When you select a genre, the screen refreshes and presents new zones to explore, such as a sampler and a listing of the most popular tracks in the given category.

- **My Library and My Playlist**—Always present on the left side of the screen are the My Library and My Playlist boxes. Here you can flag and track your favorites and build your own custom playlists.

- **Radio**—Click the Radio button in the center of the screen to bring up a set of powerful search and play controls. Check out the Listen to the Top 10 Stations list on the far right. And note that you can add stations you discover to a list in the Create a Custom Station box, as shown in Figure 6.13. Being an old hippie, I created a custom radio station list to include favorite artists such as Joni Mitchell; Jackson Browne; Crosby, Stills, Nash and Young; and Donovan. And don't miss the Station Genres area, which lists a host of choices from rock/pop to holiday/comedy. When you play your custom station, songs by the artists you selected are played in a rotating random order.

FIGURE 6.13

The Create a Custom Station feature allows you to assemble a dream team of your favorite artists and build a virtual radio station.

Step 5: Conducting Searches

You can also use Rhapsody to search for music based on the artist (or group), track, album, or composer.

Find the blue horizontal Search bar. Make sure the search drop-down box to the left of the Go button is set to the category you want to search for. In this example we'll select artist and key in The Doors (a sizzling hot band when I was in high school; see Figure 6.14). The main Rhapsody page refreshes and displays elements dedicated to the band.

From a band or artist's main page, you can check out the Artist Spotlight area, which provides a listing of the most popular tracks and various Rhapsody radio stations playing the band's music. To the left is a listing of the group's main releases (albums) in chronological order. Click on any album entry and you can see the tracks available. The red flame symbol means the track is available for purchase and download.

The editors managing the Rhapsody service, as with other online music-playing services, have provided lots of thoughtful features such as links to other musicians and groups you might enjoy if you like The Doors. These suggestions are presented in the Similar Artists box on the far right. In this case, as you can see, the editors feel I'd enjoy the Grateful Dead, Jimi Hendrix, and Love. I certainly recognized the Grateful Dead and Jimi Hendrix, but the group Love did not ring a bell. I clicked on the entry for the group Love in the

Similar Artists box and sampled their music. I've had countless hours of fun with Rhapsody and other services getting to know bands and artists new to me, thanks to this suggestion service.

Albums listed by release date

FIGURE 6.14

Rhapsody pages dedicated to an artist or group offer an extensive array of informative resources, including a chronological list of album releases.

Look above the Similar Artists box and note the Radio Plus box. Rhapsody has a virtual radio station dedicated to The Doors and similar artists. Click the Play Now button to switch to the streaming broadcast, or click Save to Library to add this station to the My Library box for future fast access.

Now it's your turn. Repeat with a band or artist of interest to you and then try searches based on the name of a song, album title, or composer.

note The first time I sat down with Rhapsody, I spent hours just clicking around seeing what was available. I encourage you to do the same with this service and others. You'll discover that some major artists are not included in the library, or they are represented with a token entry. Try a Rhapsody search for Dave Matthews Band, for example, and only a few tracks are available. Search for the Beatles and only their album *In the Beginning* is accessible. But, the range of major artists included is impressive, from Britney Spears and Madonna to oldies but goodies such as Paul Simon and Ray Charles.

Project: Explore Three Other High-Fidelity Web Music Services

Rhapsody is far from alone in the world of CD-quality streaming web music services. In this project I'll guide you to three other subscription-based services you might want to investigate and test drive, including Musicmatch On Demand, Napster, and Microsoft Radio Plus.

Time

The activities that make up this project require about one hour to fully explore each of the three services. Add one hour per service if you elect to download their trial software.

Step 1: Check out Musicmatch On Demand

When it comes to web-based music services, Musicmatch is one of the founding parents of this genre. At http://www.musicmatch.com you can download a seven-day free trial of Musicmatch On Demand to access more than 800,000 songs. To use this service you'll install the Musicmatch program, which delivers a great player, ripper, recorder, and audio tool. On the opening page look for the Musicmatch On Demand area and click the Learn more link. Three plans are available: $9.95 per month, $26.85 per quarter, or $95.40 per year.

Step 2: Meet the New Napster

Hey, this one might ring a bell. Originally, Napster was a notorious free file-swapping service millions of people around the world used to swap copyrighted digital music files. The recording industry went ballistic over Napster and ultimately legal pressure forced it off the Web. The reborn Napster is a state-of-the-art legal music purchase and download service that also offers 50 commercial-free radio stations and a library of more than 700,000 tracks and 65,000 albums representing 45,000 artists. A free trial is offered at http://www.napster.com.

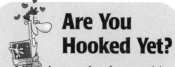

Are You Hooked Yet?

Are you a fan of commercial-free satellite radio? Check this out—you can have a web-delivered version of the channels offered by the XM Satellite Radio streamed directly to your PC via the Internet. Go to http://www.xmradio.com and search for the XM Radio Online information page. XM Radio offers a free three-day trial of its web delivered service, and it costs $3.99 a month for existing XM Radio subscribers or $7.99 per month for those who don't subscribe to the regular service.

Step 3: Explore a Service Tucked Inside of Windows Media Player

Here's one right at your fingertips. Next time you fire up the Windows Media Player (make sure you have the latest version), look at the top toolbar and on the right you'll see a Radio tab. Click this and, if you are connected to the Internet, the MSN Radio Plus page appears on the center screen. Microsoft offers a 30-day free trial. The service has 25 member-only stations in addition to free radio streams and goes for $4.95 a month or $29.99 per year.

Project: Turn Your PC into a Karaoke Machine

Karaoke is a worldwide phenomenon for a good reason. It's all about fun and laughs doing an activity that can release the inner ham or hidden talents inside of you, your family, and friends. Although using your PC as a karaoke machine to break the ice at your next party is an obvious motivation, I've found parents of young kids find sing-along karaoke a wonderful activity for rainy days.

With all its brain power, color display, and disk storage capacity, a home PC can morph to become a highly flexible karaoke machine. Add access to the Internet and in an instant you have a library of thousands of karaoke song files in every genre under the sun.

In this project you'll explore the two worlds of PC-based karaoke: free players and tunes for a budget experience, and commercial software and tracks you buy to stage a more sophisticated karaoke performance in your family room.

Time

About one to two hours to read a few articles on the vanBasco website, download its free karaoke player, fetch a few free tunes from several web-sites, and sing your heart out. Add another hour or so to download and test drive the 30-day trial version of PC Karaoke for a more professional experience.

As an optional activity, I'll show you how to purchase and download a few tunes from the PCKaraoke.com site to complete your introduction to PC-based karaoke.

Warning: At-home PC karaoke can be very addicting. Proceed only if you and your family have a strong sense of humor and reduced inhibition!

note Time out! Before we take another step, let me stress that a dedicated karaoke machine linked to your TV display is a great way to go. The purpose of this project is to show you how a PC can become a low-cost karaoke player. Die-hard karaoke fans typically opt for dedicated solutions.

The PC Karaoke software you'll experience does not, by the way, play the karaoke tracks from CDs purchased for playback in a free-standing karaoke machine. It is possible to buy special PC CD drives that can physically read traditional karaoke tracks and you can find software to work with these drives, but the entire process is too costly to warrant going down that path.

Step 1: Download and Set Up vanBasco PC Karaoke Player

1. Open your Internet Explorer browser and go to http://www.vanbasco.com. When the opening page appears, find the Articles and Awards sections. Now click Articles and spend some quality time reading the three articles. The first, *Computer Karaoke*, provides a nice introduction, with the remaining two articles being for the more technically inclined.

2. Okay, with that homework reading assignment done, it's time to download the free player. Click the Downloads link on the left side of the web page. On the Download page that follows, select the latest version of the vanBasco's Karaoke Player and click the Continue button.

3. The Download page requests you enter your email address, accompanied by a disclaimer stating that your address will not be shared with third parties. Providing your email is optional. Click the Download button to continue.

4. When the Windows File Download dialog box appears, click the Save button and then use the Save As dialog box to navigate to your downloads folder and save the file there.

5. When the download process completes, close your browser and use Windows Explorer to navigate to your downloads folder. Find and double-click the downloaded program file to start the installation.

6. Follow the onscreen instructions to install the player. Before you know it, the multiple windows of the vanBasco's Karaoke Player fill your screen.

Once installed, you can launch vanBasco by clicking Start, All Programs, vanBasco's Karaoke Player.

Step 2: Explore the vanBasco Player

Follow the steps below to play a sample vanBasco karaoke tune.

1. When the program fires up, it displays a Tip of the Session window. If you're new to the program, I recommend you click through all the miniscreens to learn valuable tips for running the program.

2. Close the Tip of the Session dialog box and locate the Player, Playlist, Control, and Piano windows.

3. Now it's time for the fun to start. Click the Play button (find the window with controls that look like a VCR). The first sample song listed in the Playlist window starts playing and the lyrics display in the window with the words highlighted in sync with the tune, as shown in Figure 6.15.

Synchronized lyrics

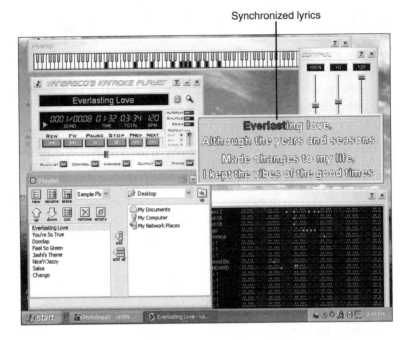

FIGURE 6.15

Karaoke programs for personal computers display the synchronized lyrics just like a dedicated karaoke machine.

Step 3: Finding Free Karaoke Files

In addition to the songs included with the free vanBasco download, you can also use its search function to scour the Internet for more free karaoke music. This activity will give you a taste of the vast amount of karaoke material just a mouse click away on the Internet.

1. Make sure you are connected to the Internet. In vanBasco's Player window, click the magnifying glass icon to open the MIDI Search screen. Enable (click) the check box Only Show Results Containing Karaoke Lyrics.

2. For training purposes, let's key in and search for a karaoke file of "Jingle Bells." I'm going to save you a bunch of time in terms of finding a file with lyrics as opposed to one with the melody only. At the time of this writing the first search result entry was for Jerry's Christmas Jukebox (the actual site address is http://wilstar.net/xmas/xmasjuke.htm). Click the underlined Jingle Bells link and you are taken to Jerry's website.

3. Scroll down the website's opening page and find the entry for Jingle Bells. Click the yellow underlined words Jingle Bells and the file

> **tip**
>
> If you want to have your vanBasco Karaoke Player display the lyrics in full-screen mode, double-click in the lyrics window. To shrink it back, just double-click it again.

automatically downloads to your PC's hard disk and begins playing on your vanBasco Karaoke Player, as shown in Figure 6.16. Now that the music file is stored on your hard disk, you can replay it any time you like.

FIGURE 6.16

The vanBasco Karaoke Player displays the lyrics of the downloaded "Jingle Bells" karaoke file along with a control panel and full play buttons, such as Play, Stop, and Rew (Rewind).

    4. Now that you've got the hang of it, try other artist and title searches using the vanBasco's MIDI Search.

Step 4: Try a Commercial Karaoke Player

Tons of free karaoke files are out there in cyberspace. But I've found it to be a bit tedious browsing through a lot of sites and links to get those with synchronized lyrics. On another front, did you notice that you can't record your voice and combine it with the karaoke music using the free vanBasco Karaoke Player? It's for all of these reasons that the next set of activities will expose you to a commercial karaoke software player with all the bells and whistles. Another benefit of the player you're about to meet is the audio quality of the commercial files is much better than the tinny synthesized ditties we just experienced. To complete the tour, you'll see what it's like to purchase, download, and play more professional-sounding files.

> **note** The PC Karaoke software is designed to play files specifically made for it. You can't use it to play commercial karaoke CDs designed for free-standing dedicated players.

    1. Point your browser to http://www.pckaraoke.com. When the opening page appears, read it from top to bottom for a quick introduction to the program you'll download.

2. Scroll all the way to the bottom of the opening display and click the Download Now button.

3. Click through any alerts warning you about downloading a program file and when the File Download dialog box appears, click Save, navigate to the Downloads folder and click Save to deposit the file.

4. When the download completes, click Run to install PC Karaoke and click through any security warning issued by the Internet Explorer browser.

5. A Download Wizard appears listing elements the program needs and the status of their installation on your PC. If your PC is running an updated version of Windows XP, the first two items (DirectX 8.1 + and Media Player 7 +) should be tagged as Installed, as shown in Figure 6.17. If your PC lacks these items, follow the onscreen instructions to update your system. To complete the installation, click the Click Here to Download Files button.

FIGURE 6.17

The Download Wizard dialog box lists elements needed to install and run PC Karaoke.

6. Accept the default directory and click the Next button when the Update Song List dialog box appears. The installation process completes with the placement of a PC Karaoke Trial Version icon on your Windows desktop.

Step 5: Start Up PC Karaoke

Now it's time to get jiggy with PC Karaoke:

1. Be sure your PC is linked to the Internet because the PC Karaoke program needs an active connection to support its web song search feature.

2. Look at your Windows desktop and find the PC Karaoke icon (it's a box with orange *PC* letters with a green *K* underneath). Double-click it and a dialog box

announces the number of days left in your 30-day trial. When asked about learning more about the full version, click No.

> **tip**
> PC Karaoke will accept whatever the Windows XP operating system recognizes as the current microphone input source. This is good news for webcam owners because it means that if your webcam microphone is currently set as the Windows microphone source, you can use it with PC Karaoke to record your voice. You may, of course, use a traditional PC microphone, too.

3. Starting the program might call up a Windows Mixer Setup window. If you own a PC microphone and want to record yourself singing along with a tune, click the Microphone Input drop-down horizontal box and change the setting from Line In to Microphone. Don't worry if the Mixer window does not appear at this point. Later, when we try out using a microphone with the program, I'll show you how to call up the Mixer and change the settings.

4. Click OK on the Mixer window and the full program elements display.

Step 6: Get to Know PC Karaoke

As shown in Figure 6.18, PC Karaoke opens with multiple toolbar and display elements you can arrange at will, using your mouse.

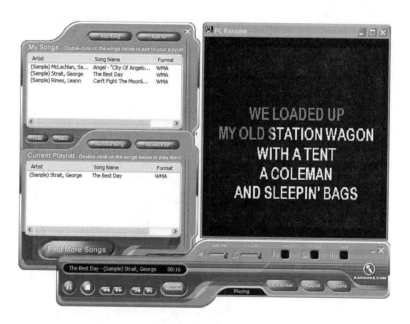

FIGURE 6.18

The PC Karaoke program displays multiple separate elements to manage your karaoke songs and control their playback.

Here's a rundown of the set:

- The large black empty window displays the words of a song in sync with the music.

- In the My Songs area on the upper-left, you'll find three songs preloaded to experiment with, including tunes from Sarah McLachlan, George Strait, and Leann Rimes.

- The Current Playlist window on the bottom consists of a list of songs you want to be played when you activate the karaoke player.

- The main control interface for PC Karaoke is located at the bottom of the screen. It gives you the usual options for playing tracks and controlling PC Karaoke.

note Notice the Format column associated with the three sample songs. PC Karaoke's sing-a-long files are in the Microsoft WMA format. As you'll soon discover, the PC Karaoke program is actually a complete end-to-end product scheme. You buy the player and it, in turn, plays special WMA format files you buy using the PC Karaoke website. The bottom line, however, is you can't use the PC Karaoke program to play the karaoke files we used with the vanBasco Karaoke Player. Those files are *MIDI format files* (a type of digital music file used extensively in electronic music creation).

Okay, enough talk! I'm not going to make you wait another second—double-click one of the three sample songs and you see it instantly loaded into the Current Playlist box below My Songs.

To start getting your funk on, double-click a track in your Playlist. In a few moments the song lyrics should appear in the main PC Karaoke window and play for 35 seconds. (This is one of the limitations of the songs preloaded in the trial version; later when we buy some PC Karaoke program compatible songs, they will play the full length.)

Step 7: Record Your Voice

A key feature found in the lower toolbar is the Record button. It's time to tune up your vocal chords and give this a try. Don't worry if you are not familiar with the three sample songs. You can play them and just recite the lyrics to get a feel for the process you're about to learn.

1. Make sure the microphone in your USB webcam is ready or plug in a PC microphone to your PC's microphone port located either on the back of your PC or, if you are lucky, on the front panel.

   Don't have a microphone of any kind? No sweat. You can readily find them at most retail electronics, office supply, or computer specialty stores for about $20 and up.

2. Make sure PC Karaoke is ready to use your microphone. On the lower toolbar, find and click the Options button. On the Options dialog box, look to the upper-left area and click the Setup Sound Mixer button. When the Windows Mixer Setup dialog box appears, make sure the Microphone Input horizontal box is set to Microphone, as shown in Figure 6.19. Click OK and OK again to close the Options window.

3. Ready? Take your mouse pointer and highlight a song in the Current Playlist box, but don't double-click it. Instead, move your mouse to the Record button and click it. The song begins just as before, but now when you start singing, your vocal

skills (or lack thereof) are being recorded. (When the 35-second limit is reached, a Listen or Save Your Recording dialog box appears. Click the Listen button and hear your voice combined with the tune (see Figure 6.20).

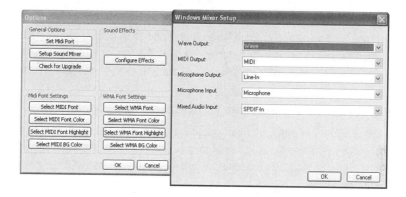

FIGURE 6.19

The Windows Mixer Setup dialog box allows you to set the sound input to microphone or line-in.

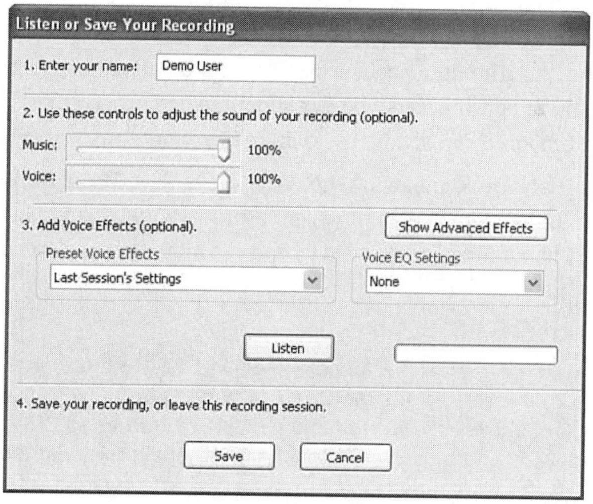

FIGURE 6.20

The Listen or Save Your Recording dialog box includes a Listen button to preview your performance. Note the slider bars to balance the volume of your voice with the background music.

4. From here you can also edit. First enter your name in the top box of the Listen or Save Your Recording dialog box and leave the Music and Voice volume control sliders alone for now. Move to the Add Voice Effects area and click the down arrow associated with the Preset Voice Effects. Play around applying a variety of settings,

such as the 60s Rock effects, and listen to the result. You can also apply equalization effects using the Voice EQ Settings drop-down menu. Don't fret if all the terms and numbers mean nothing to you, such as Low Mid Boost +6db 800Hz. Just click around and see how the EQ setting impacts your recording.

5. Your final step is to save the recording by clicking the Save button. After a brief processing window appears, you are retuned to the main program display with your recording listed in the Current Playlist. Hey, now you are shown as the artist! Double-click your entry and the player runs the song with your voice.

Step 8: Find and Purchase More PC Karaoke Songs (Optional)

For a fee of $1.99 per song, you can purchase and download PC Karaoke compatible song files. The PC Karaoke program library is extensive and it's easy to find and download songs after setting up an account using a credit card that will be used for your first and future purchases.

To search the library and purchase songs, look for the large Find More Songs button at the bottom of the Current Playlist box. Clicking this button sends you to the PC Karaoke website. Look to the far left and click the Song Search option to start up the PC Karaoke web-based Song Search Wizard. When I keyed in "The Beach Boys" in the blank horizontal search box, shown in Figure 6.21, I found that 14 songs by the group are available. You can click the little speaker icon to hear a sample of the file and then click the Buy $1.99 link to add the track to your shopping cart. The PC Karaoke Song Wizard guides you through three actions: search, review and purchase, and download.

I purchased "Help Me Rhonda" by the Beach Boys, "I've Been Working on the Railroad," and "Fly Me to the Moon." Well, it wasn't a pretty phonic experience for the family to endure, but I had a blast singing along and recording my performances.

All About CD+G

If you know someone with a karaoke machine, or if you own one yourself, you are familiar with the very affordable CD+G format CDs you can buy where music CDs are sold. A *CD+G format file* (or sometimes just referred to as CDG) cleverly combines synchronized lyrics and music. CD+G files and discs, in turn, can be decoded by dedicated karaoke machines.

Although your PC can play these discs too, you'll only hear the music. The lack of lyrics in sync with music is a big drawback, but I've still had a lot of fun using the lyrics sheets that most karaoke CD+G discs include to sing along.

If you're willing to dig in to your wallet and if you are lucky enough to have a CD+G-compatible CD drive, there are specialty software packages that enable you to rip CD+G discs and create files you may store and play back on your PC with the synchronized lyrics. One example is a $178.95 program called Hoster at http://www.mtu.com/basics/karaoke-hoster.htm.

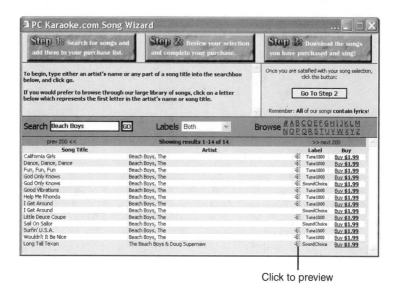

Click to preview

FIGURE 6.21

The Song Search feature offered on the PC Karaoke product website found 14 hit tunes by The Beach Boys.

What's next? The projects in this chapter showed how your PC can morph into a remarkable and flexible audio entertainment jukebox. With the exception of the karaoke adventure, the focus was on rather passive, albeit rewarding, listening experiences. Now it's time to get your creative juices flowing. In the next chapter I'll show you how to use a personal computer to serve as a multitrack home recording studio.

Turn your PC into a Recording Studio

The karaoke project at the tail end of the last chapter moved us from passive listening to active music interaction. Now it's time to crank up the creativity dial to full blast.

For the past five years I've witnessed a revolution unfolding. Millions of people around the world are using PCs to record their own musical performances and produce CDs. They're doing everything the big studios and record companies do, albeit on a much smaller scale.

I've experienced it all firsthand. My teenage son Jeff and his friends record original music, design CDs, and even sell them to raise money for their next creative venture. And they're far from alone. Chances are good your home is a prime candidate for the projects in this chapter because experts tell us that more than 50% of U.S. homes have at least one musician, and nearly half of those have two or more.

Less than ten years ago, some of the projects in this chapter would have been too demanding for a home computer to handle. For years personal computers have been a fixture in professional recording studios, but they were often custom-built and filled with very expensive special components.

Today, the whole landscape has changed with the combination of powerful brain chips, such as the Pentium 4 processors, and a new generation of multitrack software designed with consumers in mind. The bottom line—if you own a modern Windows XP-based personal computer, you have the makings of a very credible multitrack recording studio.

note In the world of music recording, *multitrack* refers to a recording comprised of two or more tracks. For example, one track for guitar, another for voice, and so on.

Do you have a teenager in the house? Does she play a musical instrument and/or have a band? If yes, you're in luck. For me, the projects in this chapter have a special place in my heart as the parent of a teenager. The hours of working shoulder-to-shoulder with my teenage son have shown me that the activities in this chapter can help forge a close and positive working relationship with your teen. And that's something many parents desperately seek when their kids plow throughout the challenging middle- and high-school years.

Okay, I'll stop preaching. Let's get down to business. The projects in this chapter will show you how to turn a PC into a basic music recording studio, one that can even record, edit, and mix multiple tracks of separate input.

The first set of projects focus on recording live performances and will show you how to

- Purchase a PC microphone and connect it to your desktop or laptop PC
- Record a single track using the Windows XP sound recording utility and a free program from the web called WavePad
- Record, edit, balance, and mix multitracks of recorded input using a free software package called Audacity
- Create a final master single-track file ready for burning on a CD

The second set of projects shifts from live performance recording to focus on composing using digital music loops. You'll learn:

- The basic concepts behind composing with music loops using a wonderful children's program called Super Duper Music Looper
- How to combine music loops with live recorded tracks using ACID Xpress

At the end of the chapter, you'll find a list of suggested hardware and software products to consider if you catch the home recording bug and want to grow. And, as with the previous chapter, free trial software downloaded from the Internet will be used whenever possible.

Starting the Habit

The projects in this chapter barely skim the surface of what is possible today when it comes to PC audio recording.

The world of audio recording using a personal computer is exceptionally rich and deep. Hundreds of hardware products and loads of software options populate the landscape of websites and stores, such as the Guitar Center chain, that specialize in meeting the needs of home-recording enthusiasts. Check out http://www.guitarcenter.com, http://www.musciansfriend.com, or http://www.musiciansbuy.com and do a search using the key word *recording* and you'll be blown away by the spectrum of goodies available, spanning price ranges from just less than $100 to thousands of dollars.

Your first exposure to the world of PC recording can be overwhelming and confusing. There are so many ways to approach the topic that it can be frustrating. My son and I were tossed into a sea of complex terms and gear right out of the gate. Everyone we talked to for advice was an enthusiast who wanted us to buy hundreds of dollars worth of software and specialty gear. All we wanted to do in the beginning was see what was possible on a shoestring budget. How we would have welcomed the exercises contained in this chapter!

To start your introduction to the world of PC recording, I'll use the same super-low cost and easy-to-understand path my son and I followed in the beginning. The exercises target recording live performances using microphones attached to your PC's existing sound system and expose you to the fun of using all-digital music loops to create music.

After completing the projects in this chapter, you might find, as my son and I did, that home music recording develops into an irresistible hobby you can enjoy for the rest of your life.

Skills and Gear Check

I have only one question—do you or one of your family members play a musical instrument or like to sing? If yes, you're ready. Don't fret if you lack musical skills. You can still do the exercises and learn the software basics by simply speaking and using household objects as makeshift instruments. And when it comes to composing using digital loops, you'll discover no prior music knowledge is required.

Materials

All of the projects in this chapter share a common need for a PC with speakers or headphones, a high-speed link to the Internet, and a PC microphone. The only other considerations are

- A table top or tripod floor-style microphone stand (less than $30).
- A mic-in jack on your computer (all modern PCs for years have included this feature).
- A pair of standard headphones.
- A CD or DVD disc recorder (also called a writer or burner) built into your PC.

- Microsoft's Windows XP operating system. All onscreen operating system illustrations, dialog boxes, and pop-up menu samples are based on Windows XP.

- Windows Internet Explorer as your browser for these projects. All references to downloading steps and dialog boxes are based on the use of this browser.

Project: Purchase a PC Microphone and Learn How to Create Single Track Recordings

In this project I'll offer tips for finding and buying a microphone designed for personal computers and show you how to connect and activate it. You'll learn how to

- Find and connect a PC microphone to your desktop or laptop computer

- How to run the built-in Windows XP sound management software to activate and adjust your microphone input

- Download, install, and use the free WavePad single-track recording program

Time

After you have purchased a PC microphone, the exercises in this project will take about two to three hours.

Step 1: Purchase a PC Microphone and Stand

Personal computer microphones come in many forms, as shown in Figure 7.1. My collection includes tiny disc-like microphones and some that look like a traditional handheld type with a ball-shaped end. Most microphones made for personal computers have a small mini-plug that looks just like the plug on the end of standard headphones designed for personal CD or handheld digital music players. This plug is designed to be inserted into your PC's mic-in jack. A host of USB-connected microphones are also available. Later in this chapter we'll learn about two other forms of higher quality microphones, those with a quarter-inch jack and the XLR models with three prongs.

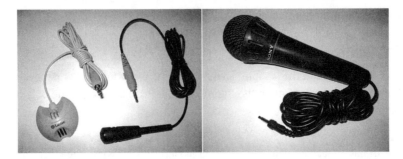

FIGURE 7.1

This collection of PC microphones includes two miniature models designed primarily for recording speech or supporting web conferencing and one that looks and feels like a traditional handheld mic.

If you need to shop for a PC microphone, here are some points to keep in mind:

- If you're just starting out, and especially if recording the spoken word is your main goal, don't buy an expensive microphone. I've had remarkable luck using microphones priced less than $30 from Sony, RadioShack, Labtec, Logitech, GE, and Plantronics.

- Go for one with a long, shielded cord. As you progress through the projects in this chapter, you'll discover that the Holy Grail of PC recording is attaining clean input. The typical PC generates a lot of electronic interference that can negatively impact the cleanliness of your recordings. A PC microphone with a long, shielded cord helps in two ways; it resists electronic interference from your PC and places the microphone away from the system for added isolation.

> **note** Before you run off to the computer supply store, check the set of accessories that came with your PC to see if a microphone was included. Do you own a computer *webcam*? These are small digital cameras that plug into a PC using a *universal serial bus (USB)* cable that often include a built-in microphone you may use for the projects in this chapter.

- Most PC microphones are designed for voice recognition or web conferencing. These models often have small plastic bases and a long stem. Or, you'll see a lot of headphone and adjustable microphone combination products ideal for web conferencing. For recording singing or the playing of a musical instrument, I recommend you buy a PC microphone that looks like a traditional handheld microphone.

- Ask for a *unidirectional* PC microphone. Because you'll be recording singing or the playing of an instrument, you want a microphone that concentrates its listening on a specific target. Unidirectional microphones do just that, as opposed to omnidirectional microphones designed to capture a total environment. I prefer a traditional handheld model and one that includes an on/off switch. Some of the recording programs used in this chapter automatically start recording sound the moment you click the Record button.

- Get an adjustable table top or tripod microphone stand, as shown in Figure 7.2. Popular outlets, such as RadioShack and Guitar Center, offer lots of choices at prices starting at less than $20 for table top models and less than $30 for tripod floor models. Whether singing or playing an instrument, it's important to avoid handling a microphone during the recording process. And, of course, a stand enables you to position the microphone for the best results.

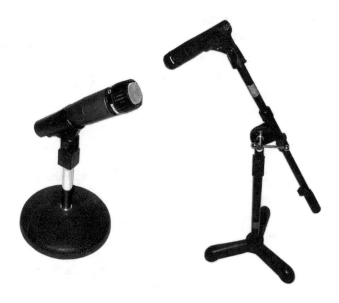

FIGURE 7.2

Microphone stands come in three styles. Shown on the left is a table top stand, with a mini version of a floor tripod model.

Step 2: Connect Your PC Microphone

If you purchased a microphone that uses a USB connection, follow the manufacturer's installation instructions. If you bought a microphone with a traditional mini–plug, the first step is to locate a small mic-in jack on the back or the front of your desktop PC. In most modern PCs, this connector is color-coded with a red plastic ring around it. You'll find it next to a hole with a green ring used to connect speakers to your PC. On a laptop, look for the same color-coded holes. If the color-coding is not present, look for the words *mic in* or a microphone symbol near one of the audio connectors. Insert your microphone plug into this connector.

Step 3: Ensure Your Microphone Is Activated

Now that you've plugged in your PC microphone, it's time to make sure the line is activated. The software utility within Windows XP that manages sound has the ability to select and control multiple recording inputs. This is important because some PCs include a blue stereo line-in hole. For our activities, we need to ensure that the microphone line is assigned as the active recording input source. Follow these steps:

1. Open the Windows Start menu and then click Control Panel.

> **note** The Windows Control Panel has two views. The default view, Category view, is the one these instructions are based on. If your Control Panel is configured for Classic View, you should click the Switch to Category View link on the upper-left area of the window.

2. When the Control Panel window opens, find and click the Sounds, Speech, and Audio Devices icon. This brings up a new window with the words Pick a Task... or Pick a Control Panel Icon displayed on the right side of the Control Panel. Look to the upper-left area and find and click Advanced Volume Controls.

3. A Volume Control dialog box now appears that looks something like a mixing board with virtual sliders for Volume Control, Wave, SW Synth, CD Audio, Line In, and PC Speaker. Open the Options drop-down menu and click Properties.

4. A Properties dialog box now appears with choices to adjust volume for Playback, Recording, or Other. Click the Recording button and note the check boxes in the Show the Following Volume Controls zone at the bottom of the window. Make sure the Microphone box is checked and click OK.

5. You should now see a Recording Control dialog box as shown in Figure 7.3. Make sure the Select box associated with the microphone is checked, and leave the volume slider at the midway position for now.

FIGURE 7.3

The Recording Control dialog box allows you to activate and set the volume level for your PC microphone.

At last you are ready to test your microphone and create your first PC recording using a mini-program bundled with Windows XP.

Step 4: Download and Install WavePad

The built-in Windows XP Sound Recorder program is a nice convenience tool for recording very simple and brief segments. I use it to capture short voice messages that I attach to email messages. Our next step introduces you to a free program you may keep and use indefinitely called WavePad. As you'll soon discover, WavePad offers more sophisticated editing and manipulation features than the built-in Windows recording program.

1. Connect to the Internet and point your browser to http://www.nch.com.au/wavepad/. This takes you to the NCH website and the host of audio products it offers.

2. On the WavePad page, look in the third paragraph and find the Click Here to Install link to download the free WavePad audio recording and editing program. NCH is making this available to you free of charge as a way to introduce you to its more sophisticated commercial products.

3. When you click the link, you might see a File Download—Security Warning dialog box. The file you are downloading is a program with an .exe file extension in its name. Some viruses are program files with an .exe extension, so Windows is trying to protect you with the warning. In this case, click the Save button and use the Save As dialog box to place the program file in your downloads folder.

4. When the download completes, I suggest you close down the Download Complete dialog box and your browser. Next, use Windows Explorer to navigate to your downloads folder and double-click the wpsetup program file. Again, for safety purposes, you might encounter a dialog box warning you that the publisher of the program file could not be verified. Click the Run button to install the program. Respond to any dialog boxes regarding license terms and the program should install and open automatically.

Step 5: Record a Vocal or Instrumental Performance with WavePad

The following set of exercises introduces you to an experience a step up from the rock-bottom basics supported by the built-in Windows Sound Recorder. First, we'll use WavePad to record an audio performance starring you speaking, singing, or playing an instrument. The next step shows you how to trim out unwanted segments in your recorded clip, add echo, reverb, fade-in, and fade-out effects.

1. If you are continuing on from the previous step, the WavePad program is already open. If not, click Start, All Programs, WavePad. Or you can go to your Windows XP desktop and find the WavePad program icon and double-click it.

2. At the bottom of the opening screen of the WavePad program, you see buttons for play, record, pause, stop, and so on. Click the large red Record button.

3. A New File dialog box now displays with the default settings of a sample rate of 44,100 and mono active. Because your PC microphone is most likely a mono model, leave the Channels setting at the Mono (Single) setting. The mysterious 44,100 number refers to the fidelity of the recording you are about to make. The higher the number, the better the quality, but also the larger the sound files it produces. For now, leave the setting at the 44,100 sampling rate. Click OK.

4. A Record Control dialog box now appears as shown in Figure 7.4. Look at the upper-right area of this dialog box and find and click the Open Windows Record Mixer button. This opens the Windows XP Recording Control dialog box showing a slider control for your microphone. Make sure the Microphone Select box is checked and set the level slider at the midway position. Close the Recording Control dialog box and return to the WavePad Record Control window.

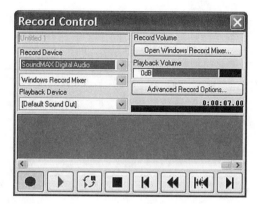

FIGURE 7.4

The Record Control dialog box provides access to the Windows Record Mixer, shows the playback volume level, and includes Record, Stop, and Playback controls.

5. Grab your microphone or place it in a holder or stand. Sing, speak, or play your musical instrument and look at the virtual microphone volume horizontal meter just below the button labeled Advanced Recording Options. If the horizontal meter bars constantly hit into the red zone, move the microphone back or reduce the microphone input volume using the Windows Record Mixer button.

   Experiment until you get a reading that hits all green with barely any crossover into the red zone. All red zone recordings are distorted. In digital recording circles, hitting the red zone is called *clipping*. Your goal is to find the right level setting for your microphone.

6. Click the red Record button and begin your performance. WavePad begins recording the moment it detects any incoming sound from the microphone.

7. When you are finished, click the square black Stop button. The long horizontal white rectangle within the Record Control window should now display the recorded wave patterns of your performance, as shown in Figure 7.5. Note how the patterns do not hit the top and bottom limits.

   This is what you want to achieve. If your recording wave patterns look like those in Figure 7.6, you need to pull the microphone back or reduce its volume, as noted above.

8. If you need to rerecord your performance, close out the Record Control window as well as the long horizontal window that floats behind it labeled Untitled 1. Answer No when a dialog box asks you if you want to save the file.

9. Repeat the steps above until you achieve a recording with good levels that you want to save.

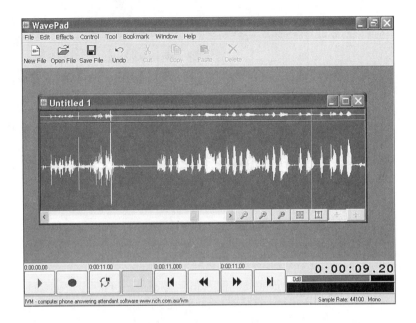

FIGURE 7.5

Taking time to adjust your microphone input volume produces wave patterns that remain within the upper and lower limits of the recording range.

FIGURE 7.6

If your recorded wave patterns look like this, your microphone volume setting is too high. Reduce the volume or move the microphone back from the source.

Step 7: Make Basic Edits to Your Recording

After you've achieved a recording with good levels, click the red *X* in the upper-right corner of the Record Control window to close it. A long horizontal window labeled Untitled 1 should appear displaying the wave patterns of your recording, as shown previously, in Figure 7.6.

Before we move on, let's save your basic, unedited recording for safekeeping. Look at the top horizontal toolbar of the WavePad program and click the Save File icon, and then use the Save Audio File As dialog box (which works just like Windows Explorer) to give your masterpiece a name and save it under your My Music folder within My Documents.

When you create a name for your file and determine the folder in which to place it, click the Save button in the lower-right corner of the Save Audio File As dialog box. This brings up a small Select Wave File Format dialog box. Accept the default settings and click the OK button. The file is now saved as a WAV format audio file which you may later play back on your PC or burn to a CD for playback on any stereo.

Now it's time to use a few of the editing tools to give you a taste for what today's audio software can do.

Because the WavePad program starts recording the moment it detects any sound coming from the microphone, my recording contained several seconds of unwanted material as I prepared to sing a few bars of "Oh! Susanna." I didn't want that to be part of the final file. To trim out the unwanted front portion, all I had to do was place my mouse pointer within the horizontal box at the starting position, hold the left mouse button down, and drag the pointer across the region to be removed. When I reach the end of the zone to be cut, I release the left mouse button and then click Edit, Cut and bingo, the unwanted segment disappears (see Figure 7.7).

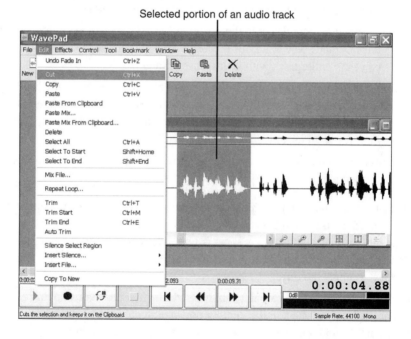

FIGURE 7.7

Using your mouse pointer to highlight portions of an audio track to remove or modify is a classic capability found in all personal computing audio-editing software programs.

Selecting the exact portion of a recording to delete can be tricky. The squiggly lines in WavePad are a graphic representation of the level of sound present at any given time in a track. A flat line indicates no sound at all.

WavePad, as with all good sound editing programs, also offers tools to make the process easier. For example, look at the bottom horizontal toolbar and find the magnifying glass icon with a plus symbol. Click it to zoom in on the wave pattern. With the deleting instructions above in mind, you can now pinpoint the exact start and end point for the segment to be deleted. Listen to the segment, however, before cutting it. To do this, click the play arrow. Playback will begin with the boundary you set on the left edge of the segment to be cut. Are your left and right cut boundaries on target? If yes, execute the deletion. If not, paint the segment again. Remember that you can zoom in very close to improve start and stop point accuracy.

> **tip** After each editing change you make and want to keep, it's a smart move to save your file. If you make a mistake or something happens to interrupt your system, your hard work will not be lost. As you invest more of your heart, soul, and time into music recordings, you'll also want to back up your edited recordings onto some form of external storage, such as a floppy disc or a USB keychain drive.

Follow the steps below to apply an echo effect to your recorded track:

1. Let's add an echo effect to the recorded track. First we need to highlight the entire track. A quick way to do this is press Ctrl+A on your keyboard. You can also just paint the entire track with your mouse pointer.

2. Go to the top menu and click the Effects drop-down menu, and click Echo. An Echo dialog box appears with two settings—Echo Time in Milliseconds and Echo Gain by Percent. Click the Preview button and see what the default settings sound like. Alter the settings until you find an echo effect to your liking.

3. Try an Echo time of 100 milliseconds and set the percentage to 25. To keep the applied effect, click OK. The edited portion now automatically plays.

Do you feel like going retro with some cool reverb effects? Highlight another portion of your recording. Go to the Effects drop-down menu and click Reverb. Just as with the Echo routine, a small dialog box appears with two reverb settings—Reverb Level and Reverb Time. Play around with the settings to find the right mix for your ears and then click OK to apply the effect.

Our final exercise in this step is to apply a fade-in effect to the beginning of the recording and a fade-out effect at the end. By now you're an expert with the highlighting mouse bit. To add a professional fade-in effect, follow these steps:

1. Highlight the first moments of your recording, go to the Effects drop-down menu, and click Fade In.

2. Preview the effect by clicking the Play button. If you like the effect, save the file. If not, return to the top toolbar, click the Edit drop-down menu, and click the first entry, Undo Fade In.

3. Apply the same steps to the end of your recorded performance for a fade-out effect.

4. Save the file if you want to make the effect permanent.

Guess what? You just did some of the basic sound-editing functions professional recording engineers use every day. Think of the possibilities. Even a basic program, such as the free WavePad, puts at your fingertips the ability to record, edit, and save audio performances on your PC hard disk. And that's just the start.

note Windows XP also includes a primitive recording program that might be easier for a small child to use. To find it, click Start, All Programs, Accessories, Entertainment, Sound Recorder.

WavePad saves your final edited recording using the standard Windows WAV format which may then be used by any CD-making program to burn a CD. Now you can use the skills you learned in Chapter 6, "Turn Your PC into the Ultimate Audio Entertainment Jukebox," to burn your WavePad file to a CD that can play on any car or home stereo. Record several more tracks and you can create your own music CD!

Project: Create a Multitrack Recording Using the Free Audacity Program

The previous project took you through the initial steps for recording audio on a PC. Now that you have a command of the basics, it's time to do a small scale version of what professional sound engineers do for a living—record, edit, and mix multiple tracks of separately recorded material (called a *mix down*) to create a final, single master track.

For this project we'll use the Audacity multitrack recording program. This free program is the creation of a team of volunteers from around the world. But don't let its zero price tag fool you. This little gem is loaded with lots of powerful features you can exploit to create impressive final productions.

This project shows you how to

- Record three tracks of live performance audio input
- Adjust the volume of each track to achieve the overall balance you want
- Apply some special effects to one or more of your recorded tracks
- Mix the three tracks down to one (that is, combine the three separately recorded elements into a new single file)
- Add new tracks to continue building your production and then combine them to one file (mix down)
- Use the final, mixed-down master audio file to create a version that plays on a stereo or handheld digital music player

 Time

Allocate about two hours to download and install the Audacity program, learn the ropes, record three tracks, edit them, apply special effects, and mix down to one master track.

Step 1: Download and Install Audacity

Follow the steps below to download, install, and set up the Audacity program:

1. Connect to the Internet and point your browser to http://audacity.sourceforge.net/. When you reach the opening page for the Audacity website, look to the large yellow box with the Download Audacity 1.2.3 link and click it.

2. The website refreshes to display a page titled Windows. Find and click the Audacity 1.2.3 installer link. The next page presented lists a number of remote computers (hosts) available to download the program to your computer. You can choose any of these, but it's usually best to choose a location near you geographically. Move your mouse pointer to the far right area of the location you've chosen and click the icon of a page with a dog eared upper-right corner (it's under the Download heading).

3. If the download process does not start, note the text at the top of the page offering an alternative link highlighted in dark blue type. In either case, a dialog box appears asking if you want to Save or Run. Click Save and direct the file to your downloads folder.

4. When the program download completes, you can close down your browser and use Windows Explorer and navigate to your downloads folder. Find and double-click the `audacity-win-1.2.3` file to install the program.

5. When the Setup—Audacity dialog box appears, click the I Accept the Agreement button, and then the Next button. Click Next when the information screen appears and Next again, allowing the program to be installed to the default `C:\Program Files\Audacity` folder. Leave the Create a Desktop Icon box checked and click the Next button, followed by clicking the Install button on the final screen display.

6. The installation process completes with the display of a dialog box asking you to click the Finish button. A small dialog box appears to select a language, with English as the default. Click OK and the Audacity program should now load and display on your PC's screen.

Step 2: Get to Know Audacity

If it's not already running, start Audacity by clicking Start, All Programs, Audacity. All of Audacity's controls and editing tools are accessible via a long horizontal toolbar zone at the top of the screen display, as shown in Figure 7.8. I suggest you take a few moments and move your mouse over all of the control icons. As you do, mini pop-ups appear identifying the function of the control icons.

The main Record, Play, Pause, and Stop buttons are self-explanatory, but there are a few special controls I really find helpful. For example, locate the slider bar with a microphone and + and – symbols on the left. This nifty tool can be used on the fly to adjust your microphone's input volume to achieve a clean, distortion-free input signal.

FIGURE 7.8

Audacity's controls and editing tools are presented in bold and simple fashion.

Before we take the next step, play around with the drop-down menus at the very top of the program and scope out the wide library of tools. Don't worry if a lot of the terms are Greek to you. I've found the best way to learn what they do is to record a test file and just randomly apply these special effects. And, of course, if you're not a man and thus are willing to read instructions, click the Help drop-down menu at the top of the screen and visit the wonderful online web guide.

Step 3: Record Three Tracks

Ever hear audio engineers conduct microphone level checks before a concert? Setting good microphone levels is essential for getting distortion-free digital recordings, as noted earlier. To conduct a microphone level test using Audacity, you first need to plug in your PC microphone. For the best results, use a microphone floor or table top stand. Then follow these steps:

1. Get your instrument or vocal chords ready and click the large red Record button at the top of the Audacity display. As you sing or play, watch the wave patterns as they scroll across the track the program automatically generates.

   The goal is to have a good strong signal pattern, but one that remains within the upper and lower edges of the horizontal track band (to avoid distortion, or what recording experts call *clipping*), as shown in Figure 7.9. Use the handy microphone control slider to raise or lower the input volume to set the best level. When you are happy with the setting, click the Stop button. To discard the test track, simply find and click the black *X* in the gray box associated with the track.

   Wait, how can you set the microphone level and play or sing at the same time? Just play, adjust, keep playing, and repeat the process until you have found the right setting. Or deputize your spouse, parent, sibling, or friend to be your recording engineer and take command of the mouse.

   With your microphone level now set, the remaining steps will help you plan and record three separate tracks.

2. Use Windows Explorer to create a folder under My Music and call it `Audacity Recording Sessions`.

3. Now it's time to plan your recording session. For example, let's say you want to sing a song accompanied by guitar. To add some extra spice, include a track for a percussion instrument, such as a tambourine. Don't have a tambourine? No problem. Clap your hands, take two sticks and bang them together, or grab a jar with popcorn seeds and use it as a shaker.

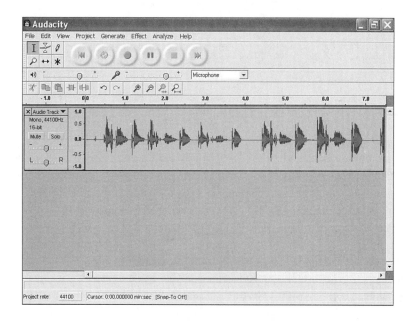

FIGURE 7.9

The microphone input slider control is used to set a good distortion-free level to create wave patterns that remain within the upper and lower edges of the track horizontal band.

4. Let's say your first track is the guitar part. Set your microphone level using the technique discussed above. Ready? Click the red Record button and Audacity automatically creates a track. Play your guitar part. Then click the Stop button.

5. Before you lay down the next track, give your masterpiece a name and save it. Go to the File drop-down menu at the top of the program and select Save Project As and then use the Save Project As dialog box to give your session a name and direct placement of your project file in the `Audacity Recording Sessions` folder I asked you to create earlier.

6. Ready to sing? Plug in your headphones using the green sound-out jack on your PC. Find the output volume slider control immediately to the left of the microphone input volume control at the top of the Audacity toolbar area. Place the volume slider to the midway position. Click the green Play button and listen to your first track play. Adjust the headset volume using the slider. Now you are ready to lay down the next track.

7. Before you click the record button, let me explain the process. What you will be doing is listening via your headphones to the first track play as you sing into the microphone. Using the headphones ensures that you will not double record the original guitar track (which would happen if it played back through your PC's speakers). Using the headphones from this point forward delivers pure isolation and avoids feedback as well.

8. Okay, lesson over. Click the Record button and Audacity automatically adds a new track directly below your first one. As with the first track, you'll now see the sound patterns appear and scroll across the new second track. When you are done, click the Stop button.

9. Get ready for a multitrack rush! Look at the controls at the top of the screen and find and click the purple double arrow symbol to the left of the Play button. This control takes you to the beginning of your recorded tracks. Now click the Play button and listen to your two tracks play simultaneously. Cool! You are now an official multitrack amateur recording engineer.

10. Repeat the process to create a third track. Use my suggestions for homemade percussion or anything your imagination cooks up. Your Audacity screen should look like Figure 7.10.

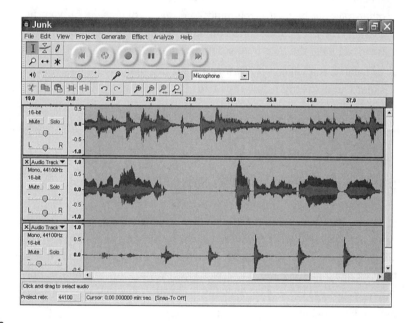

FIGURE 7.10

Using Audacity, I recorded three separate tracks, one for guitar (top), vocal (middle), and tambourine (bottom).

11. Save your work by going to the File drop-down menu at the top of the program and select Save Project. Get into the habit of saving frequently.

Step 4: Balance the Volume of Your Three Tracks

Ever see a mixing board in a recording studio? It's usually a huge panel filled with slider controls and tons of knobs and flashing lights. One function of the sliders is to set the volume level of an individual track. Imagine a mixing board for three tracks. To balance the volume between the three tracks, you would manually move the slider up and down relative to the other two tracks. Audacity, as with all other multitrack recording programs for personal computers, accomplishes this same task using virtual onscreen software controls.

As you listened to the three tracks you recorded, did one track overpower another in terms of volume? No problem. Here's how to adjust the volume of your three recorded tracks:

tip Curious about the L/R slider bar below the –/+ volume control? This tool is used to balance (or pan) relative output to your left or right speaker. This tool was very popular in the 1960s when you'd have a bass part, for example, panned full right, with solo guitar full left.

1. Look at the extreme left edge of each of your recorded tracks. Note that a gray control box is attached to the far left edge of each track. Each box includes track-specific information and controls. The Mute button silences the track, allowing other tracks to be heard. You might find this feature useful for your next recording session. The Solo button forces all other tracks to be silent. So, of course, only one track can have the Solo button depressed at a time.

2. To balance the volume of all three tracks, use the –/+ *gain* (or volume) control slider found directly below the Mute and Solo buttons. Play your three tracks together and move the gain slider control to find the right volume mix.

3. Be sure to save your file or project to ensure the volume setting is permanently applied.

Step 5: Explore Some of Audacity's Special Effects

The best way to discover the wide range of special effects Audacity offers is to experiment at will. With your three track recording displayed, use your mouse pointer and click any area not occupied by a button within the far left gray box assigned to a given track. This highlights the entire track. Now go to the top of the screen and click the Effect drop-down menu to see a list of nearly 30 effects you may potentially apply, from changing tempo and pitch to reverse and wahwah.

Follow the steps below and try changing the tempo of your recording:

1. Highlight the entire track (press Ctrl+A on your keyboard). Open the Effect drop-down menu and click the Change Tempo command.

2. In the Change Tempo dialog box that appears, move the Percent Change slider to the right and then click the Preview button to hear how the effect sounds applied to your track (see Figure 7.11). If you like, you may also alter the beat by entering different values in the Beats per Minute boxes.

3. If you like the effect, click the OK button and it is applied to the file. If you change your mind, go to the top toolbar area and click Edit, Undo Change Tempo.

FIGURE 7.11

When you click a special effect command, its dialog box appears.

Experiment with the other special effects at will. If you are doing this project with a child, record her talking and then apply the change tempo and pitch effects. And to really get a chuckle, apply the reverse effect.

Step 6: Mix Multiple Tracks to Create a Single Master Track

This process still amazes me. What you are about to do is use the remarkable computing power of your PC to combine the three separately recorded and edited tracks to create a single master track. This is a step the music geeks call mixing down.

1. Save your work created up to this point by going to the File drop-down menu at the top of the program and select Save Project.

2. Before we move on, you may have been concerned about the dead air at the front of your recorded tracks. *Dead air* refers to the amount of time from when you clicked the Record button and then picked up your guitar or started to sing. In the next step, after we mix down the three tracks, I'll show you how to trim out any dead air at the front and end of your final recording.

3. When you are happy with the volume balance settings for each of your three tracks and you've applied any special effects desired, go to the File drop-down menu and click Export As WAV.

4. A Warning dialog box appears telling you that the file is now exported into a single mono channel file. Click OK and use the Save WAV (Microsoft) File As dialog box to give your mixed-down track a name and direct its placement in the Audacity Recording Sessions folder.

5. The moment you initiate the Save function, the amount of time it takes to mix down the three tracks depends on the computing power of your PC.

6. Exit out of the Audacity program and Use Windows Explorer to go to your Audacity Recording Sessions folder to find and double-click the mixed-down track. Windows Media Player should play the file for you.

Step 7: Trim out Dead Air

As noted above, if you recorded all three tracks by yourself, chances are good there's quite a few seconds of dead air on your final mixed-down track as you first clicked the record button and then got ready to play or sing. As with the WavePad program we used earlier, Audacity makes cutting out unwanted material simple. Fire up the Audacity program, click File, Open to navigate to the Audacity Recording Sessions folder, and click it to open your mixed-down track. The single track loads and is displayed as the first track. Follow these simple actions:

1. To ensure accurate trimming at the front or back end of a file, we'll use the help of the magnifying glass tool. Look at the upper horizontal toolbar and just below the microphone volume adjustment slider you find two magnifying glass icons—one with a + and one with a – symbol.

2. Click the + magnifying glass and you'll notice that each click sequentially increases the magnification of the wave pattern. This is one of the most remarkable features of audio-editing software. The ability to zoom in on a wave pattern and with pinpoint accuracy trim portions out is something you'll grow to love!

3. Use the master file position slider (at the extreme bottom of the screen display) to move to the beginning of the file. Using the mouse pointer, click and hold down the left mouse button at the point where you want to trim and drag to the end of the area to be cut, as shown in Figure 7.12. Release the mouse button, go to the Edit drop-down menu, and click Cut. The unwanted area disappears. Repeat this process to remove unwanted seconds from the back end of the file.

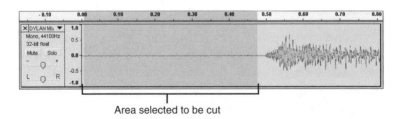

Area selected to be cut

FIGURE 7.12

The magnifying tool used to zoom in on a recorded wave pattern is a powerful feature Audacity and most audio-editing software packages offer.

4. Save the file as a new project, or use the Export As WAV command under the Edit drop-down menu to save and overwrite the previous file.

Step 8: Adding More Tracks to Your Mixed-Down Master Track

This activity is optional but very powerful. By this time you might have already realized the full potential of being able to record, edit, and mix down multiple tracks to create a single track. In our exercise, we recorded only three tracks to create a single master track. Check this out—there's nothing to prevent you from using Audacity to open up the master single track and augment it with new additional tracks. You can edit the new tracks and then mix down with the original master track to create a new master track. Wow, you could create a final production that combines lots of previously recorded tracks!

Step 9: Use Your WAV File to Burn a Music CD

Just as with the WavePad program, the final edited master file is in the .wav format. Now you can use the skills you learned in Chapter 6 to burn your Audacity final production .wav file to a CD that can play on any car or home stereo.

Project: Enter the World of Music Loops Using Super Dooper Music Looper

So far we've used a microphone to capture and edit live performances. Another extremely popular part of the PC music creation story involves building compositions using short clips, or loops, of recorded musical instruments, voices, and sound effects. A loop is a small digital audio file designed to be repeated over and over. Composing with loops is what a lot of the rap stars do in their recordings.

Loops can be created by recording voice or actual instruments. For example, a loop could be a recording of a drummer hitting a snare drum or cymbal or a pianist striking a single key. And here's the really cool part—you can buy CDs with collections of loops or buy and download loops via the Internet (or even find free ones).

Another popular way to make loops is to use an electronic keyboard attached to a personal computer using *musical instrument digital interface (MIDI)* technology. MIDI technology was developed as an international standard to enable a personal computer to interact with music synthesizers and sound cards to produce music (I'll tell you more about MIDI later in this chapter).

To ease you into this brave new world of loops, I've selected an absolutely charming program from Sony called Super Duper Music Looper. It's designed for kids as a toy but I've had hours of fun with the full purchased version, creating goofy compositions including pathetic middle-age rap songs to torture my teenage son and co-workers.

This project will show you how to

- Download, install, and play with the Super Dooper Music Looper free trial program
- Mix multiple tracks of digital music loops
- Manipulate the tempo and key of the loops

Time

Figure on about one hour to download and install the free trial demo of the Super Dooper Music Looper program, learn the ropes, play with the canned loops, and manipulate the tempo and key.

Step 1: Download and Install Super Duper Music Looper

Follow the steps below to download and install Super Duper Music Looper:

1. Connect to the Internet and point your browser to http://mediasoftware.sonypictures. com/Products/. On the opening page of the website, search for the Super Duper Music Looper area under Kids' Software. Click the Super Duper Music Looper link which takes you to a page dedicated to the product.

2. Look at the upper-right side of the page and find and click the Download Free Version link.

3. When the Download Super Duper Music Looper Xpress page appears, click the Super Duper Music Looper Xpress link to download the 18.7MB file to your PC's hard disk.

4. When the File Download dialog box appears, click the Save button and then use the Save As window to direct the placement of the file to your downloads folder.

5. After the download completes, click the Run button on the Download Complete dialog box. Click the Run button if a security dialog box appears and follow the onscreen dialog boxes to install the program, including the acceptance of the license terms and the default directory and folder settings. When the installation process completes, a dialog box appears with a Finish button.

Step 2: Run and Familiarize Yourself with Super Duper Music Looper

Click Start, All Programs, Sonic Foundry, Super Duper Music Looper XPress, or go to your Windows XP desktop and search for the Super Duper Music Looper icon. Double-click the icon and the program loads and automatically plays a 2.25 minute video tutorial using the Windows Media Player.

When the tutorial completes, the full Super Duper Music Looper program screen is displayed, as shown in Figure 7.13. Bold Play, Stop, Record, Paint, and Erase commands dominate the upper toolbar, flanked by a set of slider controls for volume, tempo, and key. The left vertical channel shows a stack of musical instruments and one special effects and microphone track. The large grid zone holds the tracks of loops you are about to create.

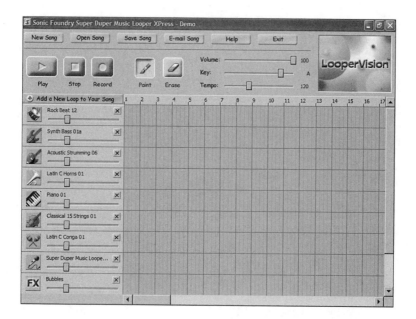

FIGURE 7.13

Super Duper Music Looper's opening screen shows instrument and special effects icons.

Step 3: Paint Loops and Play Them Back

Follow the steps below to have instant gratification building a multitrack composition:

1. Get ready for some big fun! Move your mouse over the large grid area and the pointer looks like a paint brush. Position your mouse pointer at the top of the grid within the horizontal band associated with the image of a drum labeled Rock Beat 12. Click and hold the left mouse button down and drag it to the right. As you do, a wave pattern representing the drum loop appears, as shown in Figure 7.14. Release your mouse button and repeat the process, painting other portions of the horizontal band. Now click the Play button and hear the drum beat repeat, stop, and repeat again, following your painting pattern.

2. Okay, go wild! Repeat the same process using the other loops to add as many instruments or sound effects as you like.

3. Ready for some real magic? Click the Play button, go to the upper-right area of the program display, and move the Key and Tempo sliders back and forth. You just changed key and increased or decreased the speed of all the tracks at once.

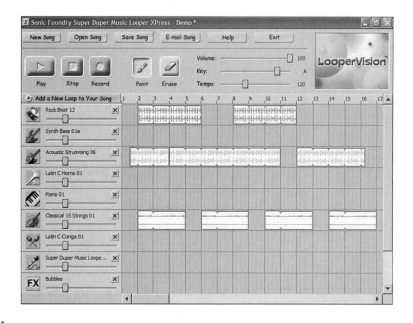

FIGURE 7.14

Super Duper Music Looper uses a fun and very intuitive paintbrush tool to lay down instrument loops.

Project: Dig Deeper into the World of Loops with ACID Xpress

Super Duper Music Looper does a great job introducing the novice, young or old, to the essential concepts behind composing music with loops. It's time to graduate to a more sophisticated experience that puts you squarely in the driver's seat. In this project we'll use Sony's ACID XPress, the free version of a world-famous program called ACID Pro, which is used by millions of digital music composers.

Are You Hooked Yet?

The demo version of Super Duper Music Looper provides a slim taste of the program's full potential. The full version of the program, which goes for $29.97, comes with more than 700 studio-quality sound effects and instrument loops. The full version also allows you to add live recordings and mix them with your loops. And that's just the start. You can mix down your compositions and save them as files that can be burned to a CD.

To purchase the product, return to http://mediasoftware.sonypictures.com/Products/ and click the link for Super Duper Music Looper. On the page dedicated to the product, click the Buy Now shopping cart icon and follow the onscreen instructions.

Using ACID Xpress you'll learn how to

- Use a point, click, and drag technique (identical to Super Duper Music Looper) to preview and build multitrack compositions (up to 10 tracks) using a demo composition

- Import additional sample compositions from the Internet

- Use a PC microphone to record a short track and integrate it with demo loops

- Save your hybrid multitrack composition to your PC's hard disk

Time

Figure on about three or more hours to download and install the free trial demo ACID Xpress 5, register online, learn the basics, download some free ACID loop compositions, edit a sample composition, and record a vocal part to create a loop.

Step 1: Download and Install ACID Xpress

1. Connect to the Internet and point your browser to http://mediasoftware. sonypictures.com/Products/. Under the Music Creation area of the web page, find and click the link for ACID XPress 5.0.

2. Spend some quality time reading the tutorials offered in the far right vertical channel of the page dedicated to ACID XPress 5.0.

3. Look at the upper-right area of the page and click the Download Free Version link.

4. When the Download page appears, select the ACID XPress English version (it's a big file weighing in at 36.3MB). When the File Download dialog box appears, use it to navigate to your downloads folder. Save the file to the folder. This places the `acidxpress5.exe` file to the folder.

5. After the download completes, click the Run button on the Download Complete dialog box. Click the Run button if a security dialog box appears and follow the onscreen dialog boxes to install the program, including the acceptance of the license terms and the default directory and folder settings. When the installation process completes, a dialog box appears with a Finish button.

6. When the Ready to Install dialog box appears, click the Install Shortcut on Desktop and click Install. A new dialog box showing the progress of the installation displays and ends with a Completing the Screenblast ACID XPress 5 Installation Wizard dialog box. Click the Finish button to complete the process.

Step 2: Register online

Registering for a free trial download is somewhat the exception and not the rule. However, in this case, it's important to follow the steps below to register because this enables you to later visit a special Sony website for registered users of ACID XPress that offers several additional loop-based compositions you can download and use.

1. Be sure you are connected to the Internet because the installation process requires you to register online.

2. Return to the Windows desktop and find and click the icon for the Screenblast ACID Xpress program, or click Start, All Programs, Sony, ACID XPress 5.0.

3. Fill in the requested information on the Register Online dialog box and click the Finish button when you are ready to move to the next step.

Step 3: Explore ACID XPress

After completing the online registration, the ACID XPress 5 program should load and open with a sample multitrack composition (see Figure 7.15). And you can always start the program by clicking the ACID XPress icon on the desktop or click Start, All Programs, Sony, ACID XPress 5.0.

ACID XPress opens with a sample multitrack composition displayed. As you let the landscape of this program sink in, you'll notice it bears some essential similarities to the Super Duper Music Looper program. Note the horizontal bands containing a series of loops strung together. To the left of each track are controls to mute, solo, and adjust volume.

Below the track control stack on the far left is a small box with a slider and beats per minute (BPM) to adjust the tempo of the composition. Below the long horizontal tracks you'll find a set of VCR-like play, record, pause, and stop controls. The lower portion of the screen is divided into two main areas—a display for three tabs labeled Explorer, Track Properties, and ACID FX (*FX* is shorthand for effects).

1. Okay, let's get right to experiencing multiple loops in action. Look for the VCR-like controls on the lower-middle portion of the screen and click the Play button. You should hear the sample composition play.

2. As the composition plays, move your cursor to the upper-left edge of the first horizontal loop track called Ugly Remnants. Find and click the exclamation mark symbol. This is the *Solo button*. Clicking the Solo button causes all the other tracks to be muted, allowing you to hear this track play in Solo mode. The circle with a diagonal line symbol (the *Mute button*) immediately to the left causes the track to be muted.

3. Each track's volume can be independently adjusted. Click the Play button and then click the Solo button for a track. Use your mouse to grab and move the volume slider left and right. This tool allows you to balance each track's volume against the others.

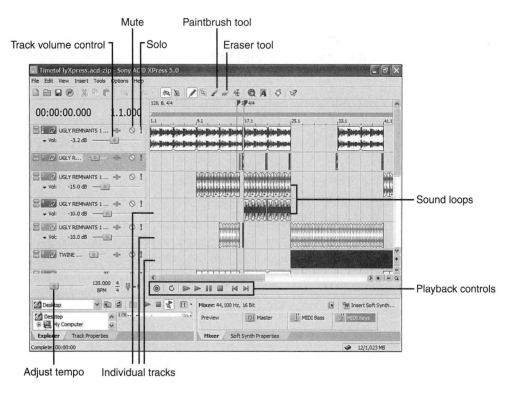

FIGURE 7.15

ACID XPress uses a layout scheme similar to Super Duper Music Looper. A host of editing controls allows you to adjust volume and tempo and apply special effects.

4. Move to the extreme upper-right area of the screen and find the vertical slider bar framed by up and down arrow symbols. Use your mouse to grab the vertical slider bar, or repeatedly click on the down arrow, to move all the way down to the bottom of the stack of horizontal loop tracks.

5. Next we'll learn how to paint a loop in a track and erase loop segments. Move your mouse pointer up to the top toolbar and click the icon of a paintbrush. Now move your mouse pointer into any horizontal track area and the point turns into a paintbrush tip. Find a track with an open horizontal zone not currently occupied with wave patterns. Place your pointer within any of the rectangles in the track and click the left mouse button. In one stroke you've added a single loop segment to the track. To repeat the loop, all you have to do is hold the left mouse button down and drag to the left or right and release when you are done.

6. Erasing a loop or string of connected loops is equally easy. Return to the top toolbar and, this time, click the Eraser button. Now move to the track you populated with additional loops and, holding the left mouse button down, erase one or more loop inserts.

There are many other features and controls to explore and I encourage you to click around and try things out. At any time you can click the Show Me How button at the top right of the main screen's toolbar to access a wonderful tutorial with step-by-step instructions for working with this program.

Step 4: Download Additional Sample Compositions

Tons of free and commercial ACID loops can be downloaded from the Internet and used with this program. Follow the steps below to download some additional canned compositions:

1. Leave your ACID XPress program up and running.

2. Make sure you are connected to the Internet.

3. Look at the upper-right area of the toolbar and click the Get Media button. This little icon shows a tiny globe with a magnifying glass over it. Click it and your browser automatically takes you to Sony's Get Media from the Web website for registered users of ACID XPress that offers free loop-based compositions you may download and use. The compositions are from its archive of weekly Eight Packs the site offers, as shown in Figure 7.16.

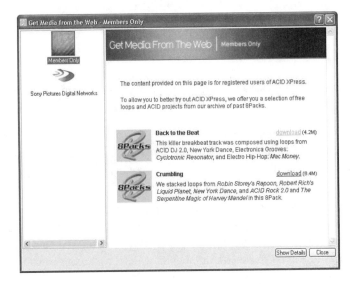

FIGURE 7.16

Sony's Get Media from the Web website offers ACID loop-based free compositions you may download and enjoy.

4. Click the Download link associated with an Eight Pack and use the Browse for Folder dialog box to create a new folder under My Music. Call the folder Sample ACID XPress Compositions. When the download completes, ACID XPress asks if

you want to save the changes made to the current composition being displayed. After you make your decision, the new composition you just downloaded is opened and displayed.

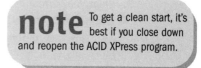

note To get a clean start, it's best if you close down and reopen the ACID XPress program.

5. Listen to the new composition by clicking the Play button. Repeat the steps above to download any other weekly Eight Packs compositions offered.

Step 5: Edit a Sample ACID Loop Composition and Add a Live Recorded Segment

In this step we'll take one of the sample compositions you downloaded earlier, manipulate the loops, and then record and edit one or more live vocal or instrument tracks.

1. Go to the upper-left, click the File drop-down menu, and look at the very bottom area for a list of the loop compositions you recently opened. Select and open one by highlighting it with your mouse pointer and clicking the entry.

2. Using the skills you learned earlier, add or erase loops in a given track, adjust volume, and so forth.

3. To add a personal live recording touch, plug in your PC microphone and ensure it's activated.

4. Move your mouse pointer to the area below the horizontal stack of loops and find the circular Record button (it will be gray until you mouse over it and it turns red). Click the Record button and a Record dialog box appears.

5. Take a moment to study the Record dialog box, as shown in Figure 7.17. If your microphone is active, you should see the green dual thermometer-like vertical shafts move up and down as the microphone picks up your voice or instrument. At the top of this dialog box is a File Name box. Leave all the other settings at their default values.

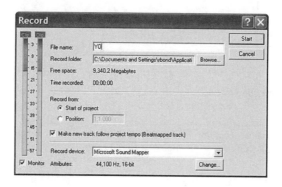

FIGURE 7.17

The ACID XPress Record dialog box monitors the level of microphone input and allows you to name a recorded clip.

6. Clear your throat or tune up your instrument and get ready to click the Record button. Your goal is to record a very short clip that can become a loop. My favorite thing to do is play with one of the downloaded loop-based compositions and record short rap vocal outbursts. It's always good for a laugh, if nothing else.

note The free trial version of ACID XPress allows up to 10 tracks so, in this example, I could add one more recorded track to the composition.

7. Click the Start button on the Record dialog box and the composition begins to play. Record your short vocal clip and then click the Stop button. Your live recorded clip has been automatically inserted as a new track at the bottom of the stack of horizontal loops. In my sample, as shown in Figure 7.18, the short clip I created called Yo was inserted as track nine, along with additional repeats created using the Paintbrush tool.

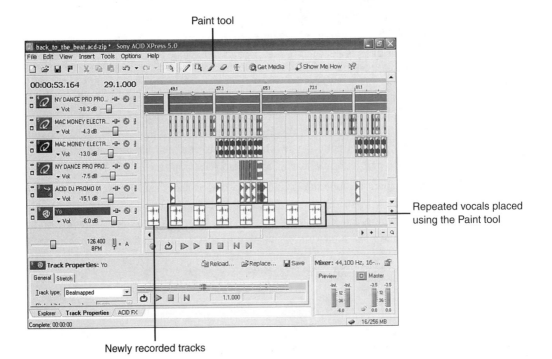

Paint tool

Repeated vocals placed using the Paint tool

Newly recorded tracks

FIGURE 7.18

The bottom track shows the short recording I created with a PC microphone. Using the paint tool, I repeated, or painted, the clip seven times following the original inserted clip.

8. After recording one or more live tracks, use the volume control in the far left box associated with the track to balance the new track with the others.

Step 6: Save Your New Composition

When you are happy with your final mix, save the new hybrid composition by going to the top toolbar and clicking the File drop-down menu and then select Save As. Use the Save As dialog box to give your composition a new name and navigate to the folder where you want to store it.

Where You Can Go From Here

I know of no other activity using a personal computer that offers more possibilities to grow and explore than recording and creating music. My goal in this chapter was to spark your appetite with a glancing taste of creating music using loops and the thrill of live, multitrack recording. From here you can take any number of steps to significantly improve your recordings. But be ready to open your wallet wide. For example, with an investment of around $500 to $700, you could buy this combination of goodies:

- A pair of better quality XLR type unidirectional microphones with shielded cables
- A commercial home multitrack recording software package that can handle live, MIDI, and loop input

Are You Hooked Yet?

What you just experienced was a limited introduction to a more sophisticated music creation program based on loops. The demo version of ACID XPress imposes lots of limitations. You may only have 10 tracks and you can't really do much with your final compositions beyond saving them to the hard disk of your PC and playing them back.

To give your loop composing tool chest a boost, you might want to purchase Sony's entry level product, ACID Music Studio. This program, which goes for $69.95, is a consumer version of the famous ACID Pro package professional artists use that sells for just less than $400. ACID Music Studio's features include

- A library of 1,000 loops
- Ability to record tracks using a microphone or *MIDI compatible keyboard* (an electronic piano instrument that can connect to a personal computer via a MIDI connector normally found on a desktop system's sound card)
- Ability to apply special effects to each track, such as EQ, reverb, and delay
- Option to mix down multitrack compositions and burn a CD or save final compositions as MP3 or Windows formats

To learn more about ACID Music Studio, return to the http://mediasoftware.sonypictures.com/Products/ website and find and click the link for the product. Also spend some time exploring the http://www.acidplanet.com website where you can buy CDs with collections of professional, royalty-free loops.

Another rewarding and rich loop-making software package you may download is FL Studio 5. Go to http://www.download.com and conduct a search for FL Studio. Follow the instructions to download the demo software. For years, this program was called FruityLoops and it is a favorite tool of the hip techno DJs in dance clubs. Renamed FL Studio, it remains an important player in this genre. It's a cool tool for creating drum and other audio loops using a MIDI-connected instrument, such as an electronic keyboard.

- An externally USB-connected recording box that can connect to XLR or quarter-inch microphone or instrument lines
- An electronic keyboard that can connect to a PC using a MIDI link or an external USB-connected recording solution equipped with a MIDI port

Following is a shopping list of suggestions and links for representative products in each of the categories just outlined. My son and I have personally used this gear throughout the past five years as we progressively improved our recording and editing capabilities.

Home Multitrack Recording Software

Seven years ago, personal computer multitrack recording software was generally prohibitively expensive and complex. The software interface assumed the user was a recording engineer. That's all in the past because today the shelves of any computer supply store, such as CompUSA, offer consumer multitrack music recording software packages starting for less than $100.

Here are three entry-level titles you might enjoy:

- Cakewalk's Music Creator ($39, at http://www.cakewalk.com/products/MusicCreator/)
- MAGIX Music Studio 2004 deLuxe ($79.99, at http://site.magix.net/index.php?411)
- Cakewalk's Home Studio Version 2 ($149, at http://www.cakewalk.com/Products/HomeStudio/)

External USB-Connected Recording Boxes

Plugging a microphone into a PC's sound card works, but you'll quickly discover that your recordings might be very noisy and weak. Standard sound cards found in off-the-shelf consumer desktop personal computers are fine for producing clear sound output, but often incorporate very limited recording capabilities. The same rule of thumb applies to laptop sound systems.

All the noise comes from the electronic gear inside a personal computer. Standard PC sound cards are not well shielded and, as a result, recordings might contain a lot of noise. And a weak recording signal might be the result of a PC sound card's lack of adequate microphone input amplification.

One way to bypass the limitations of a PC's standard sound system is to opt for an external

tip For an up-to-date listing of music recording and editing software, go to the Featured Software section of the Personal Computing area of the Intel website (http://www.intel.com). From there, click the Music and Create and Edit links and you'll find listings and links to loads of great programs.

USB-connected recording and amplifying solution. Many are available today for around $200. These products typically incorporate built-in amplifiers associated with quarter-inch or XLR line-in connectors to provide clean input from microphones capturing vocals and acoustic instruments. And some of these products also sport a MIDI connection to link to an electronic keyboard.

Well-known PC music recording companies, such as Edirol and M-Audio, make good products. Originally designed for on-the-go field recording using a laptop, they can also offer a solid solution for desktops.

Combine one of these boxes with a dynamic microphone using a shielded quarter-inch or XLR cable (jump ahead and see Figure 7.20) and you can boost the quality of your recordings considerably. Expect to pay $50 and up for a decent microphone and about $20 for a shielded microphone cable.

The M-Audio MobilePre USB box my son and I have been using lately is a typical product in this category (see http://www.m-audio.com and search for MobilePre). Priced for less than $200, the small box shown in Figure 7.19 connects directly to a desktop or laptop using a standard USB cable. It supports two quarter-inch microphone and/or electric instrument lines, or two XLR-type microphones (see the section below on microphones). A standard headphone jack is provided for monitoring, along with stereo microphone input and stereo output jacks.

FIGURE 7.19

The M-Audio MobilePre is a small, external recording solution that connects to a desktop or laptop using a USB cable.

After it's connected, the M-Audio MobilePre box takes over as your PC's sound system for playback and recording. You can connect your microphone or electric instrument to the box, adjust the volume of the incoming signal, and produce remarkably clear recordings given the modest price of the unit.

Other products in this category priced around $200 include the Tascam US-122 USB Audio/MIDI Interface box, Audiotrak MAYA44 USB, Terratek Aureon 5.1 USB, and Edirol UA-3FX USB Audio Capture and Playback Device.

XLR and Quarter-Inch Microphones and Shielded Cables

One of the things you'll quickly discover about home recording on a PC is the value of a good microphone. Equally important are shielded XLR or quarter-inch type microphone cables. As you move up from a standard PC microphone, you'll hear all about dynamic and condenser models. Better quality microphones, like the ones shown in Figure 7.20, use XLR three-prong connectors, which, in turn, use microphone cords terminating in an XLR or quarter-inch plug.

FIGURE 7.20

Quarter-inch format microphone cables have a plug at the end that looks just like the ones used for electric guitars. XLR format microphones and cables use a three-prong connector.

Dynamic microphones are used for recording sessions and live performances, whereas *condenser microphones* are used for recording only (as they are very sensitive). Condenser microphones also typically need to connect into specially powered inputs. So, your safe bet is to buy a dynamic microphone. Expect to pay at least $50 and up for good microphones.

Mixing Board to Support Multiple Input Microphone Lines

My son is a drummer and has a set of five microphones he positions to record his kit. If you need to record multiple lines at one time, a mixing board can be a quick solution. The Behringer Eurorack MXB1002 Mixer board shown in Figure 7.21 costs about $100 and supports up to 10 quarter-inch microphone and/or electronic instruments lines or five XLR lines. Most mixing boards include left and right channel quarter-inch or standard RCA composite-type connectors intended to be patched to amplified public address speakers.

FIGURE 7.21

The Behringer Eurorack mixing board is a typical example of a modestly priced solution for connecting and balancing multiple microphone or instrument lines.

One quick fix is to buy two male-to-male quarter-inch patch cables (sold in music supply stores) and link the mixing board's speaker outputs to the left and right channel input jacks of a product such as the USB MobilePre. Set the levels of the multiple microphone or instrument lines feeding into the mixer using its slider controls and then record the mixed left/right output signal using the external recording solution.

Electronic Keyboard with MIDI Interface

About eight years ago my wife bought our kids an inexpensive $100 Casio electronic piano. You could make it sound like a regular acoustic piano or, using push buttons on the top control panel, transform it to sound like imitation drums, sound effects, and a host of instruments from trumpets to violins. But on its back panel was a feature we discovered years later that gave this $100 gift a whole new reason for being!

When my son and I started playing with Cakewalk's Home Studio program, we noticed that in addition to supporting live voice or instruments, these programs could accept input from MIDI instruments. We rolled up our sleeves, did some research, and learned that most electronic pianos have a MIDI outlet designed to link to a MIDI connector typically found on the sound card of a PC. As luck would have it, our piano had just such a connector.

We dashed off to the Guitar Center store in our area, bought a special cable designed to link a MIDI instrument to the sound card, came home, and hooked it all together and in a few minutes we were banging out notes on the keyboard to create MIDI-coded tracks.

As noted much earlier in this chapter, the MIDI standard defines an interface between electronic instruments and a PC. When you input notes from a MIDI keyboard linked to a PC running a software program such as Cakewalk's Home Studio, you'll see a series of dash-like patterns appear in a MIDI track. These patterns look entirely different than the audio wave patterns a microphone produces. You can use libraries of digital instrument samples and sound effects often bundled with home recording programs to transform these dash codes into every imaginable instrument or sound effect. It's a low-cost and powerful way to add an entire orchestra of virtual instruments to your creative arsenal!

An Expensive Proposition

Warning: Turning your PC into a home recording studio can become an extremely addicting hobby—one that can consume a lot of bucks. My son and I started five years ago, plugging a cheap $20 PC microphone into the sound card of our home computer. Next we went to RadioShack and bought a $40 four-line mixer that we rigged up with a patch cable to connect into the stereo-in jack of our PC sound card. Along with the four-line primitive mixer, we purchased two $30 unidirectional quarter-inch microphones and $10 desktop stands that helped a lot. Total investment, about $100.

Five years later we have a studio set up that includes

- A powerful PC with a Pentium 4 processor with a Hyper Threading Technology brain chip, a gigabyte of RAM, and two 100GB hard disks. Total investment here, about $1,500.

- An Aardvark Audio Direct Pro 10 package that includes an advanced sound card linked to an eight microphone line-in external box. Unfortunately, Aardvark Audio has gone out of business since I purchased its gear. If you want to check it out, I'd suggest trying eBay. Failing that, there are certainly many other comparable products, including Delta 1010, 10-In/10-Out PCI/Rack Digital Recording System from M-Audio ($599.99), at http://m-audio.com; or the Layla3G from Echo Digital Audio ($629), at http://www.echoaudio.com.

- A DBX brand model 166XL compressor/limiter/gate box that prevents clipping and distortion (approximately $250).

- A collection of dynamic and condenser microphones ranging in price from $50 to $150 each.

- Lots of microphone stands and microphone line cables.

- Two self-powered speakers designed for studios (about $100 each) that connect to the Aardvark Q10 box.

- An additional video card in our PC that can support two monitors which, when combined with the PC's standard graphics card, enables support for three display monitors. We use the three displays to spread out the display of the tracks and other program elements.

- A library of powerful recording and editing software that includes such titles as Steinberg's Cubase SX multitrack software ($599, see http://www.steinberg.net), Acid Pro 4 from Sony Pictures Digital ($399, see http://mediasoftware.sonypictures.com/Products), and Cakewalk's Sonar 4 Studio ($479, see http://www.cakewalk.com).

Brace yourself because the gear and software we use represents about $5,000 worth of stuff! But wait; let me put this into perspective.

Go to any big retail electronics chain store these days and look at the rows of large screen plasma and LCD TV monitors with price tags of $5,000 or more. For the same investment you can transform your home personal computer into an amazing tool that will deliver countless hours of interactive, mind-developing personal creativity experiences for the entire family.

And I've got one more point to toss your way before I hop off this soapbox. Planning and managing multitrack recording productions is all about discipline. My son Jeff has picked up a lot of good habits so far on his journey to becoming a successful semi-pro recording engineer. I'm talking about habits such as carefully naming and storing critical files in folders with names that make sense, backing up files for safekeeping, and learning to patiently take a complex challenge and break it down into steps to be executed over time.

On the surface it might look like a fun pastime or hobby. But I'm convinced that Jeff's work with our home PC recording studio is preparing him to be a solid project manager in the workplace.

What's next? Home computers are no longer islands unto themselves. The Internet links your PC to the world, so now it's time to link your PC to others in the home and even to your TV and stereo. Next up is a step-by-step guide for creating a home network using the latest wireless technologies.

8

Enjoy Your PC's Digital Media in the Family Room

Do you have tons of digital photos, music files, and perhaps even videos sitting on the hard disks of your home PCs? Do you enjoy listening to streaming Internet music and talk radio programs but find it frustrating to have the experience tethered to where your PC resides? Wouldn't it be great to see and hear all that digital fun in the family room using the TV's big display and the power of your stereo's amplifier and speakers?

Today's ultra-versatile PCs combined with wired and wireless home networks, the Internet, and innovative adapter products that allow TVs and stereos to join in on the fun have ushered in a new age of show–and–tell possibilities. Thanks to a lot of creative engineering, the stage has been set for your home to become a place where digital content from your PCs and the Internet can flow through the air to be enjoyed anytime, anywhere, and on many forms of electronic devices.

This chapter offers two projects that will show you how to break down the Berlin wall that has separated your PC from the consumer electronics gear in the family room. The first is a rock-bottom basic project that uses inexpensive, standard audio patch cables to make a simple PC-to-stereo link to expand your listening options. The second project is for the adventurous and shows how a digital media adapter box designed for a home with a wired or wireless network can retrieve pictures, music, and video from a PC and dispense this content on a TV and stereo (preferably a home theater).

Open Wallet Alert

This chapter describes activities that require the purchase of gear ranging from standard audio and video cables (around $20) to wireless digital media adapters costing from $150 to $300. For each project or solution described, I've looked for modestly priced offerings that provide the best bang for the buck.

Skills and Gear Check

Before you jump into the projects, take a quick look below at the list of assumptions I'm making about your skills and gear.

Key assumptions:

- You have one or more Windows XP-based PCs in your home containing digital music and photo files (digital video files are optional).

- You know how to connect components to a stereo system using the necessary audio and video cables.

- For the basic wired PC-to-stereo audio link project, your target PC is located close to your stereo. Or, you have an understanding spouse or significant other willing to tolerate the snaking of cables under carpets and/or the drilling of holes in walls. If you plan to use a laptop for this project, it must have a stereo headphone jack.

- A home network is preferred for the adventurous digital media adapter project. The digital media adapter featured in this chapter can accept a wired or wireless link to a home network, but the project emphasizes going with the cutting-edge wireless route.

Project: Connect Your PC to a Stereo

Everything wireless is hot these days with the consumer electronics and high-tech crowd. And on the home front the buzz is all about wireless (Wi-Fi) networks and products designed to extend their value beyond tying PCs together to share a single link to the Internet.

I'm a huge believer in the value of wireless home networks and I've seen first hand the magic when PCs, entertainment PCs, and digital media adapters (DMAs) work in harmony to dispense digital entertainment on everything from huge TV monitors to tiny handheld computers. It's a heady topic, but I recognize not everyone can afford to run off and purchase a set of home networking gear and then spring for a DMA.

With that in mind, this project offers a low-cost introduction to the experience of playing PC-bound audio on a piece of consumer electronics; in this case, a stereo. The method outlined in this project might not be glamorous or the newest thing, but it's super cheap and it works. And after you experience hearing your collection of PC digital music pumping out of the speakers of your stereo, you might be inspired to consider building a home network and adding a DMA.

Materials

To complete this project you'll need a

- Personal computer with digital music files and a stereo-out audio receptacle (a standard feature on today's PCs used to connect to a set of speakers or headphones)

- Set of left/right stereo analog composite extension cables and a cable that converts left/right analog composite lines to a single 1/8-inch stereo jack (same male plug as used for headphones)

- Stereo system with a pair of unused left/right composite inputs (tape in, auxiliary, and so forth)

tip
Before you take another step on the composite path, check to see if your stereo and PC sound card offer a digital audio connector. The documentation for your stereo (or home theater rig) and your sound card will tell you if a digital audio option, such as *S/PDIF*, is present. If yes, that's a better way to go because there will be no drop in quality, caused by converting a digital signal to analog. Of course, you'll need to purchase the right cable to make the connection, but the result will be worth it.

Time

After purchasing the required cables, the time to accomplish this project will vary greatly. Making the link between a PC and a stereo takes only a few minutes. The wild card factor I can't predict is the amount of time needed to hide the cables running from the PC to the stereo if you elect to make the link permanent.

caution
Stay away from composite inputs marked Phono (which are used for a turn table). These inputs have different properties than all the other composite inputs and will not work for our purpose.

Step 1: Is Your Stereo Ready to Play the Game?

Check your stereo for an unused pair of composite audio inputs by looking at the back of the unit. The best candidates are labeled AUX (for auxiliary) or Tape In, as shown in Figure 8.1. If you use your DVD player to play music CDs, it's likely that the CD audio inputs are also available.

FIGURE 8.1

Look for a red and white set of audio composite inputs (for right and left stereo channels) on the back of your stereo.

Step 2: Acquire the Necessary Cables

If you're a home theater or electronics junky, it is very possible that you already have the cabling you need. If not, it's time to head off to the store and buy the standard stereo analog composite audio cable(s) needed to make the connection (see Figure 8.2). These cables are very easy to find at your local RadioShack or the electronics department in major chain stores such as Best Buy or Circuit City. Measure the distance from your PC to the stereo to determine the length of composite cable needed.

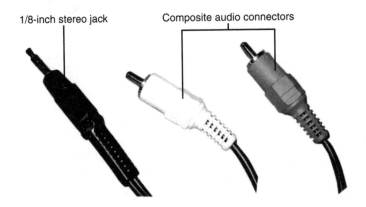

FIGURE 8.2

This Y-shaped cable connects your PC (via the 1/8-inch stereo jack) to your home stereo (via the composite red and white plugs).

Standard analog audio composite cable lengths run 3, 4, 8, and 12 feet. If you need something longer, you can "patch" multiple sets of composite cables together using female-to-female couplers (see Figure 8.3). At home I have a 30-foot cable running from a PC in our den to the stereo in our playroom.

FIGURE 8.3

If necessary, use a coupler and multiple cables to gain more cable length. A Y-adapter (right) can be used to convert composite audio cables to a 1/8-inch stereo jack.

Step 3: Connect and Test the Cable

Now that you have the necessary audio cables, your PC, and the stereo all together in the same location: Stop! Before you move a muscle, turn off your stereo and your PC. Whether you opted for the analog composite audio cable or headphone extension line route, take the left/right composite plugs at the end of your line and insert them into the left and right stereo inputs you found available on the back of your stereo system.

tip An alternative to messing around with coupling multiple composite audio cables together is to use a headphone extension cable. RadioShack, for example, offers 20-foot headphone extension lines with male to female connectors for less than $10.

Next, insert the 1/8-inch stereo jack at the other end of the line into the stereo output on your PC's sound system. To locate your PC's stereo output, look at the back of your desktop PC and find the green and red 1/8-inch female inputs (your system might also have a blue receptacle, which may not be used for this project). Some new PCs offer a set in the front as well. If you have external speakers connected to your PC, they are most likely plugged into the green input. Remove the speaker plug and connect the 1/8-inch jack for your new line to the stereo (see the following sidebar to learn how to have your speakers and extension line to a stereo share the same stereo output receptacle).

Okay, ready to go? Turn on your stereo and set the volume to very low, followed by starting up your PC. Set the stereo input to AUX, Tape In, or whatever you selected earlier. Return to the PC and start playing a music file using Windows Media Player or another audio playback program. As the music file plays on the PC, walk to the stereo and gradually increase its volume. If all went as planned, you should hear your tunes filling the family room with glorious sound. If you don't hear anything, double-check the cable connections you made and that your stereo is using the correct input device. You should also check the Windows XP volume control (usually accessed via a small speaker icon near the onscreen clock) and make sure none of the volume sliders are turned too far down.

Hearing your PC's digital music pounding out of the big speakers on your home stereo system is a moment to savor. It works, it's simple and cheap, and you can hear all the digital music files stored on your PC's hard disk or streaming live from the Internet. After the initial thrill dies down, however, you'll discover that having to control everything from your PC can be frustrating. That's where the next project steps in to offer an innovative solution for remote-controlled playback of PC content in the family room.

Having Your Audio Cake and Eating It, Too

Chances are good you had to unplug your PC's speakers to do the project above. But what if you want to keep the connection to the stereo and have your local PC speaker's working, too?

You have two options. First, check the documentation that came with your PC to see if its sound card offers two sound outputs. If it does, connect the extension line to the sound card's spare stereo-out receptacle.

If your PC sound system offers only one sound-out line, pop back to the electronics store and ask for a 1/8-inch stereo Y-cable. These gizmos, which cost about $5, allow you to plug two 1/8-inch headphone jacks into a single stereo output.

Project: Use a Digital Media Adapter to Experience Digital Media on Your Stereo and TV

At the beginning of this chapter I painted a picture of a home scenario where digital photos, music, and even videos stored on a PC could be accessed and enjoyed on consumer electronics gear, such as a TV and stereo. This project describes how to make the magic happen using a new category of products called digital media adapters (DMAs), or sometimes called Digital Media Servers.

Think of the steps in this project as more of a case history. The point here is to learn about DMAs and get a feel for what's involved with their installation and operation. This learning exercise helps you decide if purchasing and installing a DMA is a project you want to pursue.

In this project you'll learn

- What a DMA does and how it becomes a part of your home wired or wireless network
- What DMA products are available and buying tips to ensure you find the right mix of features for your family's needs
- What it's like to install and operate a DMA using the Play@TV from icube as the model

Materials

To complete this project you'll need a

- Wired or wireless home network
- A network-connected PC in your home containing digital photos, music, and video files
- A DMA box that can be incorporated into your home wireless or wired network and connected to a TV and/or stereo

Time

About three hours to set up your DMA, establish it as a member of your home network, install the media management and server software on a networked PC, and test the link.

Is This Project for You?

Before we plunge into the topic, I need to set the stage because this project is like no other in the book. First, it's aimed at readers who have a home network and want to push the envelope of their knowledge and experience. The DMAs that are the focus of this project are specialty add-on products designed primarily for a wired or wireless network, and the makers of these gizmos assume the buyer has a foundation in networking terms and concepts (and a decent wad o' cash).

Before taking another step, review the following questions to determine if you have the background and/or level of interest to attempt this project:

- Did you install your home wired or wireless network?

- Are you familiar with basic networking concepts and terms such as router, Ethernet, Wi-Fi, and IP address?

- If you did not install your network, are you willing to dig in, learn about this technology, and promise to carefully follow the instructions that come with the products described in this project?

- Are you new to home networking but interested in building one and then adding a digital media adapter at a later date?

If you answered yes to the first three questions, you are ready to tackle this project. If you answered yes to the last question, see the "Ready to Build Your Own Home Wireless Network?" sidebar. After you have a network established, return to this project.

Ready to Build Your Own Home Network?

Don't have a network? But your interest in what a DMA combined with a home network can do is piqued? Take it from me, a home network is the best way to go if you want to set the stage for shipping digital fun from your PC(s) to a TV and stereo. And a wireless network eliminates the mess of installing and hiding cables.

To build a wired or wireless network, you have two choices—pay someone to do it (using a local computer support outfit or national service, such as the Geek Squad from Best Buy) or roll up your sleeves and do it yourself. If you plan to give it a go, expect to pay around $50–$100 for a wired or wireless router and about $20–$50 for wired or wireless network adapters for each PC in the home. (Many PCs come with a wired network port built in. Some even support wireless out of the box. Make sure you know if yours does before blowing any cash.)

A great way to get a feel for what building a home network entails is to visit http://www.intel.com/personal/digital_home/home.htm and study the easy–to-understand and generously illustrated article "How to Set Up a Wireless Network in Your Home." Although the article focuses on a wireless installation, the basic concepts apply to a wired network as well.

Understanding Digital Media Adapters

Millions of consumers around the world are installing networks in their homes. The primary motivation is to connect multiple PCs, game consoles, and so forth to share a single high-speed link to the Internet. But that's just the foundation.

There's so much more a network can do, including the potential to access digital images, music, and video throughout the home. As the adoption of home networking gathers steam, clever engineers are developing innovative add-on products. *Digital media adapters (DMAs)* represent one emerging product category that leverages a home's wired or wireless network to retrieve digital content from a PC and play it back on a TV or stereo.

A DMA is a box-like device that connects to your stereo and/or TV. Its job is to use a home's wired or wireless network to retrieve digital photo, music, and video files from a PC in the network and play them back on a TV or stereo. The idea, and hence the appeal of the concept, is to make all the digital fun sitting on your PC's hard disk accessible to consumer electronics gear throughout the home.

Today's DMAs take many forms, as shown in Figure 8.4. When it comes to home networking, they all adhere to international standards, such as Ethernet and Wi-Fi (for wireless networking).

FIGURE 8.4

Digital media adapters (DMAs) come in a wide variety of sizes and styles. On the left is a Linksys Wireless-B Media Adapter WMA11b, with a Play@TV from icube shown on the right.

DMAs might conform to the most common wireless and wired networking standards, but they often differ in terms of features offered. Some DMAs offer playback of

note Manufacturers are constantly at work improving and releasing new DMA products. Don't be surprised if the examples listed here have been revised or replaced as time goes by.

- PC-based digital music only
- PC-based digital music plus specific Internet subscription streaming music services
- PC-based digital music and photos
- PC-based digital music, digital photos and video, plus Internet radio and specific Internet subscription music services

For a taste of the varied flora and fauna populating the DMA landscape, visit the following product sites and study the feature descriptions:

- D-Link DSM-320 MediaLounge High Speed 2.4GHz (802.11g) Wireless Media Player, at http://www.d-link.com
- SMC's SMCWAA-B 11Mbps Wireless Audio Adapter, at http://www.smc.com
- Linksys Wireless-B Media Adapter WMA11b, at http://www.linksys.com
- Macsense HomePod, at http://www.macsense.com
- Netgear MP101, at http://www.netgear.com
- icube Play@TV Network Media Player, at http://www.playattv.com
- Omnifi Wireless Home Stereo/Theater Digital Media Streamer, at http://www.omnifimedia.com

DMA packages typically include an adapter box with the ability to connect to a home's network, composite audio and video cables, and a remote control. All the DMAs I've worked with include a port to connect to a wired network. On the wireless side, some have a Wi-Fi network transceiver radio built-in to the body of the DMA. Others, such as the Play@TV from icube, require the addition of a Wi-Fi 802.11b wireless PC card (the same kind of card used to add wireless network capabilities to older laptop PCs).

Three Home-Tested DMA Buying Tips

1. If you decided to buy a wireless DMA, go for one that uses 802.11g wireless technology (faster than the original 802.11b wireless networking standard). Of course, in order for the benefits of the 802.11g radio in a DMA to be realized, your home network needs to be based on the same standard.

2. Here's a cyber-shopper tip that's good for any tech product. When you zero in on a candidate DMA, see if you can download the product's installation guide from the manufacturer's website. Check to see if the instructions are clear and well illustrated.

3. I've played around with many of the DMAs listed above and have found that models designed to retrieve video from a PC work, but video quality will vary widely based on the format, frame size, and so forth of the source digital video file stored on your PC. The best video playback via a DMA is achieved when it is linked to a router directly with a cable.

Either way, here's what I've experienced—some video files will play back smoothly, but in a small frame. Others might be choppy. For me, most video I've seen delivered by a DMA has been good enough to be fun, but not comparable to watching a commercial DVD.

If hearing your PC-based music and seeing your digital snaps is what you seek from a DMA, there are already great products available. If high quality video is something you want to experience, go for an entertainment PC (see Chapter 1, "Is Your PC Ready?") and place it where it belongs, in the family room directly connected to your big display and audio gear. (Or wait for the next generation of DMA to come around. The shortcomings in video quality are sure to improve.)

To illustrate what installation of a DMA entails, I've outlined the basic steps to set up the popular Play@TV DMA from icube.

Step 1: Connect the DMA to Your TV and Stereo

Most DMA installation instructions ask that you start by making a connection between the DMA and your family room TV and stereo (or home theater) . Video connection options often include standard composite video, component video, and S-video (see Figure 8.5). For sound, you'll find analog composite ports and sometimes digital S/PDIF and optical ports. Whatever path you select, it all boils down to making a physical link between the DMA and the entertainment devices.

FIGURE 8.5

Most DMAs designed to interface with a TV offer composite and S-Video ports. Some add component video inputs, too.

Step 2: Install the DMA's PC software

After making the cable connection between the Play@TV and a TV or stereo, the next step calls for the installation of two programs on the PC in your home network that contains your digital media files.

In the case of the Play@TV, the first program is called the Media Organizer. This program's job is to identify all of the digital photos, music, and videos on the server PC and create playlists and folders containing content the remote DMA can access via the network. A server program is installed next. This program's function is to manage the network connection between the PC and the Play@TV DMA.

With the Media Organizer software now installed, the next step is to use the program's wizards to gather and organize your collection of digital music, photos, and videos for use with the DMA. The Play@TV's Media Organizer software package, for example, searches a PC's entire hard drive and lists candidate content. Using onscreen wizards and menus, you can select which images, tunes, or videos you want accessible to the DMA and how to organize them into folders or playlists, as shown in Figure 8.6.

Specific software installation instructions should be included with your DMA.

Step 3: Connect Your PC and DMA

There are two ways to connect a DMA to a host (server) PC—wired or wireless. If your DMA is located within a few feet of your home network's router, use an Ethernet cable to make the link (typically included with the product).

> **tip** Composite left/right audio connectors are found on all the DMAs I've used, and the Play@TV is no exception. If your DMA is designed to interface with a TV, at the very least you should find that a yellow composite video output port is also provided (as is the case with the Play@TV). In turn, most modern stereos and TVs offer both composite and S-video inputs.
>
> If you have a high-end TV, you're likely to have other, more advanced, video connectors available. These include component inputs (with red, blue, and green connectors) and special digital connectors. Some DMAs support these connections and some don't. If yours does, keep in mind that the cables are pricier, but they also provide improved image quality.

> **note** The software model used by the Play@TV is not universal. However, the essential elements, such as a PC-based media organizing program coupled with software to enable the designated PC to act as a dispenser to the DMA (server), are found in all DMAs.

> **note** Don't feel bad if terms like router, access point, and so forth don't ring a bell. If you installed your home network, these terms might be familiar. If not, check out the glossary at the end of this book.

As most people have their TV and stereo in a family room far from where their PC(s) are located, many opt to use a Wi-Fi network to facilitate a wireless network connection. In this scenario you would follow the installation guide to tap the built-in, or add-on, Wi-Fi adapter to enable the DMA to join the home wireless network.

FIGURE 8.6

The photo album management portion of Play@TV's Media Organizer software is used to select which photo folders to make available to the Play@TV DMA.

Most DMA products offer detailed step-by-step onscreen wizards and illustrated guide booklets to make the installation process manageable for anyone who is familiar with their home network's basic components.

Step 4: Enjoy Your New Toy

Drum roll please, the big moment has arrived. If your DMA has been installed properly, is a recognized member of your home network, and you've set up its included PC software to prepare image, music, and video content, you should be ready to fly. Using Play@TV as our model, here's what the first session with a DMA generally involves:

1. Turn on the TV, stereo, DMA, and PC.

2. Set the TV to the input port connected to the DMA (for example, video line-in 1 or line-in 2)

tip If you are adding a wireless DMA to a home wireless network protected by one of the popular encryption schemes (WEP or WPA) check the DMA's installation guide for instructions on how to enter any identification and pass codes required for the DMA to join the network.

tip The Play@TV, and most DMAs, is primarily designed to retrieve multimedia content from a single PC in the home network. Consult your product's documentation to see if its media management and server software can browse the home network and retrieve content stored on the hard disks of other PCs.

3. Each time you power on the DMA, it takes a few moments to join the home network. This process ends with a display on the TV screen announcing that the connection has been established, followed by a display of the DMA's menu, as shown in Figure 8.7.

FIGURE 8.7

Play@TV's TV control screen offers easy access to the collection of music, videos, and photos compiled by the Media Organizer software.

4. Use the DMA's remote control, as you relax on the couch, to access the digital snaps, music, and videos stored on the remote PC (see Figure 8.8).

Although the installation process can be complicated, trust me, after you break down the Berlin wall separating your PC from the TV and stereo in the family room, there's no going back! If the idea of blending the worlds of your TV, stereo, PC, and Internet together into one seamless experience fires your imagination, you should also be sure to go back to Chapter 1 and review the "Introducing the Entertainment PC" sidebar.

Building your digital home on the foundation of an entertainment PC combined with a home wireless network and high-speed Internet connectivity is the ultimate digital media solution. If you go this route, you can move the DMA you purchased from the family room to another TV/stereo in the house. Using the wireless network, the new family room entertainment PC can send digital fun to, for example, a DMA now connected to the TV in the master bedroom.

FIGURE 8.8

Here's what the TV screen menu looks like as the Play@TV DMA presents icons for the music folders I made accessible. Note the options near the bottom, which allow you to search music files by album, playlist, artist, or genre.

What's next? Although you might have reached the end of this tome, completing all the projects in this book is a beginning, not an ending. There are endless ways to expand your experiences based on the activities in this book. Return to the "Are You Hooked Yet?" sidebars for any project and dig deeper. Or check out your local community college for night courses on home computing topics such as music and video production. And, of course, your local bookstore and library should have shelves of computer how-to books that focus on a specific area, such as digital photography. In the end, I've found expanding your horizon happens when you share ideas and recipes with folks on the same path of discovery. The best parting advice I have is to encourage you to seek out a local computer users group. Thousands exist worldwide and you might have one in your town. If you do, you're in luck. Often, these groups meet

Are You Hooked Yet?

If the time and/or cost of creating a complete wired or wireless home network are more than you want to tackle, there is an alternative. A few specialty point-to-point wireless products are on the market that can establish a simple PC-to-stereo wireless link.

RCA makes a product called the Lyra RD900W that you can find if you go to http://www.rcaaudiovideo.com, click Products (Audio), and select the Lyra Wireless link. Shop around. You might even find a few available for a bargain price on eBay.

D-Link also offers several packages in their Personal Air line, some of which use Bluetooth wireless technology. To learn more about these products, visit http://www.d-link.com and search for the DSM-910BT and DSM-920BT Personal Air Stereo Adapter Kits.

monthly to share ideas, new products, and projects and to help each other learn the ropes. To see if there's a group in your area, visit http://www.apcug.org, the home page for the Association of Personal Computer User Groups. At the top of the page, click the drop-down User Groups menu and select Directory, and then use the state links to see what's happening in your area. Good luck and happy computing!

Glossary

1/8-inch stereo jack   Standard male stereo plug used for headphones and other audio equipment. Most PCs have a 1/8-inch audio-out receptacle designed for speakers and headphones that use 1/8-inch plugs.

802.11b/g   802.11 refers to an international standard for wireless home or business networking, also known as *Wi-Fi*. The 802.11b standard has a transmission rate of 11 million bps (bits per second), although the 802.11g standard (now the norm for new home wireless networking gear) pumps it up to about 54 million bps. Up and coming, too, is the 802.11n that delivers 100 million bps or higher.

1394   *See* FireWire.

adware   A close cousin of spyware (*see* spyware), adware programs are downloaded (*see* download) without your permission to your PC as you surf the Web. These programs gather information about your web-browsing activities. The information, in some cases, is used to display unsolicited pop-up advertisements in the web browser.

AGP   An acronym for *accelerated graphics port*. Most desktop PCs today continue to use this technology for high-performance graphic cards that generate the display of images on a connected monitor. It is slowly being replaced by faster PCI Express technology (*see* PCI Express).

analog video tape   Common forms of analog video tape include VHS and Hi8.

AVI   Acronym for *audio video interleave*. This is a high resolution video format used for Windows-based PCs. Video-editing software packages often recommend using the DV-AVI format (digital video, audio video interleave) to achieve the best video input quality when capturing video from a camcorder linked to a PC.

bit   Stands for *binary digit*. The binary code digital computers use represents information and numbers with a series of 0s and 1s (off and on). Bits are used together to create bytes (*see* byte) which, in turn, may be used to represent numbers or letters of the alphabet.

bit depth   The amount of bits used to define a multimedia element. In digital photography, for example, a 32-bit image uses 24 bits to define the color of a single pixel (*see* pixel) with the remaining 8 bits used for control purposes. Greater bit depth translates to higher fidelity images. The same principle applies to digital audio files.

Bluetooth wireless technology   Bluetooth is a short-range wireless technology designed primarily to link peripherals (mouse, printer, and so forth) to a computer system. Bluetooth technology is also used for wireless ear-and-mouthpiece peripherals for cell phones.

browser   A software program designed to locate and display web pages. Microsoft's Internet Explorer, for example, is the browser included with the Windows XP operating system. Other well-known browsers include Mozilla, Netscape, and Firefox.

bundled software   Software provided with a hardware product, such as a personal computer or digital camera. For example, most webcams come with a software bundle that includes a photo-editing and web-conferencing application.

byte   Short for *binary term*. A byte is made up of 8 bits (*see* bit). A byte can represent in code a letter or number.

cable internet link   As used in this book, this refers to your home's TV coaxial cable acting as a carrier of high-speed digital data. It requires a cable modem and an Internet access subscription or service.

card reader   A device with slots to accept the insertion of a variety of removable memory cards, such as CompactFlash, SD, and memory stick cards.

CD   CD stands for *compact disc*. These are the discs used for music CDs and to hold PC data, programs, and multimedia content (photos and/or video). Today's CDs hold up to 700MB (megabytes) of digital information (*see* megabyte). A higher capacity disc storage option is provided by DVDs (*see* DVD).

CD burner   Slang term for a CD (compact disc) recording drive (CD-R drive). Originally, CD drives in PCs could only play prerecorded discs. A CD burner drive can read prerecorded CDs and write data to CD blanks.

CD+G format CDs   This format is used primarily for karaoke discs. The CD+G format embeds graphics and text along with audio files. A CD+G-compatible CD drive is needed for a PC to read and display the graphics elements of a CD+G formatted karaoke disc so the singer can read the words as the music progresses.

CD mix   Refers to combining multiple audio music tracks from a variety of sources to create a custom compilation. Also referred to as a *CD party mix*.

CD-R/RW   A CD-R can be burned with data using a CD burner drive in a PC. Any information burned onto the CD-R is permanent. A CD-RW may be erased and used over and over like a floppy disc.

Centrino Mobile Technology   This is a set of chips and technology developed by Intel for laptop computers. It combines microprocessors designed for mobility with other support chips and a radio for wireless 802.11a/b/g network support. The latest version of this technology package incorporates advanced audio and graphics features.

component video   Superior to composite video, component video uses separate signals for red, green, and blue. *See* composite video.

condenser microphone   As with a dynamic microphone (*see* dynamic microphone), a condenser microphone has a diaphragm. However, when sound makes the diaphragm in a condenser microphone move, it causes an electrical charge on a condenser to vary. This variation determines how sound is recorded. Condenser microphones need external power to electrostatically charge the condenser.

composite audio   The standard red and white (left/right stereo) audio cable lines that use a male plug identical to those used for a composite video line (*see* composite video).

composite video   A video cable technology that combines all the red, green, and blue elements of a video stream into a single signal.

CPU   Acronym for *central processing unit*. Refers to the main processing unit in a personal computer. Pentium 4, for example, is a CPU. Sometimes this acronym is used loosely to refer to the entire PC.

data miner   A very close relative of adware (*see* adware), data miners are little programs loaded on your PC without your knowledge or consent that gather information about your web-browsing activities. This information, in turn, is reported to marketing outfits.

dialog box   A temporary MS Windows pop-up window that presents a message or requests an action on the part of the operator.

dial-up Internet connection   A standard, slow-speed telephone line connection to the Internet via a dial-up modem. The maximum speed supported by this technology is about 50,000 bits per second (*see* bit).

digital camera   Any device that captures still images using digital codes as opposed to using film.

digital camcorder   A video recorder that captures images and audio and writes the information digitally to tape, miniDVD blank discs, or removable mini-hard disks.

digital media adapter (DMA)   A DMA is a box-like product that connects a home stereo or TV set to your home network. Its purpose is to use a home's wired or wireless network to access digital multimedia files stored on a networked PC and play them back on a piece of consumer electronics gear (stereo or TV).

digital photography versus film   Digital and film photography share one trait in common. Each records the light that passes through a lens. It's how they capture the light that separates them. When light passes through the lens of a traditional camera, it strikes the surface of a strip of film. When light passes through the lens of a digital camera, it strikes the surface of special silicon chip that makes an electronic recording of the light patterns.

digital video recorder (DVR)   A device that records TV or other video sources to DVD blanks or to a hard disk. Today's entertainment PCs, or PCs equipped with a TV tuner card, can serve as a DVR when using software designed to capture TV broadcasts or externally connected video sources (such as a camcorder) and store them on hard disk.

digital zoom   Digital zoom simulates optical zoom by cropping and enlarging a portion of a digital still image.

digitize   The act of converting an analog source or signal (such as a VHS or Hi8 analog video tape) to a digital file and format.

dots per inch (dpi)   This refers to the resolution of an image (*see* resolution). A laser printer that supports 1,200 dots per inch offers a more detailed image than one capable of 600 dpi.

download   The reverse of upload. Download is a techie term that refers to the transfer of files from a remote computer or server (*see* server) linked to your PC via the Internet. It may also be used to describe the act of transferring files from a host PC to a peripheral. For example, you might download your MP3 music files from your PC to a handheld player.

DSL Internet link   As used in this book, this refers to a high-speed connection to the Internet using *Digital Subscriber Line* technology. In a nutshell, this technology makes it possible to carry high-speed digital data using traditional copper telephone lines. A DSL modem and a subscription to a DSL service are required.

drag and drop   This refers to the use of a mouse to grab a graphical element and move it to a new location. When using the Windows XP Windows Explorer file manager program, for example, you might grab the icon for a folder (highlight an element by depressing and holding the left mouse button down) and drag it to another folder. To drop the dragged folder into the target folder, release the left mouse button.

driver   A small utility program designed to let Windows control a piece of hardware, such as a mouse, printer, disk drive, keyboard, and so on. The Windows XP operating system contains thousands of drivers for a wide range of products. When purchasing a new piece of hardware for your PC, you might need to install a driver in order for the Windows XP operating system to know how to communicate with the product.

drop-down menu   Any menu that appears to drop down vertically to form a window when a link is clicked. For example, items listed in program toolbars often present drop-down menus when clicked.

dual-core microprocessor   A single microprocessor package that contains two physical cores (or independent microprocessors). A cutting-edge PC with a dual-core processor solution gives a system two brains to boost performance (*see also* Hyper Threading Technology).

dual- and single-layer DVD   Single-layer DVD blanks can hold 4.7 gigabytes of data or video. The newer dual-layer discs offer up to 8.54 gigabytes of storage capacity.

The latest DVD burners for PCs support dual-layer blanks in either the DVD+R or DVD-R formats (*see* DVD+R *and* DVD-R).

DV   Acronym for *digital video.*

DVD   A disc, similar to a CD, with drastically improved storage capacity. Typical DVDs store from 4.7 to 8.54 gigabytes of personal video or digital data (*see* dual- and single-layer DVD). With that amount of storage, you can hold thousands of high-resolution digital photos and hours of high-quality video. A modern multimedia personal computer may be purchased with a DVD burner drive.

DVD burner   Slang for a PC drive or free-standing consumer electronics product that can record video or other digital content onto blank DVDs.

DVD+R and DVD-R   Blank DVD discs today are offered in two competing formats: DVD+R and DVD-R. First generation DVD burners for personal computers were designed to use one format exclusively. Fortunately, the majority of today's DVD burners can read and write to either format. There is a rewritable (RW) version for both of these formats.

dynamic microphone   A dynamic microphone has a diaphragm that moves in response to the vibrations created when you sing, speak, or play an instrument. These vibrations are then transformed into electrical signals. When recording using a PC, these signals are translated into digital codes.

entertainment PC A new form of home computer designed for a family room that combines the functions of a PC with a TV tuner, personal digital video recorder (DVR), and DVD/CD music and video player. Some models include an FM radio tuner. Nearly all entertainment PCs on the market today use the Media Center Edition of Microsoft's Windows XP operating system and a wireless remote control.

Ethernet An international standard for creating a local area network (LAN) to tie multiple computers together that was developed in the 1970s. The Ethernet protocol standardized how information flows within a network and underpins today's home and business computer networks.

file extension A variety of computer files are present on your personal computer. A Windows operating system-based PC, for example, will contain program files with an `.exe` extension in their name. A Microsoft Word document has a `.doc` extension, with audio files having `.wma`, `.mp3`, `.mid`, or `.wav` extensions. A file's extension determines what program can or can't use it.

file swapping Usually this refers to using an Internet file-exchange service to transfer files from one PC to another.

firewall For home computer users, this usually refers to software or hardware designed to make your Internet-connected PC invisible to outsiders. A firewall blocks unauthorized access to your PC and home network.

FireWire Developed by Apple Computer as a way to transfer digital information between a computer and peripherals (such as a digital video camcorder) at a speed of up to 400 million bits per second. You will also see this technology referred to as 1394 (the international standard name) and i.Link (Sony's term).

flash memory A form of solid state (chip) memory that holds data even when power is removed. Popular forms of removable flash memory cards for digital cameras and handheld computers include CompactFlash cards (about the size of a matchbook), postage-stamp–size Secure Digital (SD) cards, and Sony's memory sticks (about the size of a single stick of flat chewing gum).

folder On a Windows PC, files on the hard disk are organized within folders. These folders, such as My Documents, are represented graphically via folder icons. A folder might also contain subfolders.

freeware A software program distributed via the Internet free of charge.

FX Short for *special effects.*

gigabyte (GB) Approximately one billion bytes (actually it's 1,024 megabytes). *See* megabyte.

gigahertz (GHz) *See* hertz. One billion cycles per second. In computers, it generally refers to the speed of the CPU.

hacker   Originally a term for a computer enthusiast who enjoyed banging around with program code. Today, however, the term usually refers to a person attempting to maliciously break into a network.

hard disk   The main mass data storage device in a PC. In the old days PCs used floppy (flexible) individual discs to store programs and information. When higher capacity, multi-platter, rigid storage devices for PCs were introduced, the nickname hard disk was applied to these products. A hard disk can be installed inside a PC or housed in a box and connected using a USB or FireWire cable.

hertz (Hz)   Named in honor of the scientist Heinrich Hertz, this term is used to refer to cycles per second. For example, a 3.5 gigahertz microprocessor operates at 3.5 billion cycles per second.

home network   A LAN located in a residential home (*see* LAN).

Hyper Threading Technology   A technology used in most of Intel's Pentium 4 processors that causes the Windows XP operating system to think it has two independent microprocessors at its disposal to divide and conquer demanding foreground and background tasks.

icon   A graphical image representing a program, tool, folder, or function you click using a mouse.

import   Fancy geek-speak term for the act of transferring any digital file from a remote source onto your PC. The term also can mean to load a file for manipulation by a program. For example, you might import a video file stored on your PC's hard disk into a video-editing package.

instant messaging (IM)   Sending quick text messages in real-time via a web-based Internet service such as AIM, Yahoo! Messenger, or MSN.

Internet   A worldwide collection of networks that can communicate with each other using a common communications standard called TCP/IP protocol. The origin of the Internet goes back to a U.S. military project called ARPANET in the late 1960s. Ultimately its use spread to academia and then to the world at large with the advent of the World Wide Web (*see* World Wide Web).

Internet filter program   A special utility installed on a PC to manage access to the Internet. Most Internet filter programs exist primarily to block access to adult content sites.

i.Link   *See* FireWire.

JPEG   When it comes to digital photography, this is one acronym you'll find everywhere. Technically it stands for *Joint Photographic Experts Group*. The .jpg file format makes it possible for large high-resolution digital pictures to be compressed to a manageable file size for storage and especially for transport using the Internet.

Kilobyte (KB)   Approximately one thousand bytes (actually it's 1,024 bytes). *See* byte.

LAN (local area network)   Technical term for a network comprised of multiple computers linked wirelessly or via wires in a centralized location (home or business).

LCD   This acronym stands for *liquid crystal display*. LCDs are used for PC flat panel monitors, digital cameras, laptop computers, handheld computers, cell phones, and portable media players.

loop   Loops are short tracks of recorded acoustic, electric, or MIDI sequences designed to repeat. A classic example would be a drum beat loop that can be pasted together repeatedly in a track to provide a beat pattern.

malware   Short for *malicious software* and refers to a virus or other form of damaging program.

master track   The end result of a multitrack recording session and mix down operation (*see* mix down *and* multitrack recording).

megabyte (MB)   Approximately one million bytes (actually it's 1,048,576 bytes). *See* byte.

megapixel   *Mega* means million. So this term means one million pixels (*see* pixel). This word comes up when you evaluate a digital camera's performance capabilities. For example, my day-to-day digital camera can take a single photo using up to 3.2 million pixels.

Here's what several popular megapixel ranges can produce in terms of the size and quality of printed photos:

- 2.1–3 megapixels: Good 4×6 inch prints.
- 3.1–4 megapixels: Great 4×6 inch prints. Depending on lens quality and other factors, you might get good 8×10 inch prints.
- 4.1–5 megapixels: Good to great 8×10 inch prints.

memory   On a PC this can refer to RAM (*see* RAM) and sometimes a hard disk. When you hear or read *memory* associated with a digital camera, it refers to the chip(s) used to store the digital photos. There are two kinds of memory on digital cameras—built-in and removable.

memory stick   Solid state removable memory device created by Sony. *See* flash memory.

MIDI   An acronym for *musical instrument digital interface*. This is a standard for controlling electronic gear, such as a keyboard or PC sound card. The MIDI format represents musical notes using a digital code for pitch, volume, and other characteristics.

mix down   The act of combining multiple recorded audio tracks into a single master track (*see* multitrack recording).

mixing   Related to multitrack recording, this term refers to the act of combining multiple recorded sound tracks to create a new single or master track.

modem Contraction of the words *modulator/demodulator*. A modem typically takes the form of an external box or card installed in your PC that makes it possible for a computer to receive analog information via a traditional phone line and convert it to digital information a PC can digest. A modem, in turn, can reverse the process, too. The term stuck and is now applied to DSL and cable adapters used to deliver high-speed Internet digital signals to a home or business. These products, although called modems, technically are not performing a modem function.

MP3 Technically, MP3 stands for *MPEG audio layer 3*. This is an international standard for compressing digital audio files. This is the format most widely used for digital music players.

MPEG-1 and MPEG-2 MPEG stands for *Moving Picture Experts Group*, an international standards organization. MPEG-1 digital video was used for years in Asia for movie rental discs. It still lives on as a video format to create personal Video CDs (*see* VCD). MPEG-2 digital video is used on a personal computer to create homemade movie DVDs and super video CDs (SVCD). PC video-editing packages designed to create home DVD discs produce finished digital videos using the MPEG-2 format with a resolution of 720×480 pixels.

multimedia This term is applied to a computer, program, presentation, or end result that combines text, graphics, sound, animation, and/or video.

multitrack recording An audio recording comprised of multiple, separately recorded tracks. For example, a multitrack recording might have separate tracks for guitar, voice, drums, and bass.

operating system This refers to the master software program that runs your PC. Windows XP and Linux are examples of operating systems.

optical zoom Optical zoom mechanically moves the lens of a camera to bring objects closer.

PC-Cam A form of webcam that can be detached from a USB cable and used as a free-standing digital camera.

PC card About the size of a credit card, PC cards are used on laptops to expand functionality. One or two PC card expansion slots are usually provided on the side of a laptop. There's a huge range of PC cards available from products to add a wireless network capability to versions that add USB ports.

PCI In the early 1990s the Peripheral Component Interconnect (PCI) standard was established to standardize and improve the performance of PC desktop add-in cards. If you open a PC case and look inside, you'll see add-in cards plugged into a large circuit board (or the motherboard). The receptacles on the main circuit board into which a PCI card is inserted are called PCI expansion slots (*see* PCI Express).

PCI Express   The new PCI Express standard is an update to the existing PCI standard that operates at twice the speed of PCI technology (*see* PCI). If you're shopping for a new desktop PC, go for one that includes a motherboard with PCI Express technology.

Pentium 4 processor   Intel's flagship microprocessor for personal desktop computers.

Photo CD   A CD containing digital photos in a format developed by Kodak and Philips. PCs and some modern DVD players can read Photo CDs. Kodak also refers to this format as a *Picture CD*.

pixel   Here's another term you'll run into all the time. Today's digital cameras, for example, are rated in terms of megapixels (*see* megapixel). Pixel is shorthand for *picture elements*. Each digital photo is made up of tiny dots. Each dot is called a pixel. A 3.2 megapixel camera creates better pictures than a 1.2 megapixel camera.

pop-up window   Any window display that suddenly appears in the foreground of a computer display. Pop-ups might be triggered by legitimate sources, such as the operating system or a program, or by unsolicited sources, such as adware (*see* adware). Pop-up windows might appear on the main desktop screen area or within a program or web browser display.

public hot spot   A wireless network access point typically based on 802.11b or 802.11g wireless standards that is open to the public. Hot spots are found in a host of locations such as coffee shops, hotels, and airports. Public hot spots offer Internet access free or for a fee.

quarter-inch connector   A standard metal connector used for audio patch cables, electric guitars, and so forth.

RAM   Acronym for *Random Access Memory*. Inside your PC are memory sticks inserted into the main circuit board (or the motherboard). The amount of RAM you have (measured in megabytes or gigabytes) helps contribute to the overall performance of your system.

read me file   Plain text information files that often accompany programs and drivers downloaded from the Internet. These files contain installation tips, system requirements, and operational notes.

red eye   The red glow emanating from the eyes of your loved ones when you take a film or digital photo using flash is not caused by temporary demonic possession. Instead, it happens when the bright light hits the blood vessels on the retina.

resolution   A term widely used in digital multimedia to indicate in bits or pixels the level of detail. For example, a digital picture comprised of 2,048 horizontal pixels by 1,536 vertical pixels has a higher resolution than one shot at 1,600 by 1,200 pixels. The same principle applies to digital audio. A 32-bit audio file has greater fidelity than a 16-bit version.

rip   Slang term for the act of using a personal computer and its CD drive to read a track from a commercial music disc and convert it to a digital format that can be stored on a hard disk or other storage media.

ripper   A software program designed to rip tracks from a commercial music CD (*see* rip).

router   A key ingredient in a home or business network that ties two or more PCs together. A router is a box into which you may connect Ethernet cables from multiple PCs. The router's job is to facilitate the movement of data among the multiple PCs in the network. Routers are typically connected to a DSL or cable modem to make it possible for all the PCs in the network to share a single high-speed link to the Internet. *See* wireless Router.

S/PDIF   A standard developed by Sony and Phillips to send audio signals digitally. For example, you might use an all digital S/PDIF link to connect various stereo components together. Even some PCs today offer a S/PDIF audio-out option. This all-digital solution eliminates the quality loss that occurs when digital audio (from a PC, for example) is converted to an analog signal.

scanner   Scanners for consumers take many forms today. Some are flat rectangular boxes with a lift-up lid and a glass plate that operate using the same basic principles of a photocopier. A flatbed scanner is often incorporated in all-in-one printer/fax/scanner products. And there's also a crop of tiny wand-like handheld models to scan documents on-the-go. Most scanners today are

linked to a PC using a USB cable. Images are digitized and stored as files on the host PC.

screen saver   Static images left onscreen for too long on older CRT monitors could permanently burn-in an image on the phosphor on the inside surface of the glass tube. Screen savers refer to any program designed to frequently change images on a computer screen to prevent burn-in. Today screen savers are primarily used as a novelty.

scrollbar (horizontal and vertical)   A horizontal or vertical bar on the edge of a program window that contains a slider box or arrow used to pan the display up and down or left and right.

SD card   Stands for *Secure Digital*. (*See* flash memory *and* memory stick.)

server   Any computer that performs the function of delivering content upon the request of a locally or remotely connected computer. The World Wide Web, for example, contains thousands of servers dispensing web pages on demand.

Service Pack 2 or higher   Microsoft, and other software companies, issue service packs to correct problems or to add features to an existing deployed software product. At the time of this writing, Service Pack 2 was the latest collection of important bug fixes, security enhancements, and new feature additions issued by Microsoft for its Windows XP operating system (Home and Professional editions). Another related term is *patch*, which refers to a single software update/fix or smaller scale bundles of updates.

shareware   Copyrighted programs made available on a trial basis free of charge. Following a specified period, the user may opt to purchase the full version.

splash screen   The opening display on a website presented before the main page. Some computer programs also present a splash page with a company's logo, and so forth before presenting the opening menu. When you turn on your computer and for a few moments see the Windows XP logo appear, you are looking at a form of splash screen.

spyware   These are little programs that hitchhike along with downloaded files (freeware, shareware, and music files from file-swapping services). They are installed on your PC without your knowledge or consent. Their purpose is to track your activities on the Internet. The information is fed back to advertisers and others for marketing purposes. Malicious spyware can be used to gather email, password, and credit card information.

streaming music   Music transmitted in real-time via the Internet from a remote PC or server (*see* server).

streaming video   Video transmitted in real-time via the Internet from a remote PC or server (*see* server).

subfolder   A folder containing files that, in turn, is a part of a master folder.

S-Video   Short for *Super Video*. This technology uses a cable to carry video as does the composite video standard. S-Video, however, boosts image quality by dividing the video into two separate signals (color and brightness).

SVCD (Super Video CD)   A higher resolution version of the VCD format (*see* VCD).

thumbnail   A visual representation of a photo or video file stored on a PC's hard disk or other medium. Windows XP's Windows Explorer (file manager) program can display files as text entries or as thumbnails. In thumbnail mode, a small reproduction of a photo or the first frame of a video is displayed. Photo- and video-editing software programs also frequently offer a thumbnail mode to make it easy to quickly identify a given image or video file.

USB   This stands for *Universal Serial Bus*. Shortly after the standard was introduced in 1996, PCs began appearing with these high-speed ports. USB rapidly gained in popularity as it offered the flexibility to be used for printers, scanners, PC cameras, and many other external products. The intention of the USB standard was to eliminate multiple connector formats for printers, modems, mouse devices, and keyboards.

USB 2.0   USB 2.0 is the latest and fastest version of the USB standard (*see* USB). It supports data exchanges up to 480 million bits per second versus the 12 million bits per second supported by USB 1.1.

upload Refers to the act of transferring a digital file (for instance, a digital photo file) from a PC to a remote computer or server (*see* server) using the Internet. For example, you might upload a set of digital photo files from your PC's hard disk to a server of one of the many free online photo album-sharing services.

utility A program that performs a very specific function. A file-backup or disk-formatting program is an example of a utility.

VCD (Video CD) Acronym for *Video CD*. VCDs typically contain digital video in the MPEG 1 format (*see* MPEG). Most DVD players can play back VCDs.

virus A program loaded on your PC without your knowledge. Viruses are designed to hamper the performance of your PC and/or cause serious damage. Viruses can be picked up via file transfers or as email attachments.

VoIP (Voice over Internet Protocol) This refers to the use of the TCP/IP international standard for data packet communications on the Internet to transmit digital voice conversations in real-time. Several companies now offer telephone service using VoIP.

WAV This is a format for sound files that was first supported in the Windows 95 operating system. For many years it has been the de facto sound standard for PCs. Wave files have the .wav extension. Today many formats exist, including the newer .wma format from Microsoft and the international MP3 standard.

webcam A digital camera designed to be attached to a PC using a USB cable (*see* USB). A webcam may be used as a digital still camera for local snaps, as a local video recorder, or to support live two-way Internet video conferencing. Webcams are also used to broadcast live video streams from a specific location.

web radio Web radio is used to refer to several web-based audio experiences. It can apply to the streaming of live or archived audio files from a standard AM or FM station, or it can refer to streaming audio broadcasts from a web-only virtual radio station.

WEP encryption A basic form of data scrambling supported by the Windows XP operating system to help secure home wireless networks from unauthorized external access. A new form of protection, WPA (Wi-Fi Protected Access), is now gaining popularity as it provides stronger protection. *See* WPA.

Wi-Fi This term is loosely used to refer to any wireless network based on the international 802.11b or later standard. This is actually a contraction of the words Wireless Fidelity.

Windows XP (Home and Pro) Introduced in 2001, Windows XP is Microsoft's current operating system for home and general business desktop and laptop PCs. There are two versions available, Home and Pro. Windows XP is much more stable than earlier versions of the Windows operating system and the look and feel is much easier to navigate. Windows XP is also more network friendly than previous versions.

WinZip   A popular utility program designed to compress and decompress files (*see* utility *and* Zip file or folder).

wireless access point   This is a box typically used to add wireless coverage to an existing wired network.

wireless home network   *See* home network, Wi-Fi, *and* 802.11b/g.

wireless router   This is a wireless version of a router (*see* router). A wireless router connects to a DSL or cable modem to distribute high-speed Internet access to two or more PCs in a network. PCs in the network may connect to a wireless router via wireless signals or wire cables.

wizard   A series of menus and/or dialog boxes within a program designed to provide a step-by-step guide for the execution of a task. A classic example would be a wizard to help install a program.

WMA   Stands for *Windows Media Audio*. This is a compressed audio file format that Microsoft developed as an alternative to MP3 (*see* MP3).

World Wide Web   When most people informally talk about the Internet, they are actually referring to the World Wide Web. In the 1990s a new form of servers (*see* server) began appearing all over the world designed to use the Internet as a highway to share information in a friendly, menu-driven form. The scheme uses HTML-formatted documents (web pages written with a code called Hypertext Markup Language) that present text, pictures, audio, and video elements.

worms   Evil programs related to viruses. Unlike a virus, a worm program can reproduce itself and spread across a network to harm individual computers.

WPA   Stands for *Wi-Fi Protected Access*. Backed by the Wi-Fi Alliance, this 128-bit encryption standard offers greater security for home and business wireless networks than the WEP standard (*see* WEP). Key improvements over WEP include stronger data protection and improved access controls and user authentication.

XLR   A three-pin connector in a metal case used for microphones and sound patch cables.

Y splitter   A device that takes one audio or video signal and divides it into two identical outputs. An example would be a 1/8-inch audio Y splitter designed to allow a single PC audio-out port to support two separate devices simultaneously (for instance, local speakers and a line connected to a stereo).

Zip file or folder   A Zip file is one that has been compressed for faster transport via the Internet, or to reduce storage space. A Zip folder contains multiple Zip files. A zip/unzip utility is required to create and unzip these files or folders.

Index

How can we make this index more useful? Email us at indexes@sampublishing.com

More Great Titles from Que Publishing!

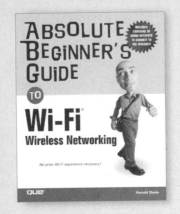

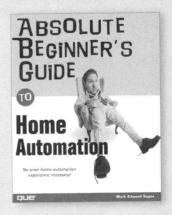

Absolute Beginner's Guide to Podcasting
by George Colombo and Curtis Franklin, Jr
0-7897-3455-9
$21.99 USA / $29.99 CAN / £15.99 Net UK
Coming Fall 2005!

Absolute Beginner's Guide to Wi-Fi Wireless Networking
by Harold Davis
0-7897-3115-0
$18.95 USA / $26.95 CAN / £13.99 Net UK

Absolute Beginner's Guide to Home Automation
by Mark E. Soper
0-7897-3207-6
$21.99 USA / $29.99 CAN / £15.99 Net UK

Building a Digital Home Entertainment Network: Multimedia in Every Room
by Terry Ulick
0-7897-3318-8
$24.99 USA / $34.99 CAN / £17.99 Net UK

Bad Pics Fixed Quick: How to Fix Lousy Digital Pictures
by Michael Miller
0-7897-3209-2
$24.99 USA / $34.99 CAN / £17.99 Net UK

iPod and iTunes Starter Kit
by Brad Miser
0-7897-3278-5
$34.99 USA